ADAPT!

Adapt!

ON A NEW POLITICAL IMPERATIVE

Barbara Stiegler

TRANSLATED BY ADAM HOCKER

FORDHAM UNIVERSITY PRESS   NEW YORK 2022

This book was originally published in French as Barbara Stiegler, *«Il faut s'adapter»: Sur un nouvel impératif politique*, Copyright © 2019 Éditions Gallimard.

Cet ouvrage a bénéficié du soutien des Programmes d'aide à la publication de l'Institut Français.

This work, published as part of a program of aid for publication, received support from the Institut Français.

Ouvrage publié avec le concours du Ministère français chargé de la Culture–Centre National du Livre.

This work has been published with the assistance of the French Ministry of Culture–National Center for the Book.

This work received the French Voices Award for excellence in publication and translation. French Voices is a program created and funded by the French Embassy in the United States and FACE Foundation (French-American Cultural Exchange). French Voices Logo designed by Serge Bloch.

Visit us online at www.fordhampress.com.

Library of Congress Cataloging-in-Publication Data available online at https://catalog.loc.gov.

Printed in the United States of America
24 23 22   5 4 3 2 1

First edition

Contents

Preface

This book would perhaps not have seen the light of day—at least it would not be the same—if I had not met Jean Terrel. For ten years, our many discussions about contemporary politics and the more academic exchanges we have had in the field of political philosophy have profoundly nourished my thinking. From this point of view, the year 2009—which was marked both by the acceleration of neoliberal reforms in the world of education, teaching, and research and by an unexpected and unprecedented mobilization of the university community—played a pivotal role both in our having met and in the genesis of this book. From the day of his having learned about this book project in 2013—during a noted workshop in Milan about political realism attended by an entire delegation from Bordeaux—Jean's confidence in this project and then his careful and thorough readings throughout all the stages of the manuscript provided invaluable support and helped me maintain my efforts up until its completion.

My debt is equally immense to Claude Gautier. Without our having met in 2015 at a memorable colloquium held in Gargnano on the shores of Lake Garda in Italy, the central question that now constitutes the heart of this book would have doubtlessly encountered problems in emerging. It was he who guided my first steps on the foreign continent of Dewey's texts and who generously put me on the path of numerous hypotheses that I am presenting here. In him, I also found an ideal reader—both thorough and generous—never relaxing his critical vigilance while also knowing how to kindly and hospitably welcome the work in progress.

For all of this, I warmly thank both of them.

This book also owes much to the participants in the master's program "Soin, éthique, et santé" at the University of Bordeaux Montaigne. My exchanges with healthcare professionals—both colleagues and students—introduced me to the ethical questions and political stories that reinforced the central question of this book. And it is this wonderful small research laboratory that motivates me to continue pursuing further health-related inquiry by confronting the hypotheses set forth here with the real-life practices of healthcare providers and patients.

The Institut Universitaire de France also granted me the ideal conditions to properly pursue this work, providing me with those moments of stasis and enclosure that have now become so rare—even within academic environments.

In the fields of philosophy and biology, I also thank Jean Gayon and Maël Lemoine; and in the social and political fields, Franck Fischbach and Christian Laval, who reread all or part of the manuscript. My thanks also go to my colleague and friend Olivier Dubos for his long-term support of the arguments defended here—notably those on the question of law.

Christian Laval and Frédéric Gros brought precious support to this book by encouraging me to submit it to Éditions Gallimard. I wish to also express here all of my gratitude to Éric Vigne for having welcomed my work into his collection and for having helped me give it its definitive shape.

Bordeaux
July 5, 2018

ADAPT!

Introduction: The Lag of the Human Species

What is the source of this widespread feeling, one that is more and more oppressive and broadly shared, of a generalized lag—itself reinforced by the perpetual injunction to adapt in order to evolve? "Evolution," they say, demands "mutations" that allow for "survival" and "adaptation" to a new "environment" that is henceforth described as unstable, complex, and uncertain, and in relation to which our societies are constantly accused of "falling behind." How can we explain this progressive colonization of the economic, social, and political fields by this biological vocabulary of evolution? To understand this widespread evolutionism and to explain its hegemony, we cannot simply cite the acceleration of technological innovations. But nor can we explain everything by the revolutionary content of capitalism, that "eminently revolutionary role" of the bourgeoisie described by Karl Marx at the beginning of the *Communist Manifesto*—for neither technology nor capitalism produces discourse about the human species and its evolution. Behind the constant lamentation about our supposed lag and behind the perpetual call for us to readapt, this book reveals that there exists something else: a political thought, both powerful and structured, that puts forth a highly articulated narrative about both the lag of the human species and its future that depends on a certain conception of the meaning of life and evolution. This dominant political thought dubbed itself, at a famous colloquium on the work of Walter Lippmann that took place in Paris in August 1938, with the name of "neoliberalism."[1]

If neoliberalism has become hegemonic in the contemporary political field, its history has been paradoxically rarely studied, and its original links with the Darwinian revolution have been completely forgotten. While neoliberal doctrines have seen an overwhelming ascent for at least a half century, it took until the 2004 publication of the Michel Foucault course on neoliberalism—held at the end of the 1970s at the Collège de France—for us to begin to finally take seriously what was actually new in this *neo*-liberalism.[2] Until this recent date, it had been systematically confounded with neoclassical economics, financialized and deregulated capitalism, and an ultraliberalism advocating a minimal state and privatized trade for all services. We are indebted to Michel Foucault for having established against all these confusions that, on the contrary, one of the principal rupture points between classical liberalism and "new liberalism" occurred through the invasive return of state action within all spheres of social life. While eighteenth-century liberals and the ultraliberals at the end of the nineteenth century advocated a laissez-faire based on the good nature of our species and of its inclinations—which are supposed to spontaneously contribute to the smooth functioning of the market—the neoliberals emerged after the Great Depression in the 1930s correctly rejecting this naïve naturalism by calling on those artifices of the state (law, education, social protection) in charge of artificially building the market to permanently ensure its arbitration according to fair and undistorted rules.

But by taking an interest principally in ordoliberalism, the German variant of neoliberalism so profoundly involved in European integration, Michel Foucault thought he could conclude that neoliberalism was essentially antinaturalism. This led him to ignore the American and evolutionary sources of neoliberalism, which depended directly on the Darwinian revolution. By doing so, he left out not only the ideas of Friedrich Hayek—whose evolutionism had been formed through a permanent dialogue with Darwinism—but also those of Walter Lippmann, whose central role in the birth of neoliberalism he had nevertheless grasped. Yet here were the elements required to discover a new properly neoliberal version of what Foucault himself had called "biopolitics": a politics oriented, as in the eighteenth century, toward the vitality of the human species—and thought of in relation to its environment—but now relying on the new gains of the Darwinian revolution.

The new genealogy of neoliberalism proposed here returns to the centrality of Walter Lippmann's work, which was the main source of the 1938 colloquium, while unveiling all that his new liberalism owes to evolutionary theory. An American diplomat, journalist, and political essayist, Lippmann (1889–1974) had a considerable influence on the political history of the United States from World War I to the Vietnam War. Among his diverse legacies, he provided the theoretical matrix for neoliberalism with his 1937 work titled *The Good Society*, around which all the "new liberals" would converge at the 1938 Lippmann Colloquium. This work is itself the result of a long political meditation on the new situation of the human species, which Lippmann judged completely unprecedented in the history of life. Indeed, for the first time in the evolution of life and living beings, a species, our own, had found itself in a situation of complete maladaptation in relation to its new environment. For Lippmann, this situation was explained by the discrepancy in rhythm between the natural inclinations of the human species, which were inherited from a long evolutionary history that had been modifying itself at the very slow rhythm of biological history, and the demands of our new environment that had been brutally imposed on us by the industrial revolution. This diagnosis leads Lippmann to his main political question: how can the human species readapt to an unstable environment that is constantly changing and completely open when its entire evolutionary history has adapted it to a stable and relatively enclosed environment—ranging from rural communities to the City-States theorized by the Greeks? How can it reconcile its vital need for stability and enclosure with the acceleration of all forms of flux and the destruction of all borders imposed by globalization? At which rhythm must the human species reform itself to reconcile its slow evolutionary history with the new demands of the industrial "great revolution"? Under the influence of Darwin, the great philosophies of life that were deployed at the turn of the nineteenth and twentieth centuries all meditated on the crisis that was triggered by this revelation of absolute flux, regarding which all forms of permanence or even stability appeared as fiction.[3] The tension between flux and "stasis"—a generic term I am putting forward to designate everything that reflects the efforts of living beings to slow down or artificially stabilize the flux of becoming—gave rise to unprecedented questions for the human species and completely renewed the political field. For Lippmann, the real question was this: How can we prevent this new tension between flux and stasis, openness and enclosure, from encouraging among the masses the rise of nationalisms, fascisms, and more generally all forms of self-retreat that try—against the course of evolution—to restore stases and to reinforce enclosures?

This new political issue, from which it seems we have not emerged and which Lippmann shared with other leading political theorists, was explicitly directed against the naturalism of Herbert Spencer and his ultraliberal excesses that were based on a bad understanding of the Darwinian revolution. For Spencer and for those we wrongly call "Social Darwinists," who had triumphed in America at the beginning of the twentieth century, the laws of evolution were supposed to mechanically ensure the transition of inert matter into an industrial society while automatically selecting only the fittest. In the political field, it therefore sufficed to let nature—and with it the natural tendencies of capitalism—take its course, which implied a categorical refusal of all artificial disturbances from the state. For Lippmann, and for many of his progressive

contemporaries who correctly understood the need to combat these ultraliberals, the industrial revolution had on the contrary created a completely unprecedented situation of maladaptation that explained all the social and
political pathologies of our time, and which were further aggravated by laissez-
faire. It was thus necessary to rethink political action as an artificial, continuous, and invasive intervention on the human species to readapt it to the needs
of its new environment. With help from the new experts in the human and
social sciences, the government had to conduct a set of large-scale experiments
that would allow it to at last overcome the lag of the human species in its own
evolution.

During this effort to rethink political action on the basis of evolutionary
questions about lag and readaptation to the environment, Lippmann crossed
paths with one of the greatest American thinkers of the twentieth century: the
pragmatist philosopher John Dewey, who was himself also occupied with
thinking about the political consequences of the Darwinian revolution—but
only to draw rigorously different conclusions. While Lippmann, and all the
neoliberals after him, theorized a regulation of society that combined the
knowledge of experts and the artifices of law, Dewey recognized experimentation as being genuine only on the condition that it was conducted by the
collective intelligence of the publics—itself inseparable from the affective dimension of all experience. While for Lippmann, and then the American neoliberals, the allocation of this role to the supposed intelligence of the public
denied the reality of evolutionary processes—regarding which the affectivity
of the masses and the human intelligence appeared as rigid, backward, and
maladjusted—for the pragmatists, contrarily, it was this joint interpretation of
affectivity and collective intelligence as a functional organ of control that was
closer to Darwin's logic. For some, intelligence was a planning faculty that,
because it denied the reality of evolution, must be switched off. For others, it
was the organ par excellence of readjustment, which alone knew how to hold
itself within the irreducible tension between the flux of the new and the stases
of the old, allowing it to relay the evolutionary logic of the living being while
amplifying it. From this long debate between Lippmann and Dewey, American
history has particularly retained the conflict from the 1920s concerning democracy—which resurfaced in contemporary America in roughly the 2000s—
opposing the defenders of a representative democracy governed from above by
experts (Lippmann) with the promoters of a participatory democracy who
encourage the continuous involvement of citizens in a collective experiment
(Dewey). Thus, by demonstrating that the famous "Lippmann-Dewey debate"
has had much greater breadth in reality—since it linked the question of the
becoming of democracy to that of liberalism while reexamining them in the

light of the Darwinian revolution—the new genealogy of neoliberalism that is proposed here reveals that John Dewey's political thought was the first great philosophical critique of neoliberalism.

Lippmann's diagnosis of the maladjustment of the human species, which led him to disqualify the intelligence of the public, relegating it to the status of the inept masses for which control would need to come from above, throws light on the contemporary widespread feeling of a perpetual lag that is endlessly whispered of by leaders. The injunctions to adapt, to catch up, to accelerate our rhythms, to leave behind our immobilism and to guard ourselves from all slowing down; the general discrediting of all forms of stases in the name of flux; and the valorization of flexibility and adaptability in all fields of life possibly find here the sources of their legitimization that are the most powerful and at the same time most ambivalent. And their strength most likely comes from being rooted not in an abstract rational choice economic theory, but in a certain conception of life, living beings, and evolution. Thus, within this framework, the sustained political conflict between Lippmann and Dewey opens a breach into which it seems urgent to plunge to renew the question about the links between flux and stasis. What is it in the human species that lags and what makes it lag? Must we think that its inherent tendencies delay the industrial environment (Lippmann)? Isn't it rather the industrial environment itself—made sclerotic and degraded under the impact of capitalism and its relationships of domination—which holds back the potentialities of our species (Dewey)? In light of the conflict between Lippmann and Dewey, the negative assessment of lag itself must be problematized. Is all lag in itself a disqualification? Must we hope that all rhythms adjust and fall in line toward a gradual reform of the human species that moves in the direction of its own acceleration? Must we on the contrary not respect the irreducible rhythmic differences that structure all evolutionary history? The real question is to know if new liberalism is correct in wanting to liquefy all stases in the name of flux, or if the tension between flux and stasis—and with it the multiplication of delayed situations, tension, and conflict—is not constitutive of life itself. It is lastly to know how, under the second hypothesis, to rethink the political field so that it confronts not only the conflict of interests but also the divergence of the evolutionary rhythms that structure all living entities.

Whatever the response may be to these questions, one better understands how neoliberalism, based on a precise and powerful narrative about the meaning of evolution, has been able to monopolize both the discourse of reform and that of revolution, condemning its adversaries for either being reactionary or conserving its vested interests or having the nostalgic hope for return (of the welfare state, of the community, of self-sufficiency)—and confining them in any case to the faction of lag. Within this very particular political context, where the conflicts surrounding a democratic government of life and living beings have never been so intense, it is time to question the respective strengths of neoliberalism and American pragmatism in order to confront the tensions of evolution and to meditate on the lags of the human species. Are there, in this long-forgotten conflict of our recent history between pragmatism and neoliberalism, fertile and not yet explored political resources to construct another interpretation of the meaning of life and its evolutions?

1

Readapting the Human Species to the Great Society

The first book by Walter Lippmann, A *Preface to Politics*,[1] crystallizes the most innovative ideas in America at the time. The originality of the work consists in mobilizing the great currents of contemporary philosophical evolutionism— embodied in the 1910s by William James, Henri Bergson, and John Dewey— toward a complete renewal of political thought, itself inspired by what was called "American progressivism." To accomplish this transformation, Lippmann begins with what he calls "human nature" and questions linked to its evolution, taking inspiration from a renewed evolutionism clearly alternative to that which Herbert Spencer tried to impose on the social and political field throughout the second half of the nineteenth century. Because if Spencer's entire intellectual enterprise did indeed already consist in refounding political and social thought on the advances of evolutionary theory, it did so on false foundations. For the new philosophy that was being established in America, it was still a matter of a pre-Darwinian biology, encumbered with mechanistic presuppositions that wrongly postulate the submission of living beings to the laws of physics and chemistry, and with the teleological illusion consisting of fixing in advance the ultimate goal (*telos*) of the evolutionary process and thereby denying its radical unpredictability. These two large errors of Spencerism will become the explicit target of the evolutionisms of James, Bergson, and Dewey. With them, Lippmann will try to draw the moral, social, and political consequences of this renewed conception of the evolution of living beings in general and of the human species in particular.

The Spencerian Target

Spencer's first mistake was to seek, for these new philosophies of life and evo-lution, the physical and chemical foundations of the supposedly constant "laws" of evolution. Against the misleading expression "social Darwinism," which is completely unsuitable for understanding Spencerism, we must recall here that the Darwinian revolution, which precisely avoided such laws founded on a system of nature, bothered Spencer more than it inspired him. But the intel-lectual and scientific shock of *On the Origin of Species* was so powerful that Spencer was in some way constrained to make room for the Darwinian hy-pothesis of natural selection in his vast system of nature—for this idea according to which a sorting takes place afterward among the multiplicity of random variations surging within the living. *The Principles of Biology* tries hard to in-tegrate Darwin's hypothesis in the great Spencerian synthesis.[2] But for Spencer, this mode of explanation of the evolutionary process is incomplete. Alongside this indirect, selective, and eliminating mechanism, which he proposes renam-ing the "survival of the fittest," he wants above all to valorize the Lamarckian mechanisms by which living beings directly adapt to their environment by a progressive improvement of their faculties that he believes to be still transmis-sible to the following generations thanks to a supposed heredity of acquired characteristics.[3] These mechanisms lead him to defend a strict biological de-terminism, according to which exterior circumstances entirely determine the life of organisms—the latter being constrained to orient all their efforts toward a more and more suitable adaptation to the environment and toward a more and more strict submission to exterior conditions.

To this strict mechanism, which removes all margin of freedom, creativity, or resistance from organisms, Spencer adds a teleological dimension: "The con-tinuous adjustment of the vital activities to the activities in the environment must become more accurate and exhaustive,"[4] until it takes the shape, with the most civilized human species, of a global division of labor, oriented toward complete specialization and a flawless coordination of all the activities of in-dividuals. The unitary law of evolutionary process that Spencer intends to find, from inorganic matter to the most "civilized" societies, cannot therefore be that of selection, because what Spencer understands as the tautological affir-mation of a survival of the fittest and of an elimination of the unfit gives no overall coherent direction to the evolutionary process. In light of the much more encompassing law of the Spencerian system, that of the passing from an indefinite and incoherent homogeneity to a definite and coherent heterogeneity, the teleological end that orients all evolution can only be that of a perfect co-operation, industrial and peaceful, in the global division of labor. In light of such a telos, the torments of competition, with the elimination of the unfit and the selection of the fittest, belong rather to a process—certainly necessary, but transitory—in which Darwin was wrong to see the principal motor of evolution.

Starting from the 1880s, in a context of the return to grace of public policies and of the role of the state in England—notably under the impetus of the liberal politics of the Gladstone government (1868–74), which he criticizes very violently in *The Man versus the State*—Spencer's political theses began a long process of decline.[5] Exported to the United States, the Spencerian version of laissez-faire was notably diffused, in the 1910s, by the sociologist William Graham Sumner, who proposed assimilating, in a single "competition for life," economic competition and the biological survival of the fittest.[6] But this trivial version of Spencerism does not take account of Spencer's own critiques against the brutal—and to his eyes typically American—vision of competition. To the American exaltation of a "savage" competition, Spencer opposes the *telos* of a fully "civilized" industrial society, defined by the peaceful and voluntary cooperation of individuals and by the perfect integration of their activities in the division of labor. If competition is a necessary transition that the state must never hinder, the ultimate end of evolution consists in the peaceful cooperation of all the members of society, which the industrial revolution will achieve when it will have arrived at its point of completion. By "industry," Spencer means therefore something entirely other than a society ruled by the "savage" relationships of predation. He defines it on the contrary as a society of voluntary cooperation, won over by specialization and coordination, and in which all forms of struggle, competition, or conflict are called on to disappear.

But even in America, and even in this "civilized" version, Spencerism meets more and more resistance at the beginning of the twentieth century. First on the political front, it is confronted by a revalorization of voluntarism and of the role of the state—in the context of the rise in power of the "progressive" movement—that is increasingly critical of the harmful effects of the unequal concentration of wealth. Enlightened America no longer believes that laissez-faire in economic matters automatically establishes harmony, the equality of opportunities, and democratic freedoms. Under the impact of social and financial crises and multiplying corruption scandals in the great political "machines" denounced by the progressives, it is in the process of realizing that on the contrary, the American promise of democracy and freedom demands a collective regulation defined by the nation. To use the language of the time, it is in the process of understanding that Big Business demands Big Government. This increasingly dominant critique of this diffuse Spencerism will have a very profound influence on Lippmann, cofounder the following year, with Herbert Croly, of the great reformist newspaper *The New Republic*.

But in America, Spencer has not only become a political target. On the philosophical front, his great evolutionary system has equally become the systematic target of American pragmatists and of Bergson, whose theories are rapidly becoming popular with the American translation of *L'évolution créatrice* (*Creative Evolution*). Refuting at the same time Spencer's adaptative mechanism and his teleological conception of the evolutionary process, Bergson, James, and Dewey strive each in his fashion to elaborate a radically renewed thought about evolution—widely inspired by the advances of contemporary biology— that intends to definitively overtake the great Spencerian synthesis. Lippmann will be one of the first in America to try to draw major political consequences from this decline of Spencerism.

He will have been preceded on this path by the British political theorist Graham Wallas.[7] It was through the seminar that Wallas gave at Harvard in 1910 that Lippmann became acquainted with the necessity of refounding evolutionism in politics. And it is this decisive meeting with Wallas that encouraged him to attempt the innovative synthesis in his *Preface to Politics* between the new anti-Spencerian naturalisms of James, Bergson, and Dewey and the social and political field—itself also in full reconstruction under the impact of the first financial, social, and political crises engendered by the concentration of great industrial capitalism. With the refutation of Lamarckian biology on one side and the first crises of American industrial capitalism on the other, all was in place for political evolutionism to be rid of Spencer's illusions.

From Wallas's 1908 work entitled *Human Nature in Politics*, Lippmann first takes up the idea that contemporary political philosophy had completely forgotten about the study of human nature—which ultimately constituted the only valuable and interesting aspect of Spencer's evolutionism. Whereas the Ancients (from the Greeks until Machiavelli) belong to a realist tradition, having known to take into account the real nature of man, with its affects and its impulses, classical and contemporary political philosophy would have been built, starting from eighteenth-century liberalism, on an idealization of human nature in the service of rational and abstract principles of justice, liberty, and equality. Certainly, Wallas recognizes, there were major contemporary attempts to reinstate human nature in the political field, whether with the utilitarian psychology of Bentham or the evolutionary sociology of Spencer. But in his eyes, the profoundly unequal social consequences of these naturalisms made them lose all credit in the political field, which widely contributed "to discredit[ing] any attempt to connect political science with the study of human nature."[8]

For Wallas as for Lippmann, this simultaneously idealist and rationalist approach of the dominant political philosophy had ultimately always only looked to conserve a balance by stabilizing the cogs of the institutions. The Darwinian revolution involves definitively breaking with this static, conservative, and repetitive conception of politics, by opposing in a realist manner the dynamism of nature and of life to the abstract approach of the classical physical sciences, which still too often serve as the epistemological model in the social, economic, and political fields. Since everything evolves, including the human species and its environment, the guiding principle of politics in the future will no longer be the respect for mechanisms regulated by rational laws—nor the abstract idea of equality, liberty, or justice—but the dynamic reality of evolution. From here on, the challenge becomes knowing how to import the lessons of evolutionary theory into politics, so as to fully implement "the infusion of the 'evolutionary' point of view" in new political practices.[9]

The Pragmatist Influence

In addition to the profound influence of Graham Wallas on Lippmann's political thought, we also see that of the great American pragmatist philosophers William James and John Dewey. His biographer recounts that while Lippmann was still a student at Harvard, he had the honor of being invited every week by William James to take tea at his Irving Street residence, the student adhering unreservedly to the teacher's lessons on the value of experimentation in the social field.[10] The 1913 work bears the mark of these exchanges and adopts from James the idea that no "credo" has absolute value.[11] Being nothing but a temporary instrument that aims to adapt a human species in constant evolution, any idea—including a moral or religious one—is necessarily provisional. No more truths can boast of being eternal.

In his 1909 conference on "The Influence of Darwinism on Philosophy," John Dewey in turn tried hard to derive moral and political lessons from this new evolutionary approach to truth.[12] For Dewey as for Wallas, the goal is indeed to import Darwinian evolutionism into the political field, and on entirely different bases than those promoted by Spencer—which William James had already fought against in his *Principles of Psychology*.[13] By supporting a naturalist conception of the mind founded on the biological relationships between the organism and its environment, James and then Dewey place themselves certainly in part in the Spencerian heritage, which wanted to break definitively from the old rationalist psychology. But by showing that the organism does not submit passively to its environment, and that there is on the contrary between them a retroactive relationship, their continuist evolutionism has nothing more in common with the mechanistic reductionism of Spencer. They defend rather a naturalism of rupture and emergence, in which all evolutionary processes are necessarily unpredictable. From this ensues a major political conclusion. Far from being mechanical and passive, the adaptation of the human species to its environment, similarly, must by its nature be creative and interactive on the social and political front as well as the psychological front. No more than other living beings, the human species cannot mechanically adapt to an already given environment. It must on the contrary create and continually transform it to submit it to its own needs.

This both biological and political critique of Spencerian adaptation seems to be, at first view, taken up by Lippmann. The real statesmen, he warns us, must not be "creatures of environment, but creators of it."[14] It is "this power of being aggressively active towards the world which gives man a miraculous assurance that the world is something he can make," the government thus becoming the active watchman of a "process of continual creation, an unceasing invention of forms to meet constantly changing needs." If he does not cite Dewey's name here, the new approach to politics that Lippmann is defending, which insists on the instrumental character of government and on the active creation of new environments, seems at least partially borrowed from the instrumentalism of the Chicago School. Like Dewey and the Chicago pedagogues, Wallas and Lippmann are indeed waiting for the pedagogical revolution initiated by evolutionary theory and evolutionary psychology to inspire an equivalent rupture in the political field. But starting from this common point of departure, Lippmann is going to advance his own contribution to the evolutionary approach of politics through a theory of the sublimation of impulses which will lead him, in reality, to conclusions incompatible with pragmatist philosophy.

The first observation that Lippmann makes, in agreement with James and Dewey on this point, is that classical political philosophy has remained blind to the reality of impulses. If the history of political philosophy has indeed wanted to concede that the citizen was also a political animal, its fundamental mistake was to believe that "undomesticated impulses can be obliterated,"[15] and that they would thus make way for the civilizing action of education, morality, and life in society. It is on this illusion that the repressive arsenal of the law rested, functioning exclusively in the mode of "taboo."[16] Impulses and desires are however the only source of true energy our species has at its disposal.[17] As potentially creative as they are destructive, our desires in themselves are "neither good, nor bad." Having the explosive power of "dynamite," they are also the unique source of all power. Rather than seeking to eradicate them by the repressive action of discipline and law, the issue from then on is how to civilize them: "the assumption is that every lust is capable of a civilized expression." Adopting at the same time the Nietzschean critique of the moral condemnation of impulses and the Freudian notion of sublimation, Lippmann then proposes redefining political action, no longer by the repression of drives by the interdictions of the law but by their rerouting toward more elevated goals: "Instead of tabooing our impulses, we must redirect them. . . . The Freudian school of psychologists calls this 'sublimation.'"

To the Spencerian confidence in the mechanical advent of civilization through the dual action of competition and of cooperation and the combined biological action of selection and the transmission of acquired characteristics—which claims to provide a scientific guarantee for laissez-faire and the withdrawal of the state—Lippmann objects in favor of the necessity of a strong government which assumes an active and voluntarist politics of the sublimation of drives:

> The creative politician . . . devotes himself to inventing fine expressions for human needs, who recognizes that the work of statesmanship is in large measure the finding of good substitutes for the bad things we want. This is the heart of a political revolution.[18]

But the whole question from now on is to know *who* can become the political operator of such a sublimation. On whom will it fall to determine what are the "good substitutes"? And who can allow oneself to condemn as "bad" "the things that we want"? Must such an evaluation—responsible for reorienting the direction of impulses—take place in a horizontal mode, by the spontaneous action of citizens and their social interactions, as Dewey will later support in his analyses of the role of the public in democracy?[19] Or will it arise on the contrary from a vertical logic, the state having to decree from above what would be the "good substitutes," as Lippmann seems here to suggest? The question is ultimately to know how Lippmann manages to reconcile two incompatible influences: the pragmatist influence, which tends rather to valorize horizontal social experimentations, and a much more vertical conception of power founded on the excellence of experts.[20]

A comparison with the Deweyan theme of the sublimation of impulses can offer the first elements of a response. Like Lippmann, Dewey himself will also grant, in *Human Nature and Conduct*, a positive and creative role to impulses. Condemning the "prohibitions" of morality, he himself will also call for their sublimation:

> Any impulse . . . may be sublimated. . . . Such an outcome represents the normal and desirable functioning of impulse.[21]

But differing from Lippmann, Dewey does not conceive of impulse as a stable entity that has solidified itself through a long evolutionary history. He presents on the contrary the new impulse that surges from each newborn as a force of deviation, of rupture, and of renewal of the human species that has nothing in common with the programmatic rigidity of animal instinct:

> Impulses are the pivots upon which the re-organization of activities turn, they are agencies of deviation, for giving new directions to old habits.[22]

The difficulty of individuation through socialization—and in particular through education—is to keep open this tension between impulse, innovative and deviant by nature, and the necessity of stable and shared habits thanks to which the individual is incorporated in the existing social environment. Until now, the vertical and oligarchic structuration of our societies, which has almost always put into opposition the elite of the educators and the mass of the educated, has on the contrary most often produced a taming of impulses, constraining them to "docility" and to "compliance":[23]

> Individuals begin their career as infants. . . . [Their plasticity] seems putty to be molded according to current designs. That plasticity also means power to change prevailing customs is ignored.[24]

In reading this text by Dewey, one can legitimately wonder if the sublimation promoted by Lippmann avoids this authoritarian and vertical conception of the education of drives. From 1913 onward, it indeed seems that neither individuals nor their social interactions appear to Lippmann capable of producing this necessary sublimation of drives themselves. Instead of defending the horizontal logic of social interactions and of the collective intelligence that Dewey will support, Lippmann on the contrary promotes the vertical logic of an "expert" state:

> In order to fuse [public opinion] into a civilized achievement, [the statesman] will require much expert knowledge.[25]

It is therefore up to political leaders, and to them alone, to ensure the advent of civilization by sublimating from above the irrepressible and tainted drives of those they lead:

> Unless the reformer can invent something which substitutes attractive virtues for attractive vices, he will fail.[26]

"Sublimating" and not manipulating, because far from being determined by the arbitrary nature of its goodwill, the "good substitutes" imposed by the government must be founded on a true science of human nature that experts in the human and social sciences (evolutionary psychology, sociology, psycho-analysis, social and political psychology) are increasingly capable of providing:

> [The statesman] need not be a specialist himself, if only he is expert in choosing experts.[27]

While, according to Spencer, the advances of civilization were spontaneously accomplished by the law of evolution and the withdrawal of the state, they now occur, according to Lippmann, through the artifices of government and ex-pertise—coinciding with the return of the state, as much in England as in America, in the economic and social field. Formulating since his first book the diagnosis of a bad natural orientation of drives that he imagines frozen by evolutionary history, Lippmann is already calling for a profound transformation of the human species by the government of experts. Thus, in this face-off be-tween Spencerian laissez-faire and the return of a strong government, a third path has been left aside: that of social transformation by collective intelligence, which Dewey will set against Lippmann's political propositions—first on de-mocracy, then on new liberalism—for nearly two decades.

The Government of Experts, between Fabian Socialism and New Liberalism

In his valorization of expertise, Lippmann adopts the ideas of the Fabian So-ciety—of which his teacher Graham Wallas had been, at the end of the pre-ceding century, an active member. Lippmann's biographer opportunely recalls that what had at the beginning attracted him toward Fabian socialism was less the passion for justice and equality than the necessity of administrating society better.[28] It is this anti-Spencerian conviction radically hostile to laissez-faire that explains his initial attraction to the Fabians with their statistics, their very detailed programs, and their insistence on a "leadership from the top." Since no "law of evolution" mechanically leads us to civilization, society must be organized and planned by relying on the "scientific method." Lippmann cer-tainly demands reform, a "radical constructive program," in his own words; but from the beginning, he remains convinced that this program can only come "from the top," liberated from the interference of the masses.[29] For the Fabian socialism that emerged in the 1880s, at the time of the complexification of social relationships by the industrial revolution, only an elite of experts can indeed—through gradual reforms coming from "the top"—lead the citizen masses toward enlightened goals.[30] These new options reflect the rise in power of the role of the social sciences with the governing classes and their increasingly close collusion with power in the figure of the "expert," whose political role Lippmann constantly amplifies in his subsequent works.

The challenge for Lippmann from then on will be reconciling his attachment to the Fabian program of a government of drives by experts with the Bergsonian and liberal critique of all forms of planning of the social order by the tools of intelligence—as expert as they may be. Disqualifying all planning ambition, the "creative evolution" described by Bergson enjoins us, according to Lippmann, to a permanent innovation that is not only personal and intimate but also social and political.[31] This valorization of innovation as open evolution, radically unpredictable and thwarting any form of planning by intelligence, later constitutes for him the heart of liberal thought, which must remain the cardinal principle of the new government. But how can he extol this creative evolution that he ties to liberalism and promote at the same time a centralized government of drives of the human species that is led from a vertical conception of "good" and "bad" that only the intelligence of experts would be able to grasp? Is the political ambition of his first political philosophy essay to rehabilitate, beyond good and evil, the drive-based energy of the human species (Nietzsche) and its creative evolution (Bergson) against the multisecular intellectualist error of political philosophy? Does it not rather have the opposite political project of placing the totality of human life and its evolution under the yoke of intelligence and of the science of experts?

The pragmatist Lippmann from the 1910s, liberal and Bergsonian, thus seems to oscillate between two incompatible options; and through them, between two contradictory conceptions of evolution. For the first option, faithful to Wallas and very close to what Dewey will support, evolution in politics implies the interactive creation of new environments that favor the deployment of the new potentialities that each citizen bears within him. Here, evolution is understood as a laboratory of experimentations, whose unfolding is at the same time open, unpredictable, and branching. For the second option, which will progressively turn out to be incompatible with the conceptions that Wallas and Dewey have of evolution, the interactions freely taking place within the public are incapable of going in the right direction. The creation of new environments favoring the growth of life must be entrusted to the will of the leaders enlightened by the science of experts—which it would be totally illusory to want to disseminate to average citizens who are structurally lagging in regard to the new evolutions. Here, evolution implies a takeover of the governed by the governing to be better able to grasp the meaning and the goal of evolution and to accomplish the readaptation of the human species to its new environment.

But the challenge from then on will be knowing what can indeed survive, with this new government of life and living beings that Lippmann is appealing for, of the liberal idea and the democratic model.

Readapting the Human Species to the Great Society

In 1914, Graham Wallas pays important critical tribute to Lippmann's first book. By dedicating his new book, *The Great Society*, to him, Wallas is clearly heralding the theories of his former student. But he is also hinting at their limits. The critique of the intellectualist postulates of political science, in which he himself had engaged in *Human Nature in Politics* and which Lippmann had amplified by referring to Freud, Nietzsche, and Bergson, calls for, as an indispensable counterpoint, a reconstruction of society by human intelligence.[32]

In Wallas's new book, Lippmann finds the theme of his 1910 seminar at Harvard: that of the "Great Society" created by the industrial revolution. For Wallas, the Great Society corresponds to a completely new situation in the evolution of the living which entails thoroughly reexamining the principles that have guided political philosophy up to the present. With the extraordinary change of scale of our living environments induced by the industrial revolution, our species—until now characterized like all others by the adaptation of its inner dispositions to the external stimuli of the environment—finds itself completely maladapted to its surroundings:

> In the Great Society the original stimuli to which our dispositions
> were adapted by the course of evolution have largely disappeared,
> and inappropriate stimuli have often taken their place.[33]

The mechanization produced by the scientific revolution indeed definitively broke the adaptative, slow, and gradual logic of evolution described by Darwin, and which still prevailed in the first forms of political communities—for example, at the time when the Greeks invented the City, and among the possible political systems, the democratic City. With the industrial revolution, the marvelous adaptation between the living and their environment gave way to a seemingly irresolvable conflict between the human species and its environment. Instead of being, as Aristotle recommended in *Politics*, a political animal perfectly adapted to the size of its city, the citizen of the Great Society finds himself completely overwhelmed by his new environment so that he is no longer even capable, not only of knowing or of understanding, but of simply perceiving.

And so once political thought has gotten rid of the intellectualist illusions of political science, elevating a priori each citizen to a rational and omniscient subject, and once it has accepted the need to take into account the evolutionary upheaval of the human species that the industrial age produced under its eyes, how can it contribute toward overcoming this pathological situation of maladaptation? This is the new political question that Wallas intends to address in *The Great Society*.

Wallas, in turn, starts from Spencer's response, which had at least the merit of asking the question in terms of evolution and adaptation. But this is to immediately remind us that the Lamarckian and mechanistic response to which Spencerism had contributed in popularizing during the second half of the nineteenth century had just been brutally challenged by contemporary biology. The recent discoveries of genetics, by denying the possibility of heredity of acquired characteristics, had definitively ruined the biological bases of the Spencerian system.[34] While Spencer believed in a mechanical and continual process of adaptation, the gap between our biological heritage, frozen by a very slow evolutionary history, and the extremely rapid transformation of our environment created a situation that was rigorously opposite to that described by his system. This new situation, bringing profound unprecedented crises, was that of a complete maladaptation between the human species and its industrial environment.

Expanding on the program that was already his own in *Human Nature and Politics*, that of a naturalist reconstruction of political science, Wallas proposes in turn an evolutionary response, itself founded on the notion of adaptation. But breaking with Spencer, he profoundly transforms the concept by highlighting its duality. Adaptation can indeed have a dual meaning: "either to educate in each generation their faculties to fit their environment, or to change their environment so as to fit their faculties."[35]

The duality of the concept of adaptation comes from the fact that it can be understood in a passive or active mode. To overcome the maladaptation of the human species in the Great Society, two very different adaptative solutions present themselves to us. The first consists in modifying "from the top" the dispositions of our species: whether by education—but that implies, if we take account of the non-heredity of acquired characteristics, restarting the effort with "each generation"; or by a eugenical politics aiming to better adapt the species to its new environment.[36] In the two cases, adaptation takes, for the human masses, a strictly passive meaning. The human species is considered as a malleable material that one can adapt without resistance to the new demands of the Great Society. But a second solution can consist on the contrary in modifying the environment itself in order to make it more adequate to the native dispositions of our species:

The main task of civilization is, therefore, to produce a new environment whose stimulation of our existing dispositions shall tend towards a good life.[37]

Here, it is no longer the existing dispositions of the species that must be modified from above. It is on the contrary, in a complete break with Spencer, who identified industry as the ultimate *telos* of evolution, the new *stimuli* created by industrial society that are declared "inappropriate" to our dispositions. Instead of producing new dispositions, and further, a new human species, it is rather about creating a "new environment" for the "existing dispositions" of our species that is more adapted to the current state of its evolution. Readaptation to the Great Society such as Wallas understands it does not therefore lead to disqualifying, as Lippmann does, the native dispositions of the human species and its supposed deficiencies. It implies on the contrary an active and creative conception of adaptation, which occurs through a transformative critique of industrial environments.

In relation to *Human Nature in Politics*, which focuses on the intellectualist mistakes of classical political science (raising the citizen to a rational subject or a calculating machine), Wallas's second book insists on the crucial role of thought and of collective intelligence—essential in his eyes for readapting environments to the needs of our species.[38] By becoming organized, thought is indeed capable of modifying the social and political organization of the Great Society and, in this precise meaning, of creating a "new environment." On the political front, the creation of this new environment can consist for example in reducing the size of representative bodies (parliaments, municipal councils, steering committees) to favor democratic deliberation in a context where oral interactions between individuals are threatened by extinction and where public opinion is more and more often produced by the "passive reading" of newspapers.[39] By insisting on the necessary interaction between the human species and its environment, which occurs through the cooperation of minds and the intensification of deliberation, it is a question of refusing the idea of a species that is malleable at will—mechanically adapting itself without resistance to the needs of industrial society.

Without waiting, Lippmann will respond to Wallas's objections by publishing in that same year a second book entitled *Drift and Mastery*.[40] Following Wallas on the one hand, he also insists on the necessity of introducing more democratic interaction in industrial society by notably promoting the rise in power of unions in big industry, a sine qua non condition of a real democratization of America.[41] Regarding the preceding work, the call for science no longer only leads to an elite of experts. It also implies a collective cooperation, deliberative and democratic, functioning in the mode of collective experimentation and of pragmatic testing, which can seem very close to what Dewey calls on his side "inquiry":

> You have to create an industrial education by which the worker shall be turned, not into an intelligent machine, but into an understanding, directing partner of business. You have to encourage the long process of self-education in democracy through which unions can develop representative government and adequate leadership. . . .
> . . . It is of necessity an educational process, a work of invention, of cooperative training.[42]

By placing the accent on education and cooperation, Lippmann also recalls, following the pragmatism of James and Dewey, the intrinsic limitations of all forms of knowledge and power:

> Anything like a central authority to guide us has become impossible because no authority is wise enough, because self-government has become a really effective desire.[43]

In the situation of "drift" created by the crisis of absolutes and traditions, but also by the epistemological fallibilism which claims that no science can ever attain definitive certitude, the only guide that can give us back a certain "mastery" over events is precisely science—but understood anew, as a collective work of cooperation and pragmatic testing through experimentation: "Mastery, whether we like it or not, is an immense collaboration."[44] It is this antipositivist and democratic conception of science, cleared of all pretension toward the absolute or omniscience, insists Lippmann, that can alone allow something like a "self-government":

> Rightly understood science is the culture under which people can live forward in the midst of complexity, and treat life not as something given but as something to be shaped. . . .
> There is nothing accidental then in the fact that democracy in politics is the twin-brother of scientific thinking. They had to come together. As absolutism falls, science arises. It *is* self-government.[45]

But alongside this call for a democratization of industrial society by pragmatic testing and scientific inquiry, which can seem very close to the social conceptions of Wallas, James, and Dewey, Lippmann conducts in this same work a very severe critique of the politics of American democrats who, from Thomas Jefferson to Woodrow Wilson, always looked to favor the small scale of political deliberation against the large collective groups of industrial society, then of Big Business.[46] We must recall here that this debate between an industrial America of large groups, with rather federalist options, and a more democratic America of small rural communities, opposed to the federal model, has divided American political thought since the Founding Fathers. In light of this context, the arguments of *Drift and Mastery* reveal themselves to be in reality very removed from the Democratic preoccupations of Wallas and much more profoundly influenced by the "New Nationalism" of Herbert Croly—which the former Republican president Theodore Roosevelt was trying at the same time to embody in a program of industrial politics, incidentally in part elaborated by Lippmann himself.[47] Because when we look at it more closely and when we return it to its political context, Lippmann's plea in favor of trade unions must not be understood, any more than the New Nationalism of Roosevelt, who was himself favorable to union leadership, as a call for the emancipation of the workers. We must rather see in it a plea in favor of the concentration of power by leaders, capitalism having everything to gain in being administered, not only by the leaders of enterprises informed by experts, but also by the most enlightened union representatives from the mass of union members.

What must be struggled against is the incurable nostalgia of Democrats for small associations—those of rural communities, small cities, and small businesses, where democracy is supposed to be fulfilled simultaneously by free deliberation, the equality of opportunities, and fair competition between small entrepreneurs—a political ideal we find perfectly summarized in the "New Freedom" program brought forth by the future Democratic president Woodrow Wilson, elected the following year against Roosevelt. To these democratic and liberal illusions, Lippmann counters—with Herbert Croly and Theodore Roosevelt, but also with the Fabian socialists—that not only the "Great Society" but also the industrial concentration of Big Business are inevitable from now on, and that it is useless to try to overcome them through nostalgic fantasies driven by "resentment."[48] Rather than dreaming of a return to original small democratic communities (Jefferson) and dismantling trusts for the profit of small business (Sherman Act, 1890), the only possible political response occurs through the regulation of large industrial capitalism by a strong government that simultaneously imposes dialogue with unions, the management of large enterprises by an enlightened elite, and the definition of the public good by science. What it is countering is ultimately the ensemble of the convictions of the Democratic Party:

> The Democratic Party is by tradition opposed to a strong central government, and that opposition applies equally well to strong national

business,—it is a party attached to local rights, to village patriotism, to humble but ambitious enterprise; its temper has always been hostile to specialization and expert knowledge, because it admires a very primitive man-to-man democracy.[49]

To the spontaneous and bucolic liberal democracy of the Democrats, Lippmann aims to oppose an entire other form of democracy and of "self-government," paradoxically led by the power of experts. Such is the dominant editorial line of the new newspaper *The New Republic*, which Croly and Lippmann launch in November of 1914 at the same time *Drift and Mastery* appears. This new political line complicates again the difficulties which *A Preface to Politics* was struggling with one year earlier. Because it is still defending an open and creative evolution, favoring innovation and the emergence of the new, does the 1914 call for a strong, centralized, and planning government with more and more antiliberal accents not risk fixing in advance what was opening toward the future? Do the science, collective intelligence, and cooperation that are supposed to ensure a political "mastery" of evolution have the vocation of diffusing and transforming themselves through all social interactions in a democracy such as Dewey understands it? Do they not rather sanction a new power: the power of experts and of specialists, enlightening that of the leaders, to be diffused to the governed from above? The question is ultimately knowing if Lippmann will manage to reconcile this new power of experts, which he hopes will indefinitely increase its grip on the human species, and the liberal affirmation of government limits—the guarantors of a free and creative evolution whose meaning and goal no one can boast of knowing in advance.

2

A Darwinian Democracy

Lippmann's political thought thus oscillates between two profoundly incompatible directions. According to the first path, the evolution of the human species in the era of the Great Society demands an active reorganization of its environment, which can only occur through an intensification of democratic processes of inquiry and collective experimentation. Understood from this angle, his evolutionism appears very close to both the pragmatist conception of democracy and the way that Dewey articulates it with Darwinism's provisions. But according to the second, the same evolution demands a massive readaptation of the human species, led from above by the expertise of leaders, and removed in principle from citizen control. In the 1920s, this ambivalence will be initially settled by Lippmann in favor of the second way. This first period will lead him to a direct critique of democracy, constituting the point of departure of what will be called in the United States, beginning in the 1990s, the "Lippmann-Dewey debate."[1]

But it remains to be seen how the Lippmannian critique of the democratic model could lead at a later stage to a new theory of democracy, a sort of "neo-democracy" that allows for Lippmann to remain within the American political tradition. This new political model will rapidly raise questions similar to those that "neoliberalism" will create a decade later. With this new conception of democratic practice, are the founding principles of liberalism and democracy reinforced or on the contrary weakened? A second difficulty is added to this first one: If Lippmann so clearly chose this second path against the first, that of directing evolution from above—which is incompatible with an evolution that is branching, multidirectional, and unpredictable—how can we understand his continuing to refer not only to evolutionary theory in general but to Darwinism in particular when rethinking democracy?

Before responding to these questions, one must recall that Lippmann's leaning in favor of the second path is explained in part by the historical context. Between the 1910s and the 1920s, World War I traumatized the global intellectual community. With its procession of destructions and massacres at an industrial scale, it shook not only the Spencerian and Victorian faith in the movement of evolution and industry that had survived from the nineteenth century but also the perspectives on the future opened up by the progressive critique of Big Business at the beginning of the twentieth century. With the extraordinary explosion of state propaganda, it had notably weakened the confidence of citizens in democracies in the long term by showing how public opinion could be manipulated. This context, which must be revisited before proceeding, explains in part the original divergence between Lippmann's and Dewey's political thought. Beyond the Lippmann-Dewey debate, it partially clarifies the nascent conflict, which begins to appear in the 1920s, between the new liberalism that will take shape during the 1930s and American pragmatism.

The Postwar Context: The Failure of Wilsonian Democracy

In 1914, war explodes in Europe. The candidate who had ardently supported Lippmann, the former Republican president Theodore Roosevelt, has lost in the 1912 elections, and it is the Democrat Woodrow Wilson who has been elected. Thanks to the expansion of the conflict in Europe, and as a result of the highly influential editorials that he edits at *The New Republic*, Lippmann will however manage to get close to the newly elected president, eventually assuming a very influential position at the summit of power, which he will then hold on and off during the entire history of the twentieth century. From 1915 onward, he defends the position of breaking with the Monroe Doctrine—according to which the United States should isolate itself unless its national interests in the narrowest sense of the term are attacked—and of the resolute entry of America into the war with the goal of imposing peace and democracy on all the nations. Like many other progressives, of whom John Dewey is in the first ranks, Lippmann supports entering the war in the name of the democratic principles embodied by America.

Having won the confidence of one of Wilson's closest counselors, "Colonel" House, Lippman finds himself entrusted, when the United States finally enters the war in 1917, with the coordination of an office responsible for elaborating American foreign policy.[2] He is successful in gathering around him about a hundred experts—specialized essentially in the human and social sciences (economics, history, geography, psychology, etc.)—who have as their mission to broadly sketch out the postwar world in which America will be called on to play a central role: that of the leader of the free world. It is within this framework that Lippmann enters History by contributing to the writing of President Wilson's "Fourteen Points," which will be responsible for summarizing the American vision for exiting the conflict. Must we see in this experience a first form of this government of experts that he has called for since his *Preface to Politics*, and that he will soon directly oppose to the democratic conception of inquiry defended by pragmatists such as Dewey? Is this the symptom of Lippmann's already antidemocratic convictions? Or does this attest on the contrary to his attachment to democracy, which the president wants to embody in front of the world?

The response to this question is still as unclear as before the war. On the one hand, it can be said that in continuity with his prewar progressive and liberal convictions, Lippmann wanted to reform American foreign policy by reconstructing it on an ambitious democratic ideal that openly extended the traditional domain of the exercise of democracy into new territories, moving from the closed society of the Nation-State to an open and globalized Great Society, reenvisioned as a "League of Nations" directed by the rule of law. Like John Dewey, Lippmann moreover quickly mobilized the same year against the attempted imposition of a restriction of liberties by the official war propaganda led by George Creel, the famous director of the Committee on Public Information (CPI).[3] Profoundly democratic and liberal, Dewey and Lippmann firmly reminded that the war was entered in order to promote democracy in the world and not to threaten it in America by jeopardizing public freedoms. The name that Lippmann's work group adopted, "the Inquiry," was not without an evocation of certain lines of thought sketched by Dewey, for whom the concept of "inquiry" implies a massive participation of the human and social sciences in political deliberation. In this context, we can better understand how Lippmann might go so far as to propose to Dewey himself that he direct a branch of the Inquiry in Moscow.[4]

But on the other hand, we can also consider that the weight given to experts by the war started a new form of power that would go in strictly the opposite direction from what Dewey expects of the democratic experience. Does not the confidential character of the work of the experts, taking place in secret and outside of all democratic control, lead straight to the "manufacture of consent"[5] of public opinions through propaganda techniques? And is it not precisely in continuation of this experience that Lippmann would soon be invited to work on a new form of propaganda that is independent from and competing with the Committee on Public Information directed by George Creel?

For Lippmann, at this point, the response arrives through the distinction between good and bad propaganda. If he accepted this mission, it was because it was not according to him "propaganda . . . in the sinister sense," but a "campaign of education addressed to the German and Austrian troops" aiming to explain the high and selfless character of the American war goals.[6] Going to Europe with a captain's rank, Lippmann thus indeed led his "propagandist" mission by inundating the German territories with leaflets calling for desertion and by conducting interviews with prisoners at the front. For the author of *A Preface to Politics*, it was an unlooked-for occasion to attempt to apply his own political hypotheses by trying to "sublimate" the drives of the enemy troops into "good substitutes" redefined by the experts. But was not the Creel commission, in its propaganda for American public opinions, also inspired by excellent intentions? And in these conditions, does not the directing of public opinion through good propaganda devised by competent experts, like that which America was experimenting with thanks to the war, provide the best model to follow in matters of government, even during peacetime?

At the time of the great Paris Peace Conference (1919), which was responsible for negotiating peace between the parties, his role as propagandist would lead Lippmann into a direct rivalry with George Creel. Intent on claiming personal glory from the end of the war, President Wilson made his entrance into Paris with a thousand counselors, who were incompetent for the most part and created immense confusion during the negotiations. Lippmann's hitherto strongly positive perception of the impact of propaganda on democracy suddenly turned into the exact opposite. All the work of the "Inquiry" and the "Fourteen Points" was trampled on by the incompetence of the official "experts." To please the Allies, the Treaty of Versailles organized the systematic and long-term humiliation of Germany by the victors. For Lippmann, this sealed the stinging failure of America's engagement in the war and preluded a period of "endless trouble for Europe"[7] —a premonitory vision shared by numerous observers at the time.

Offset from its contemporary representation, which presents the American entry into the war as the beginning of its glorious leadership of the world, the 1920s thus began in immense disillusionment. The war had been pointless, the idealist politics of Wilson lamentably failed, and the most conservative movements were triumphing. The Red Scare created by the October Revolution; the rise of the Ku Klux Klan, encouraged by the cinema of D. W. Griffith; and Prohibition, which advocated the return of censorship and moral order, were spreading throughout America. In the Europe that Lippmann was exhaustively touring at the beginning of the 1920s for his new newspaper, *The World*, democratic countries like Italy were rapidly slipping into authoritarian regimes. For Lippmann, these frightening phenomena were an invitation to reexamine our ideas, and among them, the democratic credo that the citizen is competent to participate in public affairs. In his eyes, the political shipwreck of democracies demonstrated entirely the opposite.

The Cave and Stereotypes

One of the works by Lippmann still most influential today—*Public Opinion*, which appeared in 1922—bears the mark of this profound distrust of democracy. It is in this spirit that the book opens with a long quotation from Plato, drawn from the allegory of the cave.[8] Human beings are presented here as prisoners—"by their own nature," Plato specifies—of their frozen and partial perceptions of reality.[9] Chained by nature, their perceptions are condemned to fixedness ("they cannot move," "they can never move their head"), which makes them incapable of perceiving reality in its entirety. This insurmountable fixedness of human perceptions makes up the essential content of the famous concept of "stereotype" popularized by *Public Opinion*.[10] With this neologism, Lippmann argues that our cognitive capacities are condemned to produce a fixed idea (*stereos*) of reality. Inverting the basic meaning of the Plato quotation, for which the permanent reality of Ideas holds itself above the flux of becoming, Lippmann amplifies his initial argument about the human species lagging behind the flux of events. On account of its evolutionary history and before even the emergence of the Great Society, the human species—understanding nothing of the moving nature of reality—is locked into stereotypic stases that condemn it to a structural lag regarding the always new and arriving flux. The maladaptation diagnosed by Wallas finds here its anthropological and naturalist roots. With the accumulation of stereotypes that its "nature" pushes it to produce, the structural lag of the human species behind the flux of events can only get worse in the era of the Great Society.

The second idea that Lippmann draws from Plato is that the production of stereotypes is at the same time natural and artificial. Natural in the sense that as it is inscribed within the nature of our species, it immediately gives rise to an artificial image factory, to a collective production of fictions that is evoked in Plato by the metaphor of the performance led by the sophists with its figurative images and its "screen."[11] For Lippmann, the recent experience that the entire world has just lived through with war propaganda gives a perfect illustration of the Platonic metaphor. Exploiting the stereotyped nature of the representations of the average man, national propaganda succeeded everywhere in imposing, thanks to the artifices of the great entertainment industry and to the invention of cinema, its own stereotypes on the populations.

But if Lippmann makes use of certain elements of the allegory, he completely distorts their meaning. This explains how the entire end of the story told by Plato—which describes opinion exiting toward the light of Ideas—does not figure either in the excerpt from Plato or in the rest of the work. This excision of the ending from the allegory can be explained by the fact that *Public Opinion* continues to maintain, against Platonic idealism and in line with pragmatist evolutionism, that our ideas are always simply fictions that are both provisional and necessary for our adaptation to the environment.[12] Among these necessary fictions, stereotypes are the fictive stabilizations collectively produced by cultures to guide people in what William James called the "great blooming, buzzing confusion" of reality.[13] Incapable of grasping reality in its newness and its fluidity, and responsible on the contrary for projecting a fictive stability in the flux of the real, stereotypes are by definition fixed (*stereos*). Obeying the logic of miniaturization of maps and patterns, these collective fictions are nevertheless essential for the finite capacities of perception and attention in the human species:

> The need of economizing attention is so inevitable, that the abandonment of all stereotypes for a wholly innocent approach to experience would impoverish human life.[14]

Beyond the reference to pragmatism, it is this interpretation of attention as a scarce resource—whose economy must be thought of in the sense of sparing and parsimonious management—which provides the anthropological base of Lippmann's political thought. Considered in terms of deficiency and lag, the defective nature of the human species formally denies the metaphysical illusions of Platonic idealism. But it also questions the confidence of a pragmatist like Dewey in the potentialities of the human species in general, and in its political competencies in particular. By distorting the original meaning of Plato's allegory, it takes aim at the persistence of the metaphysical idealism attached to all democratic political models, which is founded on the omniscience of the citizen-subject and on the supposed wisdom of popular will. In the history of American pragmatism, Lippmann's supposedly "realist" objection will play a fundamental stimulating role, forcing Dewey to make a philosophical demonstration of a democratic ideal freed from metaphysical idealism. This will be the task, a few years later, of his great political philosophy book, *The Public and Its Problems*.[15]

In 1922, Lippmann has thus overcome his earlier hesitations, assuming from now on a direct critique of the democratic model:

> Democracy in its original form never seriously faced the problem which arises because the pictures inside people's heads do not automatically correspond with the world outside.[16]

"The original dogma of democracy"—denying that the stases of our species produced by the political imagination lag behind the flux of the real world—affirmed on the contrary that "the knowledge needed for the management of human affairs comes up spontaneously from the human heart."[17] If metaphysics is built on the fiction of having an adequate grasp of things in themselves through the intellect (*adaequatio rei et intellectus*), contemporary political philosophy would be built, with the democratic ideal, on the parallel fiction of a spontaneous adequation between the representations of the citizen and the reality of the citizen's environment.

But how could such a fiction have been established while the reality of maladjustment only became worse under the pressure of our environment's globalization? For Lippmann, this is explained by the fact that democracy in its original form, which was born in Greece and which was then theorized by Aristotle, tried hard to limit the environment of the citizen to a small scale, imposing stasis and enclosure on the shifting environment that was also in the process of growing larger:

> The only image of democracy that would work, even in theory, was one based on an isolated community of people whose political faculties were limited, according to Aristotle's famous maxim, by the range of their vision.[18]

To deny all gaps between the flux of the real world and the stases of opinion, the Greek theories of democracy arbitrarily reduce the sphere of politics to the small scale of the perceived world: that of a City-State, the most autarkic possible regarding the rest of the world and where all public affairs are debated in one *agora*, accessible to all citizens and their capacities of perception. In a very coherent way, it is this autarkic conception of the City that is next found again in the modern theories of democracy; and particularly in the praise of Thomas Jefferson—whom the American political imagination regards as an ancestor of contemporary democrats—for the small rural communities of Virginia:

> Jefferson was right in thinking that a group of independent farmers comes nearer to fulfilling the requirements of spontaneous democracy than any other human society. . . . Jefferson drew all [the] logical conclusions. He disapproved of manufacture, of foreign commerce, . . . of any form of government that was not centered in the small self-governing group.[19]

For Lippmann, all of this explains the native hostility of democrats against the warning signs of the industrial revolution, urbanization, and the emergence of the Great Society—all symbolized by "manufacturing." It also explains why they have always valorized the bucolic countermodel of an independent and autarkic life, immersed in a wild nature still untouched by the detrimental effects of industrialization:

> When [the democrat] could not find these conditions in the real world, he went passionately into the wilderness, and founded Utopian communities far from foreign contacts. His slogans reveal his preju- dice. He is for Self-Government, Self-Determination, Independence. . . . The field of democratic action is a circumscribed area. Within protected boundaries the aim has been to achieve self-sufficiency.[20]

The problem, however, stems from the fact that this model is defined through its denial of what Lippmann considers on the contrary, like Graham Wallas, as inevitable: the brutal acceleration, in the industrial era, of the progressive expansion of the environment of the human species up until the emergence of a Great Society.

This expansion, if it was initiated by the science and technology of ancient times, was at a much more modest scale in the beginning when it was still possible to artificially counter it through the stases and enclosures of the City-State. But the industrial revolution, which began to loom in the second half of the eighteenth century, went much further. Forcing all political communities into interdependence, it compelled the human species to adjust its social and political environment to the scale of the world. What Wallas had not under-stood in 1914, and what Lippmann tries to highlight in 1922, is that such a change of scale, because it profoundly contradicts the original model of de-mocracy, which is organically linked to enclosure and stability from the Greeks (Aristotle) to the Enlightenment (Jefferson), must necessarily lead to a crisis of the democratic ideal. That when the new political environment takes on the dimensions of a globalized flux, all the democratic stases and enclosures are mechanically disqualified:

> The democratic tradition is therefore always trying to see a world where people are exclusively concerned with affairs of which the causes and effects all operate within the region they inhabit. Never has democratic theory been able to conceive itself in the context of a wide and unpre- dictable environment.[21]

The new political environment that the industrial revolution imposes— perpetually changing, complex, and unpredictable—definitively deprives the people of their sovereignty, and with it the validity of the traditional democratic model. But according to Lippmann, does this mean we are finished with democracy in general? With the observation of an ineluctable crisis in the Greek democratic model, and then of the Jeffersonian "matrix,"[22] is the democratic ideal definitively disqualified in his eyes by globalization? Or does he intend, on the contrary, following the Wilsonian effort, to attempt to refound it on new bases that are compatible with the economic, social, and political globalization of our environment?

Lippmannian Neodemocracy: From the Government of Experts to the Manufacture of Consent

The response to this is announced in the introduction of *Public Opinion*. The direct critique of the democratic model is immediately relayed there by a reconstruction of the model on a double base, at the same time elective and elitist:

> I argue that representative government, either in what is ordinarily called politics, or in industry, cannot be worked successfully, no matter what the basis of election, unless there is an independent, expert organization for making the unseen facts intelligible to those who have to make the decisions.[23]

In place of the traditional democratic model, which gives political sovereignty to the people, Lippmann substitutes a new form of democracy, where an elective base certainly remains, but where sovereignty is henceforth entirely shared by representatives and an "independent" organization of experts who are responsible for informing the decision-makers. In this respect, there is nothing in reality very new in this model, as it extends that of traditional representative democracy and its well-known difficulties—namely, how can the people (*dēmos*) be represented without its representatives confiscating its power (*kratos*) or its sovereignty in the name of their virtue or their knowledge? The newness of the model promoted here by Lippmann comes from no longer even asking this question. Representative government must on the contrary embody a clean break from those it represents, in terms of both power and knowledge.[24] Representatives must especially not resemble the mass of the represented—who are structurally ignorant and incapable of enlightened decision. Decisions must be made at an entirely other level that circumvents in principle all democratic control: that of the transmission of knowledge by nonelected experts, who avoid all elective validation, to the power of the leaders in a systematic short-circuiting of popular sovereignty.

Numerous commentators have already underlined this difficulty by insisting on the failing of democratic legitimacy in this new power of experts.[25] To this political difficulty is added, for many among them, a question of an epistemological order. For what preserves the experts and leaders themselves from the production of stereotypes and allows them to be excepted from the condition of the human species? For Lippmann, the only true privilege of leaders, whatever their limits may be, comes from being able to test their own fictions on a larger scale. This mobility of action pushes them to revise their own stereotypes by noting that what "actually happens" does not always correspond to what they "imagined."[26] When put to the test, there is always a moment where "the blind spots come from the edge of vision into the center,"[27] where the obscurity that grips each stereotype by its edges tries to reach the center of the image itself. Thus, for example, the optimistic stereotype of Spencerian evolution, which may have been useful in accounting for the industrial revolution, became completely blinding when it was a question of understanding the more negative aspects of "maladjustment" between the human species and its new environment. It is this confrontation between action and its retroactive effects on the fabric of fictions which founds, in Lippmann's eyes, the privilege of the leader, who is defined as a man of action in the public opinion—which contents itself just with thinking and feeling. But for Lippmann, this privilege can only be fully exercised on condition that it is allied with that of the researcher. Researchers alone can help leaders replace a long continuation of stereotypes, where the most recent supplants the older ones, by an entirely different form of fiction or pattern that is much more supple and adaptable to the mobile environment of the Great Society. Adopting again the lesson of the pragmatists, Lippmann considers that the testable hypotheses of science are the only patterns that allow one to avoid the fixedness of stereotypes. They alone have the necessary flexibility to keep up with the increasingly changing and vast new environment of the human species.[28]

This new alliance that Lippmann promotes between leaders and scientific experts leads *Public Opinion* to redefine democracy on entirely new bases that involve a pure and simple suspension of the question of the source of sovereignty. Adopting the pragmatist critique of the search for causality, origin, and source, Lippmann demands that we evaluate democracy in a pragmatic fashion—by its "effects" rather than by its causes, and by its "results" rather than by its source: "the democratic fallacy has been its preoccupation with the origin of government rather than with the processes and results."[29] According to him, it is the growth of the quality of life of populations and of its standards, which moreover must be regularly evaluated by an "audit,"[30] and not the capacity of a people to freely govern itself, which defines a good democratic government that is both effective and pragmatic. It is in this precise sense that democracy must aim toward "human dignity":

> If, instead of hanging human dignity on the one assumption about self-government, you insist that man's dignity requires a standard of living, in which his capacities are properly exercised, the whole problem changes. The criteria which you then apply to government are whether it is producing a certain minimum of health, of decent housing, of material necessities, of education, of freedom, of pleasures, of beauty.[31]

Foucault demonstrated that liberalism had not stopped trying to preserve these two paths simultaneously since the eighteenth century: on the one hand, that of the biopolitical increase of the quality of life, which tendentially leads toward an unbounded control of life and the living; and on the other, that of an autonomous government of the self by the self, contrarily implying the demand for limits in all government.[32] Liquidating this constitutive tension of classical liberalism, the liberal democracy promoted by Lippmann clearly sacrifices, and for perhaps the first time in its history, the claim of a free and autonomous self-government for a new biopolitical government of the human species that is independent from popular sovereignty and led from above by experts—without their definition of the "good life" ever being the issue of public deliberation.

It is not surprising that this conception of human dignity henceforth rehabilitates, against the Enlightenment thinkers, the image Kant so vigorously disqualified of a population treated by its leaders like a domestic herd.[33] For Lippmann, the population indeed constitutes an uninformed "mass" stuck in a childlike situation of dependence on authority that must rely on those "who are at the head of affairs"[34] for all decisions. Measured by the liberal ideal of the Enlightenment, this persistent dependence on authority reveals a certain resemblance of the population with a herd:

> This fact is sometimes regarded as inherently undignified, as evidence of our sheep-like, ape-like nature.[35]

But by rejecting this inaccessible Enlightenment ideal, Lippmann inverts this pejorative judgment of the masses into a supposedly realist observation on the nature of people (*dēmos*) in democracy. If they are a population whose quality of life must be improved, the people are also an amorphous mass incapable of autodetermination, on which the leaders must impose leadership from above.

Such direction of the masses by the authority of leaders again involves the contribution of experts, for whom another sphere of action opens here—one that no longer concerns the expertise of the natural sciences in prolonging the techno-scientific revolution, nor the expertise of the social sciences in producing a global growth in the quality of life, but rather a new form of expertise that can only be provided by the human sciences in general, and by psychology in particular. Its role will be to indicate to leaders how to govern the static, amorphous, and heterogeneous mass of the population—which is rigidified in its stereotypes—by leading it in the right direction: that of readaptation to a new environment that is mobile, unpredictable, and globalized.

While classical democratic theory postulates a "Will of the People"[36] that is supposed to emerge from the deliberation of more or less independent communities (the Greek City, the rural communities of Thomas Jefferson, the Nation-State), Lippmannian neodemocracy adheres to a republican tradition with often elitist accents embodied in the political imagination by another great American Founding Father, Alexander Hamilton: "In the crystallizing of a common will, there is always an Alexander Hamilton at work."[37] In this new conception of democracy, more republican and elitist than democratic, will never comes from the people, who are viewed as an "ignorant" and incompetent multitude, but rather from the summit of the elite as embodied by the great man informed by science. It is this vertical model that Lippmann tried to promote with President Wilson during the writing of the "Fourteen Points."[38]

In these examples—"in the 'Fourteen Points,' in Hamilton's project"—"names" or "words" that act as "symbols"[39] are always used. The precise function of these symbols is to relay authority from above so that the heterogeneous mass is assembled (*symballein*) into a common will. For Lippmann, this is the positive role which propaganda must play in modern and globalized democracies, in times of war as in times of peace, and which he himself sought to illustrate during his campaign as a captain in Europe.[40] In counterpoint to the three most harmful characteristics of the masses—their passivity, inertia, and heterogeneity—the action of propaganda allows for the assembly of a great machine of hierarchized power endowed with opposite characteristics: will, mobility, and the maintenance of a coherent direction. In politics, the role of *dēmos* in this new democracy is clearer from now on: it has only the "fractional" power to say "yes" or "no" at election time.[41] Its role is limited to occasionally consenting to the symbols the leaders send it, and to validate them as signals of effective rallying that allow it to gather together in a homogeneous mass. Consent is certainly a classic theme, as much for the republican idea as for American democracy. There is thus nothing very new, nor very problematic, with "wise leaders . . . seek[ing] a certain degree of consent."[42] But what is radically new is the idea of a great machine of power that is intended to manufacture, at an industrial scale, the consent of populations. This theme of the "manufacture of consent"[43] is what Lippmann strongly calls for in the renovation of modern democracies and their readaptation to the needs of the Great Society.

In this striking expression, which has remained one of Lippmann's most famous up to the present day, the term "manufacture" has not been chosen at random. Manufacturing is the symbol of the emergence of the industrial revolution, which was fiercely resisted first by the Jeffersonian democrats and then by the progressives in their nostalgic lamentations against the great machine of power. The "manufacture" of consent and not "manipulation"—because for Lippmann, there is nothing new in the creation of consent through the artifices of manipulation:

> The creation of consent is not a new art. It is a very old one which was supposed to have died out with the appearance of democracy.[44]

What is new is not the art of manipulating consent; it is the necessity of its fabrication at an industrial scale, which will henceforth have to be assumed by modern democracies as their principal political task. The experience of World War I had just demonstrated this. Not only had democracy not supplanted this art; it had considerably developed it, giving it an industrial dimension through the dual impulse of the scientific expertise of psychologists and the modern means of communication:

> [The art of creating consent] has not died out. It has, in fact, improved enormously in technique, because it is now based on analysis rather than on rule of thumb. And so, as a result of psychological research, coupled with the modern means of communication, the practice of democracy has turned a corner. A revolution is taking place, infinitely more significant than any shifting of economic power.[45]

For Lippmann, this transformation of democracy into an industrial and techno-scientific manufacturer of consent for the masses, who are obliged to adhere to the rallying symbols produced by power, was a formidable political revolution. In regard to this revolution, which had only just begun and whose future developments one could hardly have guessed, the transformation of the relationship of economic powers, on which the liberals and Marxists were wrongly focused, appeared in his eyes as a secondary question.

Here, more clearly than elsewhere, one sees how Lippmann's political thought cannot be reduced to a strictly economic or political approach. In this regard, going back to the Lippmannian sources of neoliberalism allows us, among other things, to deconstruct the now common idea that neoliberalism can be reduced either to an economic doctrine or to an arbitrary reduction of politics to the economic logics of commodification. Far from sanctioning a rise in power of the economic sciences in political thought, *Public Opinion* promotes an entirely different magisterium for the human and social sciences— namely, for the social sciences and their focus on the growth of the quality of life of populations, and for psychology and its political manufacturing of consent. From *Public Opinion* to *The Good Society*, we will see that, for Lippmann, the neodemocratic then neoliberal "revolution" that he is heralding concerns neither the relationships of production nor the redistribution of wealth. As his first books already herald, this revolution concerns an entirely different field: that of the readaptation of the human species to its new environment, led by a new type of political power that relies on the scientific competence of a new type of experts—among whose first ranks figure not economists but sociologists and psychologists.

For all these reasons, *Public Opinion* does not easily fit within the liberal tradition. Liberal societies claim to preserve the private sphere—the freedom of conscience and thought, the affective and intimate life of citizens, as well as the spontaneous course of their business on the market—from invasive interventions from the government. However, the elective and not particularly liberal neodemocracy promoted by Lippmann in 1922 places the adaptation of the human species into the hands of experts in the social and human sciences and their propaganda techniques—whose role is to shift the ways of acting, thinking, and feeling in populations in a positive direction.

But three years later, when *The Phantom Public* appears in 1925, Lippmann's position has noticeably shifted. If he still critiques the traditional version of liberal democracy inherited from the Enlightenment thinkers, his whole effort now aims to minimize the scope of political life in general, and propaganda in particular. While *Public Opinion* advocated for an inflationist power of experts and of their symbolic and technical grip on the masses, *The Phantom Public* seeks to give public consent the role—as occasional as possible—of a last resort in the case of crisis. This deflationist interpretation of democracy leads Lippmann to a definitive rupture with his teacher Graham Wallas, who deemed the work to be profoundly disconcerting for all those who hope to politically engage and work "for the good of humanity."[46] By having each person refer, for the normal course of their own affairs, to their own perspective—that of their "desires," and of their "interests"[47]—Lippmann is denying, according to Wallas, the very possibility of a common goal of the "good life" and, with it, the very *telos* which has structured political life since Aristotle.

The central question of *The Phantom Public* is how to disqualify this public and collective goal of the good life through the Darwinian revolution itself, to which Wallas, however, supposedly adhered. This Darwinian break with the Aristotelian, teleological, and maximalist interpretation of political life leads Lippmann to a complete redefinition of politics—one that is deflationist, minimalist, and strictly procedural. But starting from this, the challenge becomes that of knowing if this new path, which aligns with the classic motif of the liberal critique of government excess, will go so far as to renounce the biopolitical program of readapting the human species through the power of experts. If modern democracies are no longer based on the goal of seeking the good life, are they still legitimate in pursuing the goal of increasing the quality of life of the population and readapting the human species to its new environment? In his two books from the 1920s that seek to rethink liberal democracy, how does Lippmann articulate these two paths which have defined liberalism, according to Foucault, since its birth in the eighteenth century: that of the critique of government excess on the one hand; and that of "biopolitics"—here in the sense of the unlimited government of life and the living—on the other?

The Phantom Public or the Disenchantment of Democracy

The first lines of *The Phantom Public* are a deformed echo of the quotation of Plato from *Public Opinion* where, as in Plato's cave, citizens are still presented as passive and manipulated spectators. But breaking with the allegory of *The Republic*, these same citizens, whom *Public Opinion* described as being captivated by the mise-en-scène of the cave, are no longer able, three years later, to follow the performance. Badly seated, in the back of the audience, they are having great difficulty in hearing and seeing what is happening on stage. While the Platonic spectators, like the citizen-spectators from World War I who were fascinated by the budding propaganda industry, had an ironclad belief in the reality of the idols ("Do you not think that they would suppose that in naming the things that they saw they were naming the passing objects?"[48]), the 1925 American citizen-spectator, overcome with boredom, no longer manages to follow the spectacle of public affairs:

> The private citizen today has come to feel rather like a deaf spectator
> in the back row, who ought to keep his mind on the mystery off there,
> but cannot quite manage to keep awake.[49]

Among these "mysteries" that they can no longer manage to follow, there is the religious mise-en-scène of their own sovereignty. For Lippmann, this democratic mysticism is one of the last shadows of God, a residue of the magical and religious conception of the power of divine right that has been more or less condemned in the long term by the "disenchantment of democracy":[50]

It was said often in the nineteenth century that there was a deep wisdom in majorities which was the voice of God. . . . It was nothing but a transfer to the new sovereign of the divine attributes of kings.[51]

On this point, the epigraph of *The Phantom Public* heralds once again the premonitory lucidity of Alexander Hamilton, who in the American political imagination from which Lippmann draws inspiration had assailed from the beginning the democratic mysticism of *self-government* popularized by Thomas Jefferson. Hamilton declared as much at the Federal Convention of 1787:

> The voice of the people has been said to be the voice of God: and however generally this maxim has been quoted and believed, it is not true in fact.[52]

What has changed compared to the previous century, which was widely dominated by this democratic mysticism, is that American citizens of the twentieth century now no longer even believe in the "mystery" of their own sovereignty. Globalized, the political stage and its real sovereignties henceforth appear to them as distant, muddled, and coming from "anonymous powers."[53]

Lippmann relies here on a massive phenomenon that was an increasing worry for the political scientists of his time. In 1925, more than half of the electors abstained from voting, even in presidential elections. It was in this context that the prominent political scientist Charles Merriam tried to determine the causes of this demobilization and the methods of control that would allow for a remobilization of the electors. But if *Public Opinion* paid homage to Merriam, as well as to Frederick Winslow Taylor and his methods for reorganizing industrial work, by seeing in them two possible examples for a readaptation of populations led by experts, *The Phantom Public* highlights the ineffectualness of expertise. No study by Charles Merriam, no matter how learned, can indeed prevail against the growing disinterest of citizens in public affairs. If this phenomenon is ineluctable, it is because something irreducible in human nature resists all modification by the experts—which could moreover constitute, even if Lippmann refrains from highlighting it, a major obstacle in the project of readapting the human species to the Great Society. This irreducible element is what philosophers call "finitude" and is that which restricts the human species to having only finite time and limited attention available to it:

> [The citizen] is exhorted to conserve the natural resources of the country because they are limited in quantity. He is advised to watch public expenditures because the taxpayers cannot pay out indefinitely increasing amounts. But he, the voter, the citizen, the sovereign, is

apparently expected to yield an unlimited quantity of public spirit, interest, curiosity, and effort. . . . [One] misses a decisive fact: the citizen gives but a little of his time to public affairs, . . . he cannot know all about everything all the time.[54]

In the era of the globalization of public affairs, the finite time of our attention is literally submerged by an endless stream of news that no human attention can succeed in reunifying into a coherent synthesis:

> Modern society is not visible to anybody, nor intelligible continuously and as a whole. . . . It is bad enough today . . . to be condemned to live under a barrage of eclectic information, to have one's mind made the receptacle for a hullabaloo of speeches, arguments and unrelated episodes. . . . Life is too short for the pursuit of omniscience by the counting in a state of nervous excitement of all the leaves on all the trees.[55]

This disproportion between the limited capacities of citizens and the unlimited flux of public affairs, which is intensified by the rhapsodic and disjointed flood of information, has been simultaneously revealed and aggravated by the globalized Great Society, which has led to the decline of all the former political enclosures (City-State, rural community, nation-state). Again, *The Phantom Public* reminds us that the famous solution of Aristotle had consisted in limiting the size of the City "to suit the faculties of its citizens."[56] The democratic communities inspired by Jefferson tried hard to follow Aristotle's recommendations, but are thereby marginalized by the Great Society. This explains why when confronted by the impossibility of struggling against globalization the "orthodox democrats" of the nineteenth century "answered Aristotle's question by assuming that a limitless political capacity resides in public opinion."[57] But denying the irreducible limitation of human attention capacities was a second mistake. As such, Aristotle's question seems insoluble: "we can neither reject the Great Society as Aristotle did, nor exaggerate the political capacity of citizens as the democrats did."

If *Public Opinion* concentrated on the opposition between stasis and flux by insisting on the lag of the static stereotypes of the masses in relation to the permanent flux of change, *The Phantom Public* insists on a new tension—one centered on limit and illimitation, which it interprets as "Aristotle's question."[58] *Public Opinion* had certainly already made room for the question by recognizing the need of all "human life" to "economize attention"[59] through "stereotypes" that allow for the artificial delimiting of the open flux of events. But in 1922, this common condition for all human life had been quickly overwritten by the hierarchy between the static stereotypes of the masses and the more

mobile fictions of leaders and experts—with these testable hypotheses of experimental science being much more suitable for adapting to the flux of change.
The opposition between flux and change thus allowed the restoring of the
Platonic hierarchy, even in an inverted fashion, between the high and the low.
But in 1925, the insistence on this new opposition pair, between the psychic
enclosure of attention (the limit) and the new open and globalized society
(illimitation), now denies all hierarchy between those who govern and the
governed. For with the finitude of attention, Lippmann has encountered a
universal limitation of human nature that no expert in psychology will ever
be able to modulate.[60] Must we deduce from this that the Great Society has
made all forms of democracy obsolete, including that governed by the experts
which Lippmann was still theorizing in 1922? To know that, we must first begin
by asking if one can be freed from the limitations of human nature by eugenics
or by education.

The Influence of Darwinism on the Political Education of the Citizen

The eugenicist solution, commonly invoked at the time for improving the
capacities of the human species, is clearly rejected by Lippmann.[61] His position
can notably be explained by his personal involvement in the polemic around
psychological tests responsible for measuring the "intelligence quotient" since
1922.[62] In debates hosted by *The New Republic*, he tried hard to demonstrate
that the role of these tests was to justify social hierarchies. The idea that it was
possible to measure a hereditary or biological intelligence had for him no scientific foundation, because what these tests measured could only be a confused
mixture of the acquired and the innate.[63] To understand his rejection of eugenics, we must remember that in his eyes the human species accomplished
a dual break with its biological destiny. First under the impulse of science and
technology—which had considerably widened its environment since Antiquity,
forcing the Greeks to construct, in response to this widening, a fictively closed
public space; and then under the impulse of the Great Society, which had
made the human species definitively maladapted to its new environment that
was now widened to the dimensions of the world—definitively disqualifying
the democratic myth of the enlightened citizen. In light of this dual break, to
imagine that democratic excellence could arise from native or biological de-
terminations appears as an unfathomable naïveté.[64]

The alternative response through education is at the same time more serious
and more classic, which explains why Lippmann lingers over it longer.[65] Since
the Enlightenment, he recalls, two principal paths have been explored for

thinking about the development of the citizen. First the empirical path of encyclopedic information, which consisted in initiating the citizen into the diverse problems of the world. Then the universal path of morality, which tried to found the functioning of republics—then that of democracies—on universal moral principles. In his meticulous refutation of these two paths, we will see that Lippmann returns each time to the evolutionary sources of his political thought.

Because the empirical path, that of unlimited encyclopedic information imposed by the Great Society, collides with a necessarily limited attention capacity, it can only lead to "a sightseeing tour of the problems of the world."[66] The tension between the limitation of attention capacities and the unlimited flux of information to assimilate is intensified by another tension between the stases of scholarly knowledge and the permanent flux of change:

> The usual appeal to education can bring only disappointment. For the problems of the modern world appear and change faster than any set of teachers can grasp them, much faster than they can convey their substance to a population of children. If the schools attempt to teach children how to solve the problems of the day, they are bound always to be in arrears.[67]

The problems of the Great Society are not only much too vast and much too complex for our limited capacities of perception and attention. They also transform at a much too rapid rhythm for our static capacities of comprehension. Here, Lippmann articulates the two opposition pairs cited above: that of stasis and flux, which dominated the set of analyses in *Public Opinion*; and that of the limited and the unlimited, which is henceforth established in *The Phantom Public*. Scholarly knowledge, with the stability that academic understanding requires and the slow rhythm that pedagogical transmission demands, can only be structurally "in arrears" with the rhythm of evolution and overrun by the explosion of information.

Instead of exposing the future citizen to the unlimited, infinitely complex, and perpetually changing flux of the problems of the Great Society, it is rather "some rational ground for fixing his attention" that will need to be taught.[68] This new "pattern of thought and feeling"[69] that political science must invent and with which the schools will need to inoculate the population will have to take account of this major fact: given the limited quantity of attention that characterizes all human life on the one hand, and the unlimited quantity of problems that the globalized Great Society raises on the other, the involvement of citizens in public affairs will from now on have to be reduced to a minimum. We will later see that the retreat of the individual into his own interests is that which will provide the guiding thread of this new manner of feeling and thinking.

A few chapters later, Lippmann pays homage to Thomas Malthus as the one who best grasped "the nature of the problem" and who best understood why the Great Society was condemned to produce an exponential quantity of "problems."[70] Indeed, in light of Malthus, all problems always spring from change and originate more precisely from the differences of rhythm which make up the change. Thus, in the classic example of Malthusianism, agricultural resources increase "too slowly" in relation to a population that reproduces "too quickly." Beyond this example, whose data contain nothing invariable for Lippmann, Malthus teaches us that all problems take their root not only in change but in the differences of rhythm that compose it—or in what I later suggest naming the *heterochrony* of evolutionary change.[71] In light of this redefinition of "problem," we better understand why the emergence of the Great Society, which is defined by the multiplication of interdependent changes, can only produce an exponential growth of problems for all the living.

This reference to Malthus is not made randomly. If he is credited with having grasped the nature of all problems so well, it is also because Lippmann is in the process of reconnecting with the first Darwinian sources of his political reflection. It begins with a Darwinian story about cats and clovers which will allow Lippmann to dismiss the second path explored by the Enlightenment thinkers: that of the moral education of citizens. "To any one who finds it difficult to free his mind of the assumption that his notions of good and bad are universal," Lippmann offers the advice to reflect on "Darwin's story of the cats and clover."[72] This story recounts how the population growth of cats indirectly favors the growth of the clover population. The more elderly ladies feed cats, the more cats eliminate field mice, the more bumblebees proliferate, the more the clover is fertilized, and the more the cattle increase. From the point of view of "a beef-eating Occidental,"[73] we have here something like an intrinsically good "order" that all the involved actors have an interest in conserving. But in line with Darwin, Lippmann suggests varying the points of view and adopting, for example, that of the mouse:

> But if you are a field mouse, how different the rights and wrongs of that section of the universe! . . . For what could a patriotic mouse think of a world in which bumblebees did not exist for the sole purpose of producing white grubs for field mice? There would seem to be no law and order in such a world.[74]

Let us remark that such reasoning implies that the perspective of the occidental beef-eater loses all pretensions to the absolute. A product of evolution among others, the occidental man must understand that his point of view is a perspective as completely partial as that of the mouse. What is "good" for the consumer of meat is "bad" for the mouse, and thus, one can suppose in extrapolating from the text, for the other living beings that depend on it. He also must strip these terms of all moral or absolute content to regain their utilitarian and purely relative first meaning. What is "good," or "useful," in the struggle for survival for one organism is always at the same time "bad," or "harmful," to the survival of another. In the evolution of the living, nothing is therefore ever good or bad in itself. By revealing this plurality of viewpoints, Darwinism definitively compromises morality in general; and with it the pretensions to the absolute of all moral values without exception, whether they refer to the "patriotism" of the mouse or to the "right" of occidentals to consume bovine meat.

Throughout this history, Darwin is implicitly heralded as the one who had the lucidity to dismiss the teleological conception of evolution that had prevailed since Lamarck and that had allowed for the metaphysical idea of a transcendent good to be saved. From 1910 onward, Dewey noted that this revolution would have decisive consequences in the moral and political domain.[75] As for Lippmann, it was a question of drawing all the political consequences of this revolution. For what applies to the evolution of the living also applies to the accelerated evolution of the Great Society. No transcendent good, no permanent value, can give it its meaning or its goal—even that, which had been haloed with glory since World War I, of the "homeland." Quite the contrary. In light of the Darwinian revolution, the patriot invoking the eternal virtues and values of the Republic is compared rather to a mouse in danger of extinction, incapable of suspecting the multiplicity of perspectives that exceed its viewpoint.

Because it extends the Darwinian critique of teleology while taking aim at Spencer's teleological evolutionism, Lippmann openly pays tribute to Bergson's "creative evolution" and its contesting of the idea of a transcendent order.[76] A "highly philosophical" (and Bergsonian) "field mouse" would discard its patriotic conception of the world. It would understand that from the point of view of evolution, whose creative movement is radically unpredictable, the proliferation of cats favoring American beef-eating and putting it at a disadvantage is neither good nor bad in itself. It would realize that, like "order" and "disorder," the good and the bad are only expectations that are satisfied or unfulfilled; and that its patriotic vision only has meaning for itself—concealing the narrow provisional interests of its species in a supposedly absolute and universal moral value. And so in a few pages as dense as they are decisive, the critique of this second path borrowed from the Enlightenment thinkers—which believes that the republic and then democracy can be refounded on the moral education of the citizen—is led to its conclusion.

From here on, Lippmann will propose a strictly Darwinian interpretation of political conflicts that will exorcize once and for all his own Platonic temptation for governing from above:

> It requires intense partisanship and much self-deception to argue that some sort of peculiar righteousness adheres to the farmers' claims as against the manufacturers', the employers' against the wage-earners', the creditors' against the debtors', or the other way around. These conflicts of interest are problems. They require solution. But there is no moral pattern available from which the precise nature of the solution can be deduced.[77]

Extending the Darwinian conception of evolution into the political domain, Lippmann contests all teleological approaches to political problems. The substance of politics is precisely the "conflict of standards."[78] The farmers of the Southern states who struggle against the industrialists of the Northern states extend the biological struggle for survival in which the cats and field mice are engaged. A Darwinian conception of political evolution allows us to understand that there is no more moral legitimacy in the expectations of farmers than in those of industrialists; and more generally, in the expectations of one social group compared with another. From this point of view, taking sides with the employers (and against the workers) is as inept as doing the opposite. Thus, this refusal to take sides constitutes, in Lippmann's political reflection, a true turning point. Indeed, for the first time he questions the idea of direction in evolution, in which the industrialists of the North would be "ahead" while the farmers of the South would be "behind." It is the difference of rhythm between the South and the North which is at the source of the "problem"—with all problems always deriving, in Lippmann's rereading of Malthus, from a maladjustment of rhythms in evolutionary change. But just as Darwin would have refused to think that the point of view of the cat was intrinsically superior to that of the field mouse, or that one was more "advanced" than the other, Lippmann tries hard to consider that the rhythm of the industrial North is in no way superior to that of the rural communities of the South. This new conception of maladjustment will lead him to question one of the invariants of his previous political analyses. Since, in the inevitable conflict of rhythms and interests, the accelerated rhythms of industry with its particular interests no longer appears as being intrinsically superior to all the others, no "moral pattern" seems available for deducing the solution to these conflicts. In light of the Darwinian revolution, no expert can thus boast of grasping the direction and goal of evolution better than individuals pursuing their own interests. On the Darwinian ruins of teleology, governments can no longer claim to determine what "the good life" consists of better than the populations themselves.

But how can we then understand that, in the same pages, Lippmann demands that schools transmit "a pattern of thought and feeling" that makes the citizen capable of approaching a new problem in a useful fashion?[79] This pattern must be understood as an encouragement for citizens to fall back on the narrow sphere of their interests:

> Men make no attempt to consider society as a whole. The farmer decides whether to plant wheat or corn, the mechanic whether to take the job offered at the Pennsylvania or the Erie shops, whether to buy a Ford or a piano, and, if a Ford, whether to buy it from the garage on Elm Street or from the dealer who sent him a circular. These decisions are among fairly narrow choices offered to him; he can no more choose among all the jobs in the world than he can consider marrying any woman in the world.[80]

This description of the citizen contradicts its idealization by the theories of democracy. The citizen is above all a man struggling for his private interests, which do not aim toward the "good life" (Aristotle), nor the general interest or universal justice (the Enlightenment). Because he never tries to "consider society as a whole," it is necessary to renounce both the political model inherited from Aristotle and the contemporary idea that it would be necessary—to remedy the faults of democracy—to intensify democratic debate by generalizing suffrage and by multiplying elections. To remedy the troubles of democracy, we suppose that more democracy would be needed. This inflationist interpretation is founded on an idealized representation of the political animal, which lacks the real behaviors of the citizen. Before being a citizen, man is first and above all, if we follow the lesson of this text, a worker and a consumer; but also, it reminds us implicitly with the evocation of marriage, a reproducer. It is in these three domains—those of work, consumption, and reproduction—where his freedom to "decide" or to "choose" truly manifests itself. But these choices remain extremely constrained. If the Great Society has now taken on the dimensions of the world, individual choices can in no way operate at such a scale. Even in the time of globalization, they remain inexorably confined to the narrow sphere of their immediate environment.

It remains from here on to discover *who*, ultimately, can govern society in the era of globalization. Returning to the founding principles of classical liberalism, Lippmann will resolve the problem by considering the random struggle of these interests as the true source of the government of society:

These choices in detail are in their cumulative mass the government
of society. They may rest on ignorant or enlightened opinions, but,
whether he comes to them by accident or scientific instruction, they
are specific and particular among at best a few concrete alternatives
and they lead to a definite, visible result.[81]

Inspired by the Scottish Enlightenment, the liberals indeed taught us that
it was the random and blind logic of interests that essentially governed society.
Dismissing the experts from their governing role, Lippmann gives the power
of governing back to the masses. But these masses are not the "enlightened"
majority idealized by the theories of democracy. They are the capitalization
of all the constrained, random, and for the most part blind choices of individuals in their struggle to optimize their interests. In regard to this struggle, the
question of knowing if citizens are enlightened or ignorant is unimportant.
Recognizing both the motif of Adam Smith's invisible hand and that of the
Darwinian natural selection of accidental variations, Lippmann seeks to render
the knowledge and "Enlightenment" of the citizen fundamentally inoperative
in the spontaneous government of society.

Through the struggle of interests, society thus governs itself very well. But
this self-government, by operating spontaneously across the relationships of
production, consumption, and reproduction, passes neither through the me-
diation of politics in general nor through that of democratic deliberation in
particular. Lippmann concludes that this spontaneous government of society,
which forms the heart of classical liberalism, contradicts the foundations of
the democratic theory that idealizes popular will. For how can the struggle of
private interests move toward the collective aim of the common good? Incapable of overcoming this difficulty, liberal democracy thus began to invoke the
political conscience of each person, turning it toward a "cosmopolitan, universal, and disinterested"[82] end. But it could never explain how it managed to
convert the narrow limitation of interest (that of economic liberalism) into a
universal and unlimited disinterest (that of political liberalism).

The critique is certainly severe. But we must not see in it a definitive disqualification of liberal democracy. Because once this internal contradiction is
overcome, Lippmann's ambition will be, quite the contrary, to reconstruct a
theory of democracy that is at last compatible with the true doctrine of liberalism: that of the spontaneous government of society by the struggle of interests.
This reconstruction will happen through a complete revision of the role of
democracy. Against the inflationist interpretation that dominated classical
theories in its perpetual demand for more participation from citizens, Lippmann
presents an opposite idea that is deflationist and minimalist—one in which

consultation with electors will play a role of last resort only once all the other spontaneous forms of regulation have been exhausted. The challenge from here on will be to redefine the scope of democracy, which he claims has never stopped growing, to restrain it only to what is strictly necessary.

The role of the "pattern of thought and feeling" that political science must "trace," and that schools must teach future citizens, is precisely that which teaches us to distinguish between what concerns "specific opinion" and what concerns "general opinion."[83] Specific opinion goes back to the desire and power of individuals to modify their immediate environment in favor of their individual interests.[84] As we saw above, it is this type of opinion that participates in the self-government of society by being translated into individual choices (concerning work, consumption, and reproduction). But in the Great Society, it occurs more and more often not only that the current rules no longer allow for the spontaneous adjustment of interests, but also that no new rule manages to spontaneously emerge. This situation is explained by the multiplication of "problems" itself linked to the acceleration of changes. Certain of these problems end by degenerating into "crises." It is precisely in this case, and in this case only—when the common rule no longer permits the spontaneous adjustment of private interests and when there is the threat of domination from arbitrary forces—that "public opinion" has a role to play.[85] If the political government of society still keeps a meaning and function, it is only in these exceptional circumstances: when the scale of problems and the heterochrony of evolutionary changes become so great that world affairs no longer function and that the concerned parties no longer manage to adjust.

Yet in these moments of urgency, when as a last resort democratic consultation is required, Lippmann continues to think that the general will can only emerge from above through the symbolic work of leaders. This work essentially consists in "assembling" (*symballein*) what there is that is most common in this "heterogeneous mass of desires."[86] Detached from the clear and distinct ideas produced by this thought, the continuous and fusional mass of emotions is indeed the ideal matter for melting the multiplicity of desires into a common will. This analysis of the emotional manufacturing of the general will through the symbolic arts of propaganda clearly contests that the Will of the People is capable of thinking anything at all. Defending a both minimalist and vertical conception of political government up to its neodemocratic form, Lippmann will assert that the source of rules will never be public opinion itself, but rather strongmen in situations of crisis whom public opinion trusts for this reason. Deprived of all capacity for thinking, opinion itself clearly must not seek to redefine the rules. Its role limits it to enthusiastically and passionately supporting the leader that it feels is rising up against arbitrary powers, and who is apparently looking for a viable adjustment to overcome the crisis.[87] Public opinion finds itself thus redefined as a mass of supporters who "follow" or who no longer follow, who "align" or who no longer align, behind such and such champion depending on whether he does or does not restore respect for the rules that have been weakened in times of crisis.[88] The sports metaphor, which Lippmann will bring out more and more often in his subsequent reflections on new liberalism, is continued through a group of "military metaphors" that allow him to reconnect with one of his first themes of reflection—that of the "sublimation" of drives (A *Preface to Politics*), articulated from now on through the wartime experience of propaganda:

> I have called voting an act of enlistment, an alignment for or against, a mobilization. These are military metaphors, and rightly so, I think, for an election . . . [is] a sublimated and denatured civil war.[89]

The two mistakes of liberal democracy have been believing that this government was continuous and that it came from the people themselves. Democracy as revised by Lippmann wants on the contrary to be discontinuous and led from above by leaders: by those who know how to impose "good substitutes" (A *Preface to Politics*) to the contradictory desires of the masses, allowing them to melt together through adherence to the same "symbols" (*Public Opinion*) and the restoration of a common "rule" (*The Phantom Public*).

Composed as a multiplicity of rhythms, evolution according to Lippmann is thus characterized by a group of dyschronies that calls for leaders who are capable of resynchronizing the rhythms by "reforming the ranks":

> Events do not concur harmoniously in time. Some hurry, some straggle, some push and some drag. The ranks have always to be reformed.[90]

It is precisely here that politics in general, and public opinion in particular, have a role to play by "aligning" in well-disciplined columns behind those who manage to resynchronize the ranks better than all the others. Once again, the disciplinary and military metaphor is used in full. By breaking with the reassuring evolutionisms of the nineteenth century, the heterochrony of evolutionary rhythm is at last clearly recognized. But it is immediately interpreted as a "problem" that must be resolved, like a dyschrony or a sickness that must be "cured":[91]

> Instead of that one grand system of evolution and progress, which the nineteenth century found so reassuring, there would appear to be innumerable systems of evolution, variously affecting each other, some

linked, some in collision, but each in some fundamental aspect moving at its own pace and on its own terms.

The disharmonies of this uneven evolution are the problems of
mankind.[92]

Along with the political remedies for dyschrony, the procedural reform of
the rules—to which all legitimate public intervention must be reduced, according to Lippmann—perfectly imitates the gradual evolutionary rhythm
described by Darwin.[93] It is this mimicry of the Darwinian uniform rhythm,
equidistant between the acceleration of absolute flux and the blockage of the
status quo, that explains the systematic valorization by Lippmann of *reform*
against revolution, of *gradualism* against rupture, and of *consensus* against
conflict. Ultimately, the Darwinian reform of democracy promoted by Lippmann could be summarized as follows: to control the heterochrony of the
evolutionary rhythm of the Great Society—the bringer of conflicts, ruptures,
and revolution—through a consensual and gradual reform of the rules that
succeeds in "reforming the ranks." This military objective explains why the
political field must be, for Lippmann, purged of all conflict, divergence, rhythm,
and in the end, difference:

> Although it is the custom of partisans to speak as if there were radical
> differences between the Ins and Outs, . . . in stable and mature societ-
> ies the differences are necessarily not profound. If they were profound,
> the defeated minority would be constantly on the verge of rebellion.[94]

If differences emerge that justify electoral mobilization and the fact of
aligning "for" or "against," they must be as gradual and "slight" as Darwinian
"slight variations":

> An election rarely means even a fraction of what campaigners said it
> would mean. It means . . . perhaps a slightly different general tendency
> in the management of affairs. . . . But even these differing tendencies
> are very small as compared with the immense area of agreement, estab-
> lished habit and unavoidable necessity. In fact, one might say that a
> nation is politically stable when nothing of radical consequence is
> determined by its election.[95]

Far from valorizing heterochrony by seeing in it the source of a divergent
and creative evolution, the goal of political action according to Lippmann is
to eliminate it with the aim of imposing a consensus that restores all rhythms
to the same pace. This explains why the only differences admitted in the

political field must be extremely slight variations—the most neutral possible—
that allow for the gradual reform of the rule and move away from the specter
of conflict and revolution. Thus, when standard conflicts do not spontaneously
resolve through the struggle of interests (this is the first effect of Darwinism),
they must be resolved politically—not by debating the "substance" of the
problems, but by arriving at a procedural consensus about reforming the rule
itself in the most gradual way possible. This valorization of the gradualism
of slight variations is the second effect of Darwinism on Lippmann's political
thought. Yet how can one not see in this disciplinary curbing of all forms
of conflict not just a restriction but a depoliticization of the political field
itself?

This second effect of Darwinism sanctions, contrarily to the first, the return
in force of the vertical hierarchy between the governed and the governing.
Incapable of aiming toward something like a general interest, public opinion
can indeed do nothing other than mobilize itself behind the best leaders, who
are defined as those who propose a gradual reform of the rule that most con-
forms to procedure. But is there not a profound contradiction between this
hierarchical conception of reform and the Darwinian conception of evolution,
which on the contrary grants the tendency of providing favorable slight variations to all organisms without exception? In reality, and the later work of Lippmann will more clearly confirm it again, the democratic evolutionism that he
is seeking to promote turns out to be widely dependent on the teleological
conception that Spencer had of the direction and goal of evolution. For if public
opinions must mobilize themselves behind good leaders, it is by following the
logic of the division of labor, according to which those who are better placed
to decide are the best specialists in the matter:

> There is least anarchy precisely in those areas of society where separate
> functions are most clearly defined and brought into orderly
> adjustment.[96]

For if the Great Society, by multiplying changes and striking down enclosures, is causing the problems of the world to explode in an exponential way,
it is also responsible for resolving them better through an increasingly orderly
adjustment of the division of labor. Here emerges, with the return of experts,
a third and last argument in favor of a complete depoliticization of the government: politics must not only be reduced to exceptional situations and must not
only eliminate divergence and conflict; it must also reduce itself to the most
specialized competency possible for experts in their own field. Revised by
Darwinian gradualism and the Spencerian teleology of the division of labor,

the readaptation of the human species to its new environment, which is complex and perpetually changing, can at last do without a common aim of the good life. Better: it definitively wards off the risk that such a collective evolutionary aim of the living in general, and of the future of our species in particular, would open the path to divergences or conflicts; in short, to "radical differences."[97]

3
The Biological Sources of the Conflict

Starting from the diagnosis of a crisis of democracy in industrial societies, Lippmann thus intends to propose a radically new political model—a new form of democracy where three major mutations are articulated, each breaking with the dominant democratic model. First, that of a government of experts, which breaks with the postulate of the omni-competence of citizens. Then, that of a manufacture of consent which assumes the production of good stereotypes through well-oriented propaganda that aims for the readaptation of the human species to its new environment. And last, that of a minimalist and purely procedural democracy which claims to overcome the heterochrony between evolutionary rhythms and to clear all forms of conflict through a gradual reform of the rules, imitating the homogeneous rhythm of Darwinian slight variations and of their natural selection. Lippmann's proposition will have a large influence on American political thought and, more widely, on the training of elites throughout the world. But it will also give rise to a lively debate, which still lives on today, between his political model and the pragmatist conception of democracy theorized by John Dewey during the first half of the twentieth century.

At the Sources of the New Debate on Democracy: The Lippmann-Dewey Debate

For Dewey, it would be certainly excessive to present Lippmann as a dangerous antidemocrat.[1] His critique of the classical conception of democracy, which imagines citizens as being capable of deciding on all state affairs, is on the contrary perfectly legitimate. For both Dewey and Lippmann, it is indeed urgent to reconstruct the democratic model to the scale of the challenges of the industrial and globalized Great Society. But on closer inspection, profound fracture lines are already pointing to the horizon. In his recensions of Lippmann's two books on democracy, Dewey is already formulating a series of in-depth objections against him, among which is a reflection that Lippmann judges "publicity in relation to the public" much too superficially and completely misunderstands the "organization of society."[2]

On the base of this dual disagreement, Dewey will put forward an entirely different democratic model. Against the government of experts he will first object that democracy involves the systematic usage of "inquiry," reinterpreted as the social sharing of knowledge and its being tested collectively. Next, against the manufacturing of symbols through propaganda he will oppose that the publics must reclaim the means of "communicating" between themselves in order to reform the living tissue not only of social issues but of the "community." Last, to the minimalist, procedural, and intermittent conception of democratic consultation he will object that democracy must on the contrary extend into all the dimensions of human life and that it must explicitly confront the question of values, ends, and common goals of the political community. Such are the well-known broad dimensions of what Americans henceforth will call the "Lippmann-Dewey debate," which Dewey initiates in 1927 but which will only make its mark more than a half century later in 1990s America.

The debate originated in the field of communication studies, whose beginning is generally dated to the publication of James Carey's book, *Communication as Culture* (1989).[3] Seeking to relaunch the old conflict between descriptive research (invoking Paul Lazarsfeld) and critical research (reclaiming the heritage of Theodor Adorno and the Frankfurt School), James Carey asserts he has rediscovered the American sources of the debate.[4] While Lippmann's theories were accused of supporting an "administrative" self-claimed "apolitical" research of mass media, Dewey's were presented as the matrix of all critical and politically engaged research. In this reconstruction, Lippmann appeared as the founding father of communication studies while also being the one who had skewed its theoretical foundations from the beginning. By focusing on objectivity and the neutrality of information, he indeed encouraged all his successors to miss the most essential dimension of communication, which Dewey on the contrary so well understood: that of communication as *culture*.[5]

The discussion opened by James Carey very quickly overflowed these disciplinary concerns to spread throughout contemporary political debate. A decade earlier, without mentioning the debate between Lippmann and Dewey,

Noam Chomsky had popularized in a very critical fashion the notion of the "manufacture of consent."[6] Lippmann already appeared there as the defender of neutral and objective research, incapable of recognizing the effects of domination linked to expertise. A little later, and in the rather somber political context of the 1990s (that of the First Gulf War and of its extensive manipulations of the media), Christopher Lasch greatly expanded the Lippmann-Dewey debate.[7] Adopting Carey's analyses, he maintained that the Lippmannian model of neutral, objective, and expert information had largely contributed to destroying the very conditions of democratic debate, as Dewey understood it, which involved the lively and active participation of citizens themselves in the inquiry. From this point on, everyone's stances continued to harden, the whole question being whether Lippmann's ideas were those of a "true" democrat.[8] For James Carey's opponents, the terms of the Lippmann-Dewey debate, which he had in reality entirely created, were ideological through and through. They were explained by the decline of critical theory in the 1980s in the wake of the crisis of Marxism, for which Carey had tried to hurriedly substitute a new critical model that was supposedly provided by Dewey and arbitrarily opposed to Lippmann.

To these polemics around expertise in democracy was joined a second controversy. In the context of the pragmatic turn, the question of whether Lippmann was a true democrat was progressively mixed in with that of whether he belonged to the pragmatist movement—with pragmatism itself being more and more considered as a positive ideological marker.[9] For Carey, Lippmann makes the fundamental mistake of maintaining the classical interpretation of knowledge, which he still perceives in a passive way as akin to a spectacle or representation. In doing so, he misses the epistemological break that pragmatism initiates, as much with idealism (with its permanent insistence on vision in Plato, then representation in Descartes) as with classical empiricism, where the subject of experience is never just a passive spectator. He does not grasp that Dewey's philosophy rightly consists in breaking with this conception of knowledge founded in a spectator subject:

> If we see that knowing is not the act of an outside spectator but a participator inside the natural and social scene, then the true object of knowledge resides in the consequences of directed action.[10]

He does not understand that knowledge, placed from now on in the much wider field of experience, becomes an engaged relationship of interaction with the environment whose specific feature consists in aiming toward the active control of consequences. Yet the detractors of the Lippmann-Dewey debate argued, against James Carey, that Lippmann was precisely adhering to this pragmatist conception of knowledge and experience. And at first glance, the examination of the texts seems to prove them right. Lippmann, as previously mentioned, highlights very clearly that the knowledge of experts is always provisional and limited and that it must, in this respect, be ceaselessly evaluated through experimentation. From this point of view, political action must be entirely rethought, no longer starting from its causes (sovereignty, general will), but starting from its consequences.[11] With this proposition, Lippmann stretches a theory that he had already found in a book by Dewey dated from 1915, *German Philosophy and Politics*, into the political field:

> In an experimental philosophy of life, the question of the past, of precedents, of origins, is quite subordinate to prevision, to guidance and control amid future possibilities. Consequences rather than antecedents measure the worth of theories.[12]

With this pragmatist approach to political experimentation, Carey's opponents protest that we are very far off from a dangerous "government of experts" that would claim objectivity and omniscience.

These arguments are certainly admissible. But their weakness comes from their saying nothing of what constitutes the major divergence of Lippmann's model from Dewey's, and more broadly from the pragmatist movement. Lippmann's entire political model indeed rests, we have begun to see, on the distinction between leaders, who are considered as the only truly active agents, and the masses produced by the Great Society, who are viewed as inert, amorphous, and passive. Certainly, Lippmann takes care to not essentialize these roles by recalling that each of us—according to each given situation—is either a leader, in the sense of being active in our domain, or a passive member of the masses, in the sense that there are others than ourselves who have expertise in the situation. But we are going to see that such a model supposes a dualism of metaphysical origins between activity and passivity, against which Dewey will strive to methodically oppose the biological sources of all experimentation—and with them, what he calls the "genetic and experimental logic of Darwin."[13]

The Biological Sources of the Debate

Lippmann systematically reduces the public to the "public opinion," understood as a passive entity cut off from all possibility of action. Lacking all "general will," the public must be considered as a "mass": a malleable material which must always be better readapted to the situation. In terms of a large country, this implies that the population becomes the passive and consenting target of the knowledge of experts responsible for readapting it in an optimal manner to the demands of the industrial revolution. In those of a company, this means that all experimentation—like the putting into place of a Taylorist type of work organization, to use an example invoked by Lippmann (and criticized by Dewey)[14]—is conceived of and then exclusively controlled by the leaders. They are themselves assisted by the counsel of experts who, in a well-structured company, will also include the union representatives who are most enlightened. All other scenarios mistake the real characteristics of opinion, of the masses and of the base, by giving them the capacity to articulate an autonomous and coherent will that is beyond simple "consent" in a phantasmic way. If we follow Lippmann's logic, we would find the same division of roles within a health establishment, for example, with the patients merely "following" the prescriptions of the caregivers and giving their passive consent to the experimentations of which they are ceaselessly the objects.[15] If his model lays out in principle the political necessity not only of gathering the consent of patients but also of its "manufacturing," it nonetheless excludes patients from participating in the collective discussion about the ends of the experiment itself, for which they do not have the required technical knowledge and which only the collective deliberation of experts can determine.[16]

At every turn, we have seen that the hierarchy is justified through the theory of the cognitive lag of the human species behind its own evolution as it henceforth confronts an open, mobile, and more and more complex environment. While the masses are confined to the inertia of their stereotypes, the leaders are supposed to have—thanks to their own leadership—a much broader overview of the Great Society, the rapidity of its mutations, and the maladjustment of the stereotypes of the population. It is this difference of views on the flux of evolution that justifies the Lippmannian government of experts. But instead of viewing this, in a somewhat conspiratorial fashion, as a secret room where a handful of counselors clandestinely decide the fate of the world, it should be viewed rather as the generalization of a way of structuring social organizations, where the hierarchy between those who direct the experimentation and those who are its passive and complying targets must restore itself each time and in each given local situation.

These different forms of social organization are precisely those that Dewey never stopped deconstructing, considering that it was they, on the contrary, who were lagging behind evolution. For Lippmann, we have seen, it is the passive mass of the human species that structurally lags, because of its stereotypical nature, behind the flux of evolution, which only the most active are able to grasp. For Dewey, on the contrary, it is exactly this way of thinking about lag that *lags* behind the evolution of the human species and the liberation of its potentialities. Because through the hierarchical distinction between the active subjects and passive subjects of experimentation, Lippmann disconnects the two dimensions, active and passive, from all vital experience. This disconnection reactivates the metaphysical dualism criticized by Dewey, which places the passivity of sensation and the activity of thought into opposition instead of thinking about their articulation. This dualism further reinforces itself through an inverted opposition that associates the passive contemplation of ends (through the knowledge of experts) and their active implementation (through the work of the industrious masses). For Dewey, this triply dualist approach to experimentation—which separates thought and the needs of the body, opposes knowledge with action, and disconnects implementation of the means from deliberation about the ends—raises patterns of ossified thought that are all inherited from metaphysics and are not up to the standard of the scientific and technical age of experimentation.

All these philosophical dualisms themselves descend from an old social hierarchy, already theorized by the Greeks, between the superior classes, who have the leisure of contemplating disinterested ends (*otium*), and the inferior classes, who are subjected to material work and the needs of the body (labor).[17] We henceforth better understand what is lagging in the evolution of our species. Metaphysics in general, and that of Lippmann in particular, does nothing but legitimize the social organizations that have become perfectly maladapted to what experimentation has required since the scientific revolution of modern times—and in this respect, corresponding closely with the Lippmannian definition of stereotype. For Dewey, the lag is not therefore an intrinsic disposition of the masses. It is rather these former dualist and hierarchical ways of thinking that lag, in two ways, behind evolution. Not only, as we have just seen, behind what the industrial age of experimentation—launched by the evolution of science and technology—now demands. But also, as we will now see more precisely, behind what biology has taught us of experience in general and of its leading role in the history of the living.

For what Lippmann was lagging behind and ultimately missing was not only the evolution induced by the industrial revolution, but also the "genetic and experimental logic" that Dewey considers as the great lesson of Darwinism. Beyond the invocation of the model of experimentation, invented by the scientific revolution in the seventeenth century with all the methodological refinement for which it is known, Dewey indeed takes a step further. He relies on biology itself to affirm that all experience in general involves—well before the appearance of the experimental sciences—the continuous articulation between its active and passive dimensions:

The organism is not a spectator facing the screen of the world that is bombarding him with raw data, he is an actor who takes part in the world. The concept of "participation" has a biological origin and it will irradiate as much in the questions of knowledge . . . as in the questions of value (participative democracy).[18]

In light of these analyses, it is the metaphysical dualism of our old ways of thinking that is going to appear as what blocks not only the evolution of the human species (and its experimentations), but the evolution of the living in general by destroying the very conditions of all vital experience.

Disqualifying in a single gesture classical idealism and empiricism, contemporary biology has indeed taught us, on the one hand, that knowledge was one of the functional modalities among others in the vital experience; and on the other, that the vital experience itself was at the same time active and passive:

> The effect of the development of biology has been to reverse the picture. Wherever there is life, there is behavior, activity. . . . [The] adaptative adjustment . . . is not wholly passive; is not a mere matter of the moulding of the organism by the environment. Even a clam acts upon the environment and modifies it to some extent. . . . It does something to the environment as well as has something done to itself. . . . The living creature undergoes, suffers, the consequences of its own behavior. This close connection between doing and suffering and undergoing forms what we call experience. Disconnected doing and disconnected suffering are neither of them experiences.[19]

By defining experience as the connection of activity and passivity, Dewey's *Reconstruction in Philosophy* uses some analyses already developed in *Democracy and Education* almost to the letter:

> The nature of experience can be understood only by noting that it includes an active and a passive element peculiarly combined. On the active hand, experience is *trying*—a meaning which is made explicit in the connected term experiment. On the passive, it is *undergoing*. When we experience something we act upon it, we do something with it; then we suffer or undergo the consequences. We do something to the thing and then it does something to us in return: such is the peculiar combination. The connection of these two phases of experience measures the fruitfulness or value of the experience.[20]

Against the strictly passive and atomized experience of classical empiricism, Dewey thus opposes not the inverted mirror of a purely active experience, but the new idea of an *interactive* experience, where the active and passive phases intimately connect to each other to form a continuous and bound totality:

> Understanding experience from the biological point of view is first to consider it in terms of the interactions of a living organism with its environment, of undergoing and doing. . . . If the child will be able to learn from experience, it is precisely because it is already a connection of doing and undergoing-in-consequence-of-doing and not a chain of intermittent events disconnected from each other.[21]

This description of experience as interaction with the environment, where the processes of biological adaptation are neither purely passive nor only active but always at the same time active and passive, is for Dewey part of what he calls the "genetic and experimental logic of Darwin":

> Just because life signifies not bare passive existence (supposing there is such a thing), but a way of acting, environment or medium signifies what enters into this activity as a sustaining or frustrating condition.[22]

It is this "experimental logic" that makes up in his eyes the core of Darwinism, and which allows him to rethink all forms of experience in general, from nature to society, in a nonmetaphysical way that is itself a bearer of unprecedented social transformations. We understand better now in what way Dewey could think that by transforming "the logic of knowledge" the Darwinian revolution would also transform moral, political, and religious conceptions:

> The *Origin of Species* introduced a mode of thinking that in the end was bound to transform the logic of knowledge, and hence the treatment of morals, politics and religion.[23]

Because for Dewey, as for William James, the Darwinian revolution first involves registering the group of human activities, and with them knowledge, within evolutionary history. By opening the doors of the "kingdom of plants and animals" and, with them, those of the "garden of life," it is Darwin who first brought knowledge to its true function: that of better adapting the most complex organisms to their environment.[24]

However, we must recall here that Spencer already promoted an adaptative interpretation of knowledge in his 1855 *Principles of Psychology*. In this sense, the imputation of this discovery to Darwin can seem quite vague, since it seems to be inspired rather by the spirit of the times, steeped in evolutionism and dominated by the idea of a necessary adaptation of the living to their environment that was already present in Lamarck. But Dewey, who adopts an old William James idea here, is in reality much more rigorous in his reading of

Darwin than one would believe at first glance.[25] While for Spencer adaptation consists of passive submission to the conditions of the environment—which conserves the passive subject of knowledge while also biologizing it—for Darwin as interpreted by James and Dewey, it supposes on the contrary a complex interaction involving a multiplicity of retroactions between the organism and its environment. We henceforth better understand why Dewey imputes the transformation of the logic of knowledge to Darwinian evolutionary theory and to it alone:

> The development of biology . . . with its discovery of evolution . . . displace[s] the notion that [knowing] is the activity of a mere onlooker or spectator of the world. . . . For the doctrine of organic development means that the living creature is a part of the world. . . . If the living, experiencing being is an intimate participant in the activities of the world to which it belongs, then knowledge is a mode of participation.[26]

The expressions "biology" and "evolution" must not be understood here in a vague and general sense. An entry Dewey contributed to *A Cyclopedia of Education* (1911) establishes that those terms designate Darwin's influence (and not that of Lamarck or Spencer) on philosophy very precisely. For, contrary to what Spencer maintains, the organism is in no case modeled by the environment like putty. On the contrary, it actively takes the initiative, offering a new action to its environment, whether in a completely blind fashion (as with random Darwinian variation in general, and instinct in particular), or in a more intentional way:

> In lower organisms, this trying out of the agent in the world of things is blind and instinctive; in higher organisms, in man as he progresses in civilization, it is deliberate and purposive; it involves a forecast of consequences that may follow and the endeavor to manipulate the means requisite to produce these consequences. But in both cases there is some outreaching effort to modify the environment in the interests of life.[27]

This last sentence is crucial. It signifies that if Dewey sees immense value in this difference between organisms as rudimentary as a mollusk and the intelligent beings that we are, it would be a mistake to overestimate the difference between random variation and intelligent forecast to the point of removing the latter from the natural kingdom and the Darwinian explanatory model. Certainly, scientific experimentation is more robust than an approach by trial and error, which is itself much more effective than simple variations of blind and random instinct. But in all these cases, the essential lesson of Darwinism is confirmed. Everything can be explained by the effort (conscious or not, intentional or blind, no matter) "to modify the environment in the interests of life." Such is the true "nature of the intellectual transformation initiated by Darwinian logic."[28]

By recalling that "things" themselves also shape all particular intelligence in return, Dewey additionally indicates that the active dimension of vital experience is not sufficient for realizing Darwin's experimental logic. For what Darwinian evolutionary theory is studying is also in return the set of consequences (or the passive dimension) of these attempts—which were, to begin with, at the organism's initiative:

> The organism has, so to speak, to stand the consequences of its acts. Its actions in modifying things about it modify the conditions which affect its own existence; these changes may be not only unforeseen, but also out of harmony with the direction of its actions. Nevertheless the agent has to suffer or undergo these results.[29]

To transcribe Dewey's analyses into a well-known Darwinian vocabulary: if it is the spontaneous variation of the organism that is initiating the experience (assuring its active dimension), the organism must always undergo in return the effect of that modification (which is the passive dimension of experience) in the sense that its "fitness"—its differential capacity to protect itself and to reproduce—will have the tendency either to increase or to decrease under the impact of the effect that "things" have on it in return. While variation relates to the active dimension of experience, natural selection relates to its passive dimension. In this sense, Darwin is telling us that all organisms always undergo in return, and in a passive mode, the consequences of the experiences that they themselves initiate with their environments in an active mode.

In relation to vital experience in general, knowledge can only modulate in another way the necessary retroaction between the active and passive phases of the experience. It is this retroaction which henceforth forbids all dualist interpretations of the act of knowing. In light of Darwin's "genetic and experimental logic," philosophy has thus learned something essential about the "logic of knowledge"[30] itself: it has had to recognize that there is neither a purely active subject that can claim to construct or constitute in a sovereign way the objects of its environment (like the Cartesian ego, then all the versions of the transcendental subject) nor a simply passive subject, which lets itself be impressed by its environment like putty taking the shape of its surroundings (the sensible subject of classical empiricism). No more than there is, as Lippmann believes, a society divided between active subjects, who alone think of the ends of experience, and passive subjects, who limit themselves to passively and trustfully consenting to the experimentation that has been thought up for them. Rather, all knowledge that follows the experimental logic of Darwinism is at the same time active and passive, elaborating itself through complex chains of retroaction between activity and passivity.

For Dewey, the intelligence of superior organisms thus makes no break with Darwinian logic. It only makes the selection filter more complex by introducing the possibility of countering its (purely passive) effect with a new test (relaunching a new and this time active phase of experience). In regard to random variation, animal intelligence allows for a better fulfillment of the functional, and in this very precise sense, "teleological" dimension of all adaptation:[31]

> Interest shifts from the wholesale essence back of special changes to the question of how special changes serve and defeat concrete purposes; shifts from an intelligence that shaped things once for all to the particular intelligences which things are even now shaping.[32]

Following the rearticulation of the passive and active dimensions of experience, this is the second major consequence of Darwinian experimental logic on philosophy. By substituting the absolute ends of metaphysics with the functions of adaptation and its "values" ("useful," "harmful," "good," "bad"), it now only knows one sole field of experience: the always relative, local, and situated ends of naturalism—which apprehends all experience (from that of the mollusk to that of intelligent beings) as that of an organism that is itself also always situated relative to local ends and never in relation to an "end in itself." Such is the principal gain of "the influence of Darwin on philosophy":

> Philosophy forswears inquiry after absolute origins and absolute finalities in order to explore specific values and the specific conditions that generate them.[33]

For Dewey, far from intelligence causing a break with the Darwinian conception of evolution, it thus very exactly adheres to its logic, even amplifying it in a sense. By better controlling the return effect of natural selection, it allows for the extension of its "cumulative"[34] logic if it is applied. This makes possible at the same time something like an "improvement" (Darwin)[35] or like a "growth" (Dewey), without there being any "progress" in the sense that the teleological conceptions of evolution (Spencer, Lamarck) understand it—which involve the illusory fixing of transcendent and absolute ends that are supposed to give the evolutionary process all its meaning in advance.

If Dewey's Darwin can disorient today's reader, it is ultimately because he marginalizes the question of the nonheredity of acquired characteristics that was so important for the Modern Synthesis—which tried to reconcile the

Darwinian hypothesis with the Mendelian and then Weismannian bases of modern genetics, themselves resting on the strict separation between the *germen* (the genotype) and the *soma* (the phenotype). What truly interests Dewey is not this rupture between two modes of transmission (genetic on the one hand, somatic and/or cultural on the other) that will historically restore all its strength to the hypothesis of natural selection. It is rather, and like Darwin himself, the question of transmission in general to the extent that it allows for a cumulative process that reconciles the stability of the old and the emergence of the new. In the full "eclipse of Darwinism" (1890–1930),[36] Dewey pays homage to Darwin less for the general hypothesis of natural selection—which was then being attacked on all sides—than for his cumulative conception of evolution, which he manages to combine with an interactive, open, and multilinear understanding of evolutionary processes. To the defenders of natural selection, Dewey moreover attributes the same reductionist temptation as that of determinist psychologists who believe that all psychological processes lead back to first instincts:

> It is like saying the flea and the elephant, the lichen and the redwood, the timid hare and the ravening wolf . . . are alike products of natural selection. There may be a sense in which the statement is true; but till we know the specific environing conditions under which selection took place we really know nothing.[37]

Rather than understanding the living as a material that is predictable and calculable by the same general formula, Dewey prefers to take from the Darwinian hypothesis of selection its ecological sense of diversity, which comes from a precise study of the complex and unpredictable interactions between organisms and the diversity of their surroundings. In this widened framework, natural selection coupled with genetic mutation appears only as a process among others, which the other modes of transmission and selection—education and culture—only enrich and make more complex.

This reinterpretation of what Dewey calls "Darwinian logic"[38] thus gives a new meaning to adaptation in general and to the readaptation of the human species to its new environment in particular. Instead of organisms passively bending to the demands of their environment, all readaptation involves an active and continuous interaction between organisms and their environment:

> Continuity of life means continual readaptation of the environment to the needs of living organisms.[39]

Yet on this point, Lippmann decides to take a view entirely opposite from Dewey's, confining himself without realizing it within the same metaphysical assumptions as those that underlie Spencer's evolutionism. For Lippmann, life involves on the contrary the passive readaptation of organisms to the final demands of the environment—of which the *telos* is set in advance as being the global division of labor, and which is imposed as a metaphysical "end in itself" exempted by principle, and for this same reason, from all forms of collective discussion. It is this Spencerian assumption that allows Lippmann to separate those who think up the experience (the ends) and those who apply it (the means), as it separates those who initiate the experience (the experts and leaders) and those who undergo it (the base, the mass of ordinary citizens).

For Dewey, this separation necessarily produces a break between the experts and the needs of the social body; and, more generally, a complete disconnection between the active phases of experience and its passive phases, which is aggravated ceaselessly by the dimensions of the *Great Society*:

> A class of experts is inevitably so removed from common interests as to become a class with private interests and private knowledge, which in social matters is not knowledge at all. . . . No government by experts in which the masses do not have the chance to inform the experts as to their needs can be anything but an oligarchy managed in the interests of the few. And the enlightenment must proceed in ways which force the administrative specialists to take account of the needs. The world has suffered more from leaders and authorities than from the masses.[40]

Rethought of based on Darwin's logic, which unveils the necessary connection between these two phases of experience, all social experimentation—for example, the putting into place of new Taylorist-type work rhythms—would imply on the contrary that it is those who are affected (here, all workers rather than their only representatives) by the different phases of experimentation (conception, control, evaluation, etc.) that lead them. Experts certainly bring an indispensable technical contribution to all experimentation, but they have no legitimacy in keeping the deliberation of its ends and the control of its means to themselves. If we continue with the biomedical example, this means it would be necessary to abandon the vertical relationship which in many ways still prevails between the experts who, from the height of their knowledge, illuminate with their "enlightened information," and the patient who merely gives their "consent"—"enlightened" uniquely by the scientific information that comes from above.[41] Instead of this vertical model, it would be a matter of establishing that this enlightenment also and maybe initially comes from the problem itself: that the "needs" of the patient, like the "needs and social troubles" of the public, must mobilize for themselves and evaluate by themselves the collective utility of the specialized knowledge elaborated by experts.[42]

This is not to exclude the knowledge of experts, nor to produce it in their place. It is rather about collectively controlling its possible political and social usages:

> What is required is . . . the ability to judge of the bearing of the knowledge supplied by others upon common concerns.[43]

We henceforth understand better the organic link, which was so surprising at the beginning, that Dewey declares between Darwin's evolutionary logic and the most participatory forms of democracy:

> [Democracy and Education] connects the growth of democracy with the development of the experimental method in the sciences, evolutionary ideas in the biological sciences, and the industrial reorganization.[44]

But contrary to the dominant Darwinism, it is certainly not, in Dewey's view, the play of egoism and altruism—which are considered as "instincts" or as hereditary "traits"—that allows us to register cultural and social transmission within Darwinian nature.[45] In Human Nature and Conduct (1922), Dewey indeed argues that the categories of egoism and altruism—like all the instincts listed by evolutionary psychology, as well as all the fixed motives that economic science gives to its agents—lack the indetermination or what he calls the native "plasticity" of "impulse" in the human child. The latter only stabilizes progressively in "disposition" and does so by virtue of "habit," which itself emerges from complex interactions with the group. Such is the true constitutive tension of the evolution of our species. Rather than resulting from the atomic shock between egoistic and altruistic traits, it occurs through the dual tendency toward impulse, deviant and innovative, and habit, conservative and stabilizing. For Dewey, this resolutely interactive approach, by refusing to give itself original causal forces, is much more faithful to the experimental logic of Darwin. Also, it is rather the organic link between the active and passive phases of the experimental logic described by Darwin, relayed to human animals by the tension between the innovation of "impulse" of newcomers and the stability of the shared "habits" of the group, which founds Deweyan naturalism and which allows it to disqualify all the social and political disconnection between those who act and those who submit as well as the hierarchical opposition between innovation (which should be reserved for leaders) and stability (which should be the archaic character of the masses).

Rethought of on these Darwinian bases, the role of new democracy must from now on consist, according to Dewey, of doing the precise opposite of that which Lippmannian neodemocracy advocates. It must rearticulate the passive and active dimensions of political experience at the same time as the necessary tendencies to innovation and stability, which the Great Society and then the government of experts have not stopped opposing. Yet such a mission forces us to consider the lags in rhythm of evolutionary time no longer as dyschronies to be eliminated but as a source of fecund tension that is indispensable to the emergence of a new political space of conflicts and dissensions. From this point of view, the lag of the human species must be completely reevaluated. If "the force of lag in Human life is enormous,"[46] it is not just that which seals the deficiency of our species. It is also an opportunity for the human species, making both possible and necessary this new political space of conflicts—which expands the biological struggle between the diversity of interests, values, and rhythms of change, all while profoundly modifying it.

Thinking of the lag of the human species no longer only as a flaw but also as an opportunity for its evolution involves first refuting the gradualist vision of evolutionary rhythm of both Lippmann and Darwin himself. It is in this context that Dewey will promote what I call the *heterochronies* of evolutionary time—which I suggest understanding in a much more expanded sense than the restrained one that the biology of development gives it. By "heterochrony," we here understand not only the strict meaning of the term, of which neoteny—the developmental delay of an organism in regard to its sexual maturity—is one of the most famous examples; but also all the forms of rupture in the evolutionary rhythms recognized henceforth by evolutionary theory, at the forefront of which figures the theory of "punctuated equilibrium," which contests Darwinian gradualism by arguing that evolution most often oscillates between a long period of stasis and a short period of acceleration.[47] If Dewey himself could not be aware of these recent discoveries, we will see that, differing from Lippmann, he knew perfectly well to anticipate this nongradualist polyphony of the evolutionary rhythms of the living, even going so far as to see in it the driving force of all social and political transformation. Through the theme of heterochrony, we are going to see that Dewey thinks of this transition from the biological to the political in terms of both continuity and rupture. In continuity with the history of life, since social and political change itself also supposes a diversity of rhythms potentially in conflict; and in conflict with it, since in the case of the human species, the aggravated problems of heterochrony are going to progressively be seen and addressed in an unprecedented manner: through the emergence of a common "attention" and of a collective intelligence of the public, which will strive to collectively respond to the multiplication of "problems" (Malthus)—that is to say, the phenomena of "maladjustment" and of "maladaptation" (Wallas) that inevitably generate evolution.

Gradualism and Heterochrony

This explains why the first chapter of *The Public and Its Problems* defines the public in a dual relation of continuity and rupture with experimental Darwinian logic. The continuity comes here from the fact that the two phases, both passive and active, are present within all the public's actions:

> The public consists of all those who are affected by the indirect consequences of transactions to such an extent that it is deemed necessary to have those consequences systematically cared for.[48]

Like all living organisms, the public is itself also the agent of an experimentation, involving at the same time a passive dimension ("the public consists of all those who are affected") and an active response ("that it is deemed necessary to have those consequences systematically cared for"). But in order for something like a public to emerge, an entirely unprecedented element in relation to biological association must arise: the individuals in question must feel that the interactions of the other agents affect them in an "enduring" and "serious" manner without a satisfying response to the problem having been found yet.[49] Indeed, what allows for the emergence of a public is not only the fact that the transactions between several organisms can indirectly affect other organisms exterior to the transaction. Such a possibility was already one of the principal lessons of *On the Origin of Species*, that which would open the path to an ecological approach to biological interactions.[50] But in order for a public to form itself, the organisms exterior to the transaction must also *feel themselves* affected in a "serious" way; they must go through the passive phase of experience in the mode of a "problem," a "conflict," or a "trouble" to the point that they feel the need for an active response, of which they notice together the lack or delay in making. It is the fact of being passively and indirectly affected by the interactions of others ("the public consists of all those who are affected"), doubled by the correlative conscience of a necessary yet deficient control of the consequences ("that it is deemed necessary to have those consequences systematically cared for"), which constitutes the "difference" of human associations for Dewey, and which explains both the emergence of the public space and the birth of politics:

> When we consider the difference we at once come upon the fact that the consequences of conjoint action take on a new value when they are observed. For notice of the effects of connected action forces men to reflect upon the connection itself; it makes an object of attention and interest.[51]

This is one of the aspects of the lags that structure the evolutionary history of the human species. By multiplying the delays between the passive and active phases of vital experience, it makes the political field at the same time possible and necessary—which Dewey analyzes first and before all as a new space of reflection for the intelligence of the living, who are constrained to socialize in a common attention and in a collective intelligence.

If biological experience begins through a blind activity (random variation) of which the organism then feels the consequences in a passive way (through the effect of selection), social and political experience begins by an indissolubly passive and active phase, where the passive and common hardship of a problem and the active and collective search for a solution are in both intimate connection and painful disjunction. This is what explains for Dewey that the state or the government is never already there, but must be searched for and reconstructed:

> By its very nature, a state is ever something to be scrutinized, investigated, searched for. Almost as soon as its form is stabilized, it needs to be re-made.
>
>   Thus, the problem of discovering the state is not a problem for theoretical inquirers. . . . It is a practical problem of human beings living in association with one another. . . . It demands power to perceive and recognize consequences of the behavior of individuals joined in groups and to trace them to their source and origin.[52]

Dewey thus draws political consequences from Darwinism that are strictly opposed to those Lippmann defends. Indeed, for the Lippmann of *Phantom Public*, we remember that politics, public discussion, and democratic experimentation needed to henceforth be kept to the minimum: to that of the procedural respect for the rules in case of crisis. All the rest of the time, the individual was sent back to his private choices regarding consumption, production, and reproduction, which were supposed to assure an optimal and spontaneous self-government of society. For Dewey, the return of this deflationist definition of the scope of politics in general, and of democratic government in particular, reactivates the liberal fantasy of the "naked individual,"[53] which contributes to dissolving publics in order to atomize them into a plurality of desires and individual choices without any link between them. In his eyes, this reactive return to classical liberalism, by preventing the communication of the public with itself and by favoring its atomization, is another "old idea" that lags behind evolution. Far from the public being, as Lippmann argues, apathetic by nature, for Dewey it is on the contrary this type of dominant idea that participates in the destruction of the affective dimension of collective experience, to the point that it also produces complete *a-pathy* in public opinion:

> At the outset, [individualism] was held by "progressives." . . . Today the industrial-property regime being established, the doctrine is the intellectual bulwark of the standpatter and reactionary. . . . The irony of history is nowhere more evident than in the reversal of the practical meaning of the term "liberalism." . . .
>
> Political apathy . . . is a natural product of the discrepancies between actual practices and traditional machinery.[54]

What Lippmann ultimately does not understand is that without the transmission of the social and political experience through the communication of the public with itself the human species will be condemned to remain in the clumsy fumbling of trial and error.[55] Yet it is precisely this blind fumbling that Lippmann's supposedly pragmatic Darwinism is celebrating in *The Phantom Public*.[56] By blocking the production of inquiry and its diffusion, the intermittent, minimalist, and procedural conception of political action prevents the cumulative and continuous evolution discovered by the experimental and genetic logic of Darwinism. As Dewey argues,

> Public opinion, even if it happens to be correct, is intermittent when it is not the product of methods of investigation and reporting constantly at work. It appears only in crises. Hence its "rightness" concerns only an immediate emergency. Its lack of continuity makes it wrong from the standpoint of the course of events. . . . Only continuous inquiry, continuous in the sense of being connected as well as persistent, can provide the material of enduring opinion about public matters.[57]

By reducing Darwinism to a gradualist conception of evolution by slight variations, Lippmann retains only one of the most fragile—and today one of the most discussed—postulates in contemporary Darwinism.[58] In light of this new divergence, it appears clearly that the trivial presentation of pragmatism as a fumbling series of trials and errors, undertaken by a multiplicity of atomized individuals who tend to be liberated from the shackles of politics and spontaneously govern themselves by local adjustments, rests on a profound misinterpretation. With this misinterpretation established, the inclusion of Lippmann in the pragmatist movement seems definitively compromised. Far from valorizing the dyschronies already diagnosed by Malthus—seeing in them, like Dewey, the source of a divergent and creative evolution—the goal of political action according to Lippmann is to eliminate them in order to impose a gradualist consensus that resets all the rhythms to the same pace. This explains why the only differences allowed in the political field are very slight variations that are the most neutral possible, allowing for the gradual reform of rules and warding off the specter of conflict and revolution. Such must be, for Lippmann, the effect of the Darwinian revolution on the political field: converting democracy, which has been reduced to a minimum by the Darwinian government of interests, into a simple procedure of gradually improving the rules, which has itself been purged from the risks of conflict.

For Dewey, on the contrary, the lag of old forms of political organization behind the emergence of new publics makes the accumulation of conflicts inevitable and explains the regular onset of ruptures and revolutions:

> Progress is not steady and continuous. . . .
> . . . To form itself, the public has to break existing political forms.
> . . . The public which generated political forms is passing away, but the power and lust of possession remains in the hands of the officers and agencies which the dying public instituted. This is why the change of the form of states is so often effected only by revolution.[59]

We find here Dewey's refusal to accuse the public of blocking the flux of change in the name of its supposed "static" and "stereotypical" nature. For him, it is on the contrary the old forms of power, to which the rulers cling, that prevent the self-organization of a new public and that need to be broken. Let us remember that this is the first form of "lag" with which Dewey confronts Lippmann. To this lag of institutions and social organizations behind the needs of the public is added a second form of lag: that of "ideas" which most often reflect the hierarchical rigidities of social organization. Yet for Dewey it is clear that Lippmann's political thought exactly embodies these two modalities of lag.

But to these pejorative variations on the theme of lag, we are beginning to see that Dewey added others—affected this time by a positive coefficient and illustrating the argument, which itself also breaks with Lippmann, of a "force of lag."[60] It is in this context that we must understand the famous Deweyan analysis of habits. Reviving the analyses of *Human Nature and Conduct*, *The Public and Its Problems* (1927) recalls first that, in the context of an exponential acceleration of industrial rhythms, the stability of "habits" and the rooting of "attachments" remain indispensable in the forming of a public that communicates with itself:

> A community must always remain a matter of face-to-face intercourse. This is why the family and neighborhood, with all their deficiencies, have always been the chief agencies of nurture, the means by which

dispositions are stably formed and ideas acquired which laid hold on the roots of character. . . . Vital and thorough attachments are bred only in the intimacy of an intercourse which is of necessity restricted in range. . . .

. . . There is no substitute for the vitality and depth of close and direct intercourse and attachment.[61]

Here, what is stabilizing and lagging behind the acceleration of the fluxes is revealed to be vital for the pursuit of any collective experience. Expanding the analysis of habits, the Jeffersonian demand for establishing roots in local "communities" where living face-to-face relationships allow "communication" around what is "common" also establishes itself as a positive image of lag.[62] Far from scorning, as Lippmann does, the democratic ambition that Americans borrow from Jefferson in favor of the elitist path chosen by Hamilton and Madison, Dewey argues that the pursuit of a political experience in the context of globalization involves solutions being found to articulate the global scale of the Great Society and that of the necessarily local democratic communities. Because it is accompanied by a quest for the "Great Community"[63] at the global scale, this anchoring at the local level clearly has "nothing to do with a passist and romantic return to pre-modern society."[64] It signifies rather that the new path will only be able to look for and potentially find itself in the difficult articulation—that is certainly yet to be invented—between the local and global scales of problems.[65]

Such an articulation necessarily occurs, in his eyes, through the affirmation of the necessary lag of these decelerating *stases* behind the *flux* of change:

There is something deep within human nature itself which pulls toward settled relationships . . . [toward] ties with others, which reach to such depths that they go below the surface of conscious experience to form its undisturbed foundation. No one knows how much of the frothy excitement of life, of mania for motion, of fretful discontent . . . is the expression of frantic search for something to fill the void caused by the loosening of the bonds which hold persons together in immediate community of experience.[66]

Confirming the solidarity of the concepts of community and communication, this necessary lag of all community behind the flux of change finds itself at the heart of the Deweyan analysis of communication, which entails "signs" and "symbols" that he interprets as so many stases, stabilizations, or slowdowns of flux:

Only when there exist *signs* or *symbols* of activities and of their outcome can the flux . . . be arrested for consideration and esteem, and
be regulated.[67]

Only then does something like a temporality that is stabilized, articulated, and
regulated by the memories and expectations of the collective experimentation
begin.[68]

But the whole difficulty of this stabilization of flux by the stases of the symbolic world comes from having to stop it without seeking to block it or oppose
it. If the stabilization of flux, which is undertaken by this new medium interposed with signs and symbols, originates from the native tendency to inertia
and stability, this tendency must not cut itself off from the mobile environment
to which it must precisely adjust. Instead of seeking to reject it, the stabilization
of flux by habits and the symbolic world must on the contrary help us evaluate
and regulate it.[69] Under the dual constraint of stasis and flux, enjoined at the
same time to lag and to acceleration, the human species thus finds itself caught
between two dangers: between the danger of a denial of flux by the world of
significations and symbols that the multisecular history of morality and metaphysics has so well illustrated and the opposite but just as threatening danger
of a flux hostile to all forms of stases—borne by the emergence of the industrial
and globalized Great Society:

Enormous organization is compatible with the demolition of the ties
that form local communities and with substitution of impersonal
bonds for personal unions, with a flux which is hostile to stability.[70]

A flux hostile to stasis, and a stasis that refuses the irreversibility of flux—such
is the dual pitfall to avoid. Against these harmful oppositions, the affirmation
of a tension at the same time threatening and necessary between flux and stasis
forms the tragic background of Dewey's thought.[71]

By interpreting the constitutive tension between flux and stasis as the both
dangerous and necessary condition not just of the human species but of all
forms of life, Dewey thus considerably complicates the question of its lag:

Nature is characterized by a constant mixture of the precarious and
the stable. This mixture gives poignancy to existence. If existence were
either completely necessary or completely contingent, there would be
neither comedy nor tragedy in life. . . . The significance of morals and
politics . . . have their source and meaning in the union in Nature of
the settled and the unsettled.[72]

While Lippmann systematically takes the side of a homogeneous and gradual flux in regard to which all stasis sees itself disqualified as archaic and

lagging—and all lag itself as a negative symptom of a deficiency—the social and political evolution that Dewey strongly calls for is on the contrary fundamentally heterogeneous, recognizing the irreducible heterochrony of evolutionary rhythm in the widened sense of the word, comprising the group of rhythmic discrepancies (ontogenetic, phylogenetic, social, and political) that form the uncertain and conflictual tissue of all evolutionary history. Here maybe, and beyond the caricatured vision of a Dewey who is too naïve, idealistic, and optimistic, opens a fecund path for grasping the tragedy of politics that roots itself in the poignant character of all forms of life.

To conclude, all that Dewey retained from the "experimental logic" of Darwin ultimately finds itself lost through the gradualism of slight variations. Yet if, as we have seen, it is more and more openly contested by certain Darwinians, gradualism has not in one sense ceased to harden in the most "orthodox" version of contemporary Darwinism. The gradualist postulate certainly comprises a decisive advantage, since it not only meets the dominant standards of the natural sciences—to which Darwin himself was very attached—but also mobilizes their powerful prediction tools by opening the path to an always finer mathematical modeling of the living. But for Stephen Jay Gould, it tends to also regard organisms as a "putty" that is subjected to the blind mechanism of selection. It is this conception that triumphs today in the excesses of the Neo-Darwinism of Richard Dawkins and Daniel Dennett—the latter not hesitating to thus summarize "the Darwinian core idea," in head-on opposition with what Dewey could retain from his "genetic and experimental" logic:

> An impersonal, unreflective, robotic, mindless, little scrap of molecular machinery is the ultimate basis of all the agency, and hence meaning, and hence consciousness, in the universe.[73]

Denying the interactive relationship of the organism with its environment—that which involves a duality of phases, active and passive, during the experimentation, and with them, a polyphony of evolutionary rhythms in perpetual tension—this conquering version of contemporary Darwinism clearly takes the side of a passive, mechanical, and even automatic conception of adaptation. This is what explains that when it claims to register the human experience, with its teleological functions of control and anticipation, within the logic of Darwin, Neo-Darwinism reduces it to a blind and strictly gradual mechanism of variation and selection that proceeds in an automatic and algorithmic mode. Because he questions this gradualist conception of evolutionary rhythm—and with it the passive, mechanistic, and automated approach to adaptation that it presupposes—at the same time as the atomist postulate that assumes already formed individuals, Dewey thus anticipates in his fashion certain aspects of the revised Darwinism of Gould, who will suggest more than a half century later cutting these three postulates from *On the Origin of Species*.[74] From this point of view, we can consider that the Deweyan conception of evolution, which resists the triple hegemony of gradualism, adaptationism, and the liberal postulate of individualism, appears in many ways to be more innovative, and maybe also more solid, than Lippmann's dogmatic Darwinism.

Instead of fixing in advance the *telos* of evolution, as Lippmann ultimately does after Spencer, in a global division of labor where all human activities would be supposed to mechanically adjust themselves to each other while obeying the uniform and gradual cadence of industrial rhythms, Dewey draws from the Darwinian revolution three rigorously opposite consequences. Branching, evolution does not follow in advance any *telos*, but explores entirely on the contrary a multiplicity of directions that are at the same time coherent, cumulative, and divergent. Heterogeneous, incompatible with the uniform rhythm demanded by industrial cadences, and unable to be reduced to a simple gradual and procedural reform of the rules, it will never overcome the heterochrony of evolutionary rhythms. Unpredictable, its only meaning will always remain the production of "radical differences"[75] by contributing to the liberation of the new potentialities that each newcomer brings; and with this, by taking on the risk of collective confrontation about the ends that, together, the publics can hope to aim toward in common.

4

Toward a New Liberalism

From the debate between Lippmann and Dewey, 1990s American communication studies only remembered the confrontation—that is still alive today—between two incompatible models of democracy: one led by experts and leaders, the other by publics and their problems. But they missed the other dimension of the debate: that which bears on the future of liberalism in the context of the 1930s crisis, and a question that has become strikingly relevant again. With the Great Depression, liberalism was confronted, as everyone knows, by one of the most serious crises of its history. But this crisis in reality finished off its slow disqualification which had begun at the end of the nineteenth century. The 1929 financial crisis, then the economic, social, and political crises in which—in its wake—the world was sunk during the 1930s, inflicted a scathing refutation of the liberal belief in the spontaneous harmonization of economic and social interactions. In consequence of this growing discredit, the massive failure of economic liberalism led to a progressive abandonment of the emancipating ideals of early liberalism for the benefit of an authoritarian takeover of societies. It was in this unsettling context that Dewey published *Individualism Old and New* (1930)[1] and then *Liberalism and Social Action* (1935),[2] while two years later Lippmann published *The Good Society* (1937), which would inspire the great "Lippmann Colloquium" that took place in Paris the following year. These three books and this colloquium would have a common aim: to critique a liberalism in crisis in order to reconstruct it on entirely new bases—to invent a *new liberalism*. Yet by launching this ambitious political project, Dewey was also going to open a new stage of the Lippmann-Dewey debate in which it would be Lippmann who would be forced to respond this time. Through his response, there would be not only two opposed models of democracy, but two opposed conceptions of liberalism that continue to confront each other today—dividing our dominant model of liberal democracies without our even being aware of it.

The Other Lippmann-Dewey Debate:
The Disagreement about Liberalism

For Dewey, Lippmann sees nothing of the "reversal" of meaning that liberalism underwent in the course of its history. Whereas in the second half of the eighteenth century liberalism had given itself the historic mission of promoting the liberation of the new, during the nineteenth century it in fact became the instrument of domination par excellence of conservative forces.[3] It is this reversal which culminated at the end of the century in the status quo defended by Herbert Spencer's laissez-faire and his phobia of the State. To the social hierarchy between the leisure classes and the working classes, which goes back to Greek antiquity and to its old manners of thinking, was added a more modern version of lag, where conservatism progressively concealed itself in the celebration of mobility, acceleration, and innovation. In the name of liberalization, everything was organized so that the dominant classes conserved their advantages acquired thanks to industrial concentration. While in most countries the term "liberalism" became more and more clearly associated with the defense of dominant interests, only the United States—which in the wake of Spencer continued to associate it with social progress—started to lag behind on this point by continuing to designate "progressives" as "liberals."

It remains to be understood how such a reversal could take place and to account for the paradoxical character of the industrial revolution—promoting the liberation of the new while provoking the blockage of evolutionary movement. For Dewey, the reasons for the blockage must be sought in the neoliberal conception of the individual. His critical analysis starts from the observation of a profound incoherence. The industrial Great Society, with its immense impersonal forces favoring concentration, made individuals incapable of participating in the course of social affairs, and yet at precisely this moment they were asked to become the agents of economic and social progress.[4] The industrial revolution, in the name of permanent innovation, created in its turn, like the old dynasties of the ancien régime, immense collective stases frozen in "a new set of customs and institutions."[5] All throughout the nineteenth century, the industrial revolution recreated stases just as restrictive as those it had liquidated, henceforth simultaneously controlling—like the old "dynastic interests"—the political power and the modes of life of populations. The new stases turned out to be even more restrictive since they, by affecting "thought" and "desire," imposed processes of deindividuation and transformed individuals into "interchangeable" and "standardized units." If he is right in noting them, comprehension of these processes of massification completely escapes Lippmann, who does not see the emergence of the masses as a historic phenomenon in which liberalism has rightly had a central responsibility. For Dewey, relying on the liberal belief in a "naked individual" to struggle against the domination of the masses and their inertia, which is ultimately the political program of *The Phantom Public*, amounts to making two mistakes at the same time. The first denies the evolutionary blockage induced by liberalism. The second denies the role of liberalism in the processes of deindividuation that characterize the Great Society. While Lippmann postulates that all publics reduce themselves in essence or by nature to a mass, Dewey counters by indicating the historic role of liberalism in the processes of massification.

This last paradox, that of a deindividualizing individualism, is explained by a major error of liberalism that Lippmann adopts in turn, and that one could summarize as the *atomist postulate* of its naturalism:

> The idea that there is something inherently "natural" and amenable to "natural law" in the working of economic forces, in contrast with the man-made artificiality of political institutions. The idea of a natural individual in his isolation possessed of full-fledged wants, of energies to be expended according to his own volition, and of a ready-made faculty of foresight and prudent calculation is as much a fiction in psychology as the doctrine of the individual in possession of anteced-ent political rights is one in politics.[6]

Here, Dewey takes aim at both the naturalism of classical liberalisms and the utilitarian anthropology that Jeremy Bentham progressively imposed on liberal thought. Yet we remember that Lippmann himself, in the wake of Graham Wallas, had already begun this dual critique.[7] From the 1910s onward, he criticized the belief of classical liberalism in a natural law of harmonization as much as he did the rationalist postulates of utilitarianism, which give the individual the capacity for rationally calculating pleasures and pains. Against this fiction and relying on Freud, he countered with the obscure and largely unconscious character of desire, of which only the most superficial part can potentially be resolved into a conscious goal of achieving pleasure. For all these reasons, this Dewey quotation cannot, at first glance, be taking aim at Lippmann and seems rather even to go along with him—except that in *The Phantom Public*, the latter returns to the same postulates of classical liberalism in spite of his initial criticism of them. If he does not explicitly reduce the individual to a machine that rationally calculates its costs and benefits, he does give him a ready-made faculty of executing good choices in terms of work, consumption, and reproduction. The Lippmannian individual is thus finally understood, as in classical liberalism, on the grounds of an atomist postulate: like the atom, it is a ready-made and isolated unit that precedes society and its interactions. If public opinion is an amorphous mass, the first elements that compose it— individuals and their preferences—precede the mass itself, as atoms precede their relationships. What Dewey criticizes in liberal naturalism is clearly not that it refers to nature to understand society. He himself will claim such a naturalism until the end. What he rejects is the atomist naturalism that classical liberals, utilitarians, and Lippmann himself too often maintain—which presupposes ready-made and law-abiding individuals—while Darwinism enjoins us to abandon such postulates.[8]

The confrontation between these two naturalisms is made plain in *Human Nature and Conduct*. While liberal naturalism starts from an atomic individual that is supposed to precede its interactions, Dewey's naturalism interprets individuation as a process that involves a continuous interaction with the environment—with the natural environment in the case of biological individuals and with the social environment in the case of human individuals. For human beings, if the environment that matters most to human beings is that formed by the activities of other humans, this comes from the fact of their great dependence during childhood.[9] It is what gives habit a central place, which must nevertheless be understood in continuity with nature. Like biological functions, the habits of the human animal are means and tools of using and incorporating the environment. Yet we have seen that the biological interaction between random individual variation and adjustment to the environment took on a new form with the human animal: that of the necessary interaction between impulse and habit, between the tendency to deviation and newness (impulse) that any child bears and the equally necessary tendency to adjust to the habits of its social group. For Dewey, impulses are the pivot of reorganization and the agents of deviation that alone can give new directions to habits. To reiterate, in the human species impulses are what take over from Darwinian variation and assure the evolutionary "renewal" of the species and its social transformations.

Like the Darwinian interaction between variation and adjustment to the environment, the tension between habit and impulse is resolved each time in a singular and unpredictable manner that no law of evolution will ever be able to calculate or predict. It is for this reason that Dewey can say that utilitarianism, with its mathematics of pains and pleasures, assumes a permanent world that denies the evolutionary reality of our species.[10] Singular individualities emerge, or do not, from these unpredictable interactions between impulse and habit. They appear when variation and adaptation manage to articulate themselves to each other, allowing life to evolve. But they fail when variation is maladapted, and when, with humans, the necessary tension between impulse and habit transforms into open conflict, preventing the newcomer from being individuated. For the human species to renew itself, habits must indeed be sufficiently "plastic to the transforming touch of impulse."[11] Morality, specific to the human species, emerges precisely from this perpetual tension between habit and impulse that is always on the point of entering into conflict, and which must be constantly rearticulated for this reason.[12] By extrapolating from Dewey's analyses, we can go as far as saying that evolution takes a tragic turn with the human animal even before the emergence of politics—that of a never-resolved tension between flux and stasis. For if habit tends toward inertia, to being fastened to rigid stases, how can impulse play its role of renewal or liberation of evolutionary flux?[13] In light of such a naturalism, individuation appears henceforth as an eminently fragile and precarious result that is never guaranteed in advance and that involves the delicate articulation of a multiplicity of conditions. This is what Lippmann does not understand: that by renewing the atomist postulate of classical liberalism and assuming individuals to be ready-made, he is missing the tragic and constitutive tension of the human species between stasis and flux that is itself indispensable for the emergence of politics.

For Dewey, it is this misinterpretation of classical liberalism that has created the famous antinomy between the individual and society in which all political thought has been enmeshed since the nineteenth century. It is because it had, as its origin, this atomic individual that liberalism made the emergence of the social fact enigmatic. But there is nothing enigmatic about the fact of society. Society is only a human modality of "association"—a phenomenon that is itself universal since we find it in all of nature, as much physical as biological.[14] Liberalism proceeds backwards. It assumes a ready-made individual and then asks how an association emerges, while for Dewey, human association is an already given evolutionary and natural fact—the whole question being precisely of knowing in which conditions individuals can emerge. As *Human Nature and Conduct* already declared, the problem is not so much knowing how the individual mind forms social groups but of understanding how these interactive established arrangements form and nourish different, that is to say individuated,[15] minds. Ultimately, the question is not knowing how individuals make groups, but how groups make individuals.

Far from being given at the beginning, the emergence of individuals is thus always a consequence, the result of complex and fragile processes of individuation that are precisely the focus of pragmatist inquiry. This explains why Dewey rejects both liberal "individualism" and organicist "collectivism," which make the same symmetric mistake: that of opposing the individual and soci-ety.[16] If individuals no longer manage to emerge, it is not the social fact itself that is at issue, but the domination of a sole mode of association that deprives the newcomers of the expression of their potentialities. This risk not only threatens old societies, which tend to curb the innovative potentialities of individuals through the shackles of "family, clan, and church." It also char-acterizes, and maybe much more, liberal society, which makes "one form of association"—the economic association—prevail over all the other forms of interaction.

This domination of economic association is already criticized in *Human Nature and Conduct*. Liberal naturalism—by freezing impulse in a series of "instincts" beginning with the instincts of property and competition, and po-tentially finishing with the altruistic instinct of cooperation—completely misses the plasticity of human nature, which is continually invented in the tragic tension between impulse and habit.[17] For Dewey, this list of instincts is a set of ad hoc hypotheses destined to justify a mode of social organization that cor-responds with nothing real in human nature. We henceforth understand better how the fatal "reversal" of liberalism into its opposite proceeded. By making the economic institution of property and the taste for competition prevail over all other interactions in the name of supposed natural instincts, liberalism profoundly misinterpreted the much wider potentialities of impulse. Claiming to liberate evolutionary movement from innovation by emancipating individ-uals from the shackles of society, it progressively hobbled them in still more binding restraints, going so far as to standardize their manners of feeling and thinking. In this sense, it is liberalism itself, and not the state or society, that has contributed to the destruction of impulse, the massification of individuals, and the blockage of evolution.

Toward a New Liberalism

This long reminder allows a better understanding of why, even before the eruption of the crisis of 1929, Dewey puts two individualisms into opposition: one "new" and the other "old."[18] *Individualism Old and New* willingly disturbs the opposition. Sometimes it is the individualism of classical liberalism, that which emphasizes profit and competition, which Dewey presents as an old obsolete individualism. In this case, the old liberal individualism must be overtaken by a new individualism that liberates the evolutionary potentialities of individuals again. Sometimes, on the contrary, it is the old American ideal of "equality of opportunities" that Dewey presents as the old individualism, that which blossoms precisely through the articulation of impulses and habits, and which was covered over and lost through the atomistic "new individualism" of property and competition.

This oscillation must lead us to distinguish not two, but at least four individualisms; or if we prefer, four moments in the history of liberalism clearly distinct from one another, even if they more or less hybridize throughout the eras. The first of these moments is that of the medieval conception of the individual soul, from which liberal atomism and its "ready-made" individual draw inspiration. The second is that of the "equality of opportunities," which for Dewey so well captured the driving force of impulse in the evolution of the human species—particularly in the American political thought of the Founding Fathers. The third moment is that of the liberal and atomistic individualism of competition and profit, which progressively covered over and then finally destroyed this liberalism of potentialities. Finally, the fourth and last moment is the "new individualism" which remains to be invented—that which will again make possible the articulation between the impulse of individual potentialities and habits, allowing us to incorporate our new industrial environment. Here is the "deepest problem of our time": that of "constructing a new individuality consonant with the objective conditions under which we live."[19]

A few days before the October crash (we are in September 1929), Dewey sketches out a new idea. Far from predicting the end of liberalism, he rather calls for the *invention of a new liberalism* which adopts the old liberal ideal of a liberation of opportunities while making it compatible with our new industrial environment. If the Jeffersonian and liberal ideal of the "equality of opportunities" must remain, the problem of its reconciliation with the new industrial environment—which is totally different from the small agrarian communities of which Jefferson was thinking—remains open indeed. Whereas the individualism of pioneers had to struggle against the barren and savage space of the wilderness—in a local environment and in face-to-face relationships—the new individualism must consist of "the controlled use of all the resources . . . of science and technology" that the industrial revolution created.[20] The idea that underlies this "new individualism" is thus absolutely not to escape the industrial world to cultivate our own garden and restore the enclosures of self-sufficiency.[21] It is rather to understand that the only garden that we have to cultivate is "the industrial world . . . in which we live"—a world which we must no longer accept to passively endure, but with which we must finally begin to interact.

This necessity of inventing a new liberalism becomes still more explicit five years later in *Liberalism and Social Action*. The call for a re-founding of liberalism forms in particular the object of the second chapter of the work, entitled "The Crisis of Liberalism."[22] In sharp contrast with the preceding analyses is the now detailed program of liberalism's reconstruction. But this new program confirms the prior analyses. As in his 1920s works, Dewey continues to interpret the errors of classical liberalism—which he always carefully distinguishes from its outrageous later version uniquely centered on profit—starting from its initial misinterpretation of individuation: that of the atomist postulate.[23] The naturalism of old liberals, by adopting the Newtonian model of a "decomposition into atoms" that are themselves passively submissive to universal laws, chooses a model that certainly suits—up to a certain point—inert matter but cannot account for life and its evolutionary processes.[24] In contrast with this obsolete naturalism, the new liberalism must integrate a more adequate model of comprehension of the living based on what was initially promoted by the Darwinian revolution: that of a laboratory where new hypotheses are incessantly tested.

It is precisely in this context, that of a much more rigorous grasp of both nature and its experimental methods, that Dewey advances the central notion of "planning."[25] This call for planning is surely explained in part by the historical context—that of the increasing importance of economic and social planning due to the Great Depression. But beyond the fact that, as we will see right away, his judgment of Roosevelt's New Deal is broadly very critical, this positive reference to planning can, for a pragmatist like Dewey, surprise at first glance. Is not planning, on the one hand, claiming to predict or calculate—which can recall the mathematizing ambitions of utilitarianism; and on the other, imposing a centralized government, which seems to contradict the model of participative and decentralized democracy promoted by Dewey? In addition, what can be liberal in planning if it imposes the return of a centralized and authoritarian state? These different difficulties are resolved if we grasp the precise and rigorous meaning that the notion of planning takes on in the context of pragmatism. For Dewey, the plan is never linked to an infallible calculation functioning with mathematical certitude. It is rather the result of a hypothetical projection of the intelligence whose role is precisely to try, through an approximate knowledge of causal series, to control the consequences. Intelligence regains here its Darwinian and adaptative meaning. Its function is to modify and reconstruct its environment rather than passively submit to it like atoms obeying the laws of nature. Instead of producing mathematical certitudes, the plan is the projection of "possibilities," which is exactly the operating mode of the experimental method.[26] Opposing at the same time the mathematical calculation of utilitarianism and a laissez-faire that abandons the experimental control of consequences for a supposed preestablished harmony, planning is thus a construction—the "construction of a new social order"—which must be tested in an experimental manner, just as we test any hypothesis since the scientific revolution of the classical age.

   This second aspect of the plan allows for a response to the second objection. The planning intelligence for which Dewey calls in the political and social domain cannot be that of a vertical power like that of a centralized state. As experimental intelligence, it can only be collectively put to the test; and in this sense, can only be effective in a democratic and decentralized mode. This precise concept of planning—which is very different from that of the New Deal—indeed imposes "separating the idea of social planning and that of a nationalization of the economy."[27] It is this necessarily collective, democratic, and decentralized dimension of the experimental method that allows for planning corrected this way to join in the liberal tradition, while Roosevelt's centralized planning is linked rather to a state capitalism that is itself founded on the centralized government of experts.

   In contrast with this planning liberalism, which promotes collective intelligence as the only legitimate agent in all planning, all "the tragedy of earlier liberalism," says Dewey, comes from its misinterpretation of intelligence, of which it missed the intrinsically collective nature:

> It is the tragedy of earlier liberalism that just at the time when the problem of social organization was the most urgent, liberals could bring to its solution nothing but the conception that intelligence is an individual possession.[28]

   Breaking with this atomist conception of intelligence, the liberal planning promoted by Dewey is that of a "cooperative experimental intelligence" that itself involves a "socially organized intelligence."[29] This precision shows that Dewey in no way yields to any form of bucolic spontaneism—that of a spontaneous self-organization of social life that would not need collective structure and political institutions. According to him, socially organized intelligence must necessarily be supported with a "legislation" and an "administration," and thus a group of "institutions"[30] that not only helps publics better control the consequences of the relations of production (as in *The Public and Its Problems*) but even goes so far as to make possible "the collective appropriation of the means of production"—which was not as clearly an issue in the 1927 book.[31] By combatting legislation favorable to the concentration of wealth, and by substituting legislation that attacks state capitalism at its roots, the goal is indeed to assure material security for everyone that allows for the "ideas of liberty, individuality, and of freed intelligence"[32] to be made real. Far from being opposed to socialism—which has been arbitrarily reduced by Lippmann to an authoritarian collectivism—the new liberalism promoted by Dewey here approaches what he will later designate as "the essential core of socialist thought: that only by the overthrow of a profit-economic system can the freedom of production and exchange [Lippmann] postulates be brought about."[33] The new liberalism must also at the same time lead a critique of economic capitalism and a critique of the concentration of what we will later call "cultural capital" in the hands of the elites. To do this, it must make use of political and juridical institutions to foster new forms of sharing both material and cultural wealth. It is in this precise sense that liberalism must become "radical": it can no longer be satisfied, as social democracy believed for so long and as the partisans of "social liberalism" still believe today, with simply regulating the abuses of capitalism, and must rather *collectively* reconstruct *at its root* (*radix, radices*) the institutional framework acting as the basis of economic and cognitive organization. Which implies, in the first place, struggling against all institutions that allow state capitalism and the government of experts to continually reinforce each other.

Adopting the socialist heritage of the critique of capitalism while distancing itself from the Marxist demand for a revolutionary rupture, Dewey continues to speak—like Lippmann in *The Phantom Public* and then like Roosevelt and his New Deal—the gradualist language of reform.[34] But in relation to Lippmann's procedural and minimalist reform, which proceeds only by slight imperceptible variations, as with the palliative half-measures of the New Deal, which seek to regulate the ravages of capitalism to better ensure its perpetuation, the reforms of radical liberalism assume the irreducible heterochrony of evolutionary processes—within which a "gulf" is regularly formed between the real and the possible.[35] If liberalism is at the service of evolution, and if evolution itself is grasped in all its heterochrony, it can thus only be "radical":

If radicalism be defined as perception of need for radical change,
then today any liberalism which is not also radicalism is irrelevant
and doomed.[36]

The fact that heterochrony is irreducible indeed requires liberal reforms to be not procedural but radical and reconstructive.

Dewey discovers here the tension that I qualified above as tragic—in the sense that it is at the same time perilous, necessary, and insoluble—between stases and flux; and in the categories of his naturalism, between habits and impulses. As this tension makes lag both permanent and necessary, Dewey here reactivates the theme of the "strength of lag" in the human species:

We are always possessed by habits and customs, and this fact signifies
that we are always influenced by the inertia and the momentum of
forces temporally outgrown but nevertheless still present with us as a
part of our being. Human life gets set in patterns, institutional and

moral. But change is also with us and demands the constant remaking of old habits and old ways of thinking, desiring, and acting.[37]

Contrary to what a too-rapid reading of these lines could lead one to think, Dewey is not playing the new against the old here, no more than he is affirming the superiority of creative impulse over routine habit. Linking these analyses to those of *Human Nature and Conduct* allows us to ward off this misinterpretation. If "the effective ratio between the old and the stabilizing and the new and disturbing"[38] continually modifies itself, the duality of this dual condition is "always" imposed: "the old and the new have forever to be integrated with each other."[39] In this text, as in the preceding texts, stasis and flux continue to be, like habit and impulse, the dual condition of all human life in general, and of social life in particular: "what is happening socially is the result of the combination of the two factors, one dynamic, the other relatively static."[40] Yet this reminder will allow Dewey to advance an entirely new definition of liberalism, whose historic mission would have precisely been the "adjustment" of this dual condition from the beginning:

> There is always an adjustment to be made, and as soon as the need for it becomes conscious, liberalism has a function and a meaning. . . . The necessity for adjustment defines the office of liberalism.[41]

Such would be in reality—independently of all atomist postulates and all hypostases of the instinct of property and competition—the veritable political meaning of liberalism: that of allowing the human species, which in the eighteenth century is for the first time becoming collectively aware of the fact of evolution, to confront the heterochronies of evolutionary rhythm and to optimally readjust the old and the new. Let us remember that the term "adjustment" was already found in Wallas's writing and that we will often see it again in that of Lippmann. Let us also remember that while Wallas considered that adjustment could only be produced by collective intelligence, Lippmann ultimately maintained, against his mentor, that adjustment took place spontaneously through economic interactions in general and the division of labor in particular. Such was, in the main, the meaning of Lippmann's return to classical liberalism. For Dewey, on the contrary, radical liberalism enters the scene when there is a problem of adjustment that precisely no longer manages to be resolved by itself or spontaneously by economic and social interactions alone. This explains why liberalism appeared in the eighteenth century—when evolution accelerated so much that we became aware of "maladjustment," of the lag in other words of the human species behind its own possibilities:

Lag in mental and moral patterns provides the bulwark of the older institutions. . . . Here is the place where the problem of liberalism centers today.[42]

But because classical liberalism did not understand its true mission, because it is enmeshed in an atomist individualism that led it to laissez-faire, this readjustment never occurred—with liberalism's reversal into its opposite even aggravating maladjustment. This is why the radical liberalism "of today" must at last assume its historic role by making education its first concern:

> When . . . I say that the first object of a renascent liberalism is education, I mean that its task is to aid in producing the habits of mind and character, the intellectual and moral patterns, that are somewhere near even the actual movements of events. It is, I repeat, the split between the latter as they have externally occurred and the ways of desiring, thinking, and of putting emotion and purpose into execution that is the basic cause of present confusion in mind and paralysis in action.[43]

In light of this text, liberal readjustment first supposes a policy of reeducation. Yet such a redefinition of liberalism produces a head-on collision with its classical definition. Is there not in this program of reeducation of habits and patterns of thought, in this project of producing new manners of thinking, desiring, and feeling for the human species, an unsettling transgression of one of the founding principles of liberal societies—that the government must not under any pretext seek to govern consciences and inner lives? In addition, by flaunting the program of a reeducation of human species patterns, does not Dewey restore the Fabian then Lippmannian project of a readaptation of the human species to the demands of the industrial Great Society, itself led from above by the power of experts? The fundamental question is how Dewey arrives at reconciling his two definitions of liberalism: on the one hand as a readaptation to the industrial Great Society, which seems at first glance to bring it closer to the first political projects of Lippmann; and on the other as the liberation of the potentialities, capacities, and creative impulse of individualities, which on the contrary intends to act as a bulwark against the Lippmannian government of experts. To take up an alternative already theorized by Wallas, is it a matter of readapting the human species to its new industrial environment, or rather of readapting this environment itself to the creative potentialities of individuals?

The first question supposes that we define liberalism as noninterference in the inner lives of individuals. Yet such a definition renews the atomist postulate criticized by Dewey, which considers thought as an already present reality that has been deposited in the inner core of the individual soul. In reality, individuals and their thoughts emerge from collective conditions in which education plays a central role. Like the intelligence of which it is the forming condition, it has no other mission than finding the right place between two dangers: that of curbing impulse through the rigidity of group habits; or, on the contrary, that of unleashing impulse without successfully articulating it into habits:

> The office of intelligence in every problem . . . is to effect a working connection between old habits, customs, institutions, beliefs, and new conditions. What I have called the mediating function of liberalism is all one with the work of intelligence. This fact is the root, whether it be consciously realized or not, of the emphasis placed by liberalism upon the role of freed intelligence as the method of directing social action.[44]

If classical liberalism insisted so much on freedom of thought, it thus was not—contrary to a current misinterpretation—so that the individual would withdraw into their inner self and then into their atomic preferences, but on the contrary to foster the socialization of intelligence in the public space, which is alone capable of ensuring the renewal of society. As this text shows, intelligence, education, and liberalism ultimately occupy exactly the same "mediating function" between old and new, a function that will only take a clearly political form with liberalism at the time when, starting from the second half of the eighteenth century, the human species will begin to collectively face its own evolution.

As in *Human Nature and Conduct*, the articulation of the old and the new works toward the liberation of the creative potentialities of individuals:

> Social change is . . . a fact. . . . Changes that are revolutionary in effect are in process in every phase of life. Transformations . . . are occurring so swiftly that imagination is baffled in attempt to lay hold of them. Flux does not have to be created. But it does have to be directed. It has to be so controlled that it will move to some end in accordance with the principles of life, since life itself is development. Liberalism is committed to an end that is at once enduring and flexible: the liberation of individuals so that realization of their capacities may be the law of their life. It is committed to the use of freed intelligence as the method of directing change.[45]

If the beginning of the text seems to announce, as in Lippmann's political program, a necessary readaptation of the human species to the acceleration of changes, the following oppositely concludes with a necessary control of the flux of change through intelligence, which itself serves the realization of the capacities of individuals. The liberation of impulse thus remains in this matter the only worthy "end" and the only "law" that is established; and Dewey does not hesitate in seeing in it the only end that is in agreement with the "principles of life." While Lippmann advocates for the passive readaptation of the mass of the human species to the demands of industry, like a putty that must be molded into the frame that is imposed on it from the exterior, Dewey's whole effort consists in reminding us on the contrary that the industrial revolution was initially the fruit of collective intelligence. As for "adaptation" and "adaptability," two conceptions of "flexibility" confront each other here—upon which it would be much in the interest of our current era, which is saturated with this vocabulary, to meditate. While the Lippmannian version of flexibility supposes a passive mass of individuals subject to an already known end—the acceleration of all fluxes and the dissolution of all enclosures inherited from the past working toward a globalized division of labor—his pragmatist version only allows for "enduring and flexible" ends that are, in other words, working toward the liberation of the unprecedented creative potentialities that all individuals without exception bear but can only reveal in a collective framework that supports them instead of destroying them. Such is the true meaning of "new conditions." Far from being an incomprehensible framework for the average individual that would overwhelm their cognitive capacities and that experts would have to impose on them from above, we must always recall that "the new forces generated by science and technology"[46] were initially the product of the socialization of the intelligence of the individuals themselves—that socialization itself serving the full development of their capacities. Ultimately, *Liberalism and Social Action* historicizes the anthropological analyses of *Human Nature and Conduct* while remaining faithful to its general outlines. The articulation between habit and impulse becomes the articulation between old habits and "new conditions"—those of an expansion of socialized intelligence that precisely makes possible, and better than ever, the liberation of the creative capacities of impulse.

This explains why Dewey takes up again, in this part of the text, his virulent critique of the conception Lippmann forms of the "average individual" as a passive element of a mass that would need to be readapted from above:

> The contempt often expressed for reliance upon intelligence as a social method . . . is due to the identification of intelligence with native endowments of individuals. In contrast to this notion, I spoke of the power of individuals to appropriate and respond to . . . an environment in which the cumulative intelligence of a multitude of cooperating

individuals is embodied. . . . Given a social medium in whose institutions the available knowledge, ideas and art of humanity were incar-
nate, and the average individual would rise to undreamed heights of
social and political intelligence.[47]

We henceforth understand better why the first mission of liberalism occurs
through education—interpreted as what makes possible the socialization of
intelligence—and a public policy of the provision of knowledge in a group of
institutions and collective mediations that personify and embody it. And we
also understand better why in these conditions the struggle of new liberalism
against capitalism must initially be a struggle against the confiscation of
knowledge and cultural capital by the elites or the "oligarchy."[48] Because the
struggle for the reappropriation of the means of production passes first—and
much more than Marxism understood—through a struggle for the reappropriation of knowledge; or in other words for the reappropriation of the *means of
experimentation*:

> There does not now exist the kind of social organization that even per-
> mits the average human being to share the potentially available social
> intelligence. . . . Back of the appropriation by the few of the material
> resources of society lies the appropriation by the few in behalf of their
> own ends of the cultural, the spiritual, resources that are the product
> not of the individuals who have taken possession but of the cooperative
> work of humanity.[49]

Contesting the reverse dualism of Marxism, which places the material reality
of "the infrastructure" in opposition to the ideological inconsistency of the
"superstructure," Dewey affirms here that the root of expropriation is found in
the hierarchical relationship to knowledge, which destroys the possibilities of
a socialized intelligence. These analyses allow him to rehabilitate the political
model of democracy, and to reconstruct its link with liberalism on new bases,
against its dual disqualification by Marxism and by Lippmann:

> It is useless to talk about the failure of democracy until the source of
> its failure has been grasped and steps are taken to bring about that
> type of social organization that will encourage the socialized exten-
> sion of intelligence.[50]

The source of the failure of democracy is neither that it ideologically concentrates on superstructures (Marx) nor that it puts the cognitive incompetence
of the masses into power (Lippmann). Its failure comes rather from the collective organization of the modes of production of knowledge—which, at the

advanced stage of capitalism, is concentrated like all the other "accumulated wealth" in the hands of a minority.[51] It is this concentration of wealth that is at the same time material, cognitive, cultural, and spiritual in the hands of a few that explains the fatal reversal of liberalism into its opposite—leading to the destruction of the conditions of possibility of the industrial revolution, and with it, to the blockage of the extraordinary liberation of potentialities that it had made possible.

For all these reasons, new liberalism must necessarily come about through a new industrial democracy in which the publics will not be satisfied by merely attending rational debates that are respectful of procedures and "aligning" behind a fair-play "leader" in political competition; no more will they confine themselves to "participating," as we say today, in debates of ideas. Participatory democracy according to Dewey is not in any way reducible to its trivial current version—that of "debate participation" or of a simple preliminary "consultation" of citizens in preparation for the final deliberation of the deciders. It means, in a much more "radical" fashion, that the publics themselves, and no other authority in their place, must lead social experimentation:

> The idea that the conflict of parties will, by means of public discus-
> sion, bring out necessary public truths is a kind of political watered-
> down version of the Hegelian dialectic, with its synthesis arrived at by
> a union of antithetical conceptions. The method has nothing in com-
> mon with the procedure of organized cooperative inquiry which has
> won the triumphs of science in the field of physical nature.[52]

In this context, we better understand Dewey's call for new "planning" as well as the very surprising, at first glance, inclusion of "control" and of "plans" in the historical missions of liberalism. As we have seen, planning here has nothing in common with either the nationalization of the economy in the Soviet style or a society administered from above by experts in the fashion of the Fabian Society or the New Deal. First and foremost, it implies the social-ization of intelligence in the model of "inquiry," and through this, the emer-gence of a society able to self-govern by "continually planning" itself.[53]

The mistake of historical liberalism was believing that this self-government could be left to blind economic interactions that proceed by trial and error like Darwinian slight variations. Taking an opposing view from this long liberal tradition, in which contemporary interpretations of Adam Smith's invisible hand and Darwin's natural selection continued to hybridize, Dewey's natural-ism chooses, we have seen, to leave aside this atomistic aspect of Darwinism and to highlight the emergence of the collective intelligence in the control of consequences. Because far from removing the human species from nature, human intelligence amplifies and perfects the experimental movement of life itself—which Dewey understands, following *On the Origin of Species*, as a laboratory where new evolutionary possibilities ceaselessly self-experiment. It is on the bases of this naturalism that Dewey arrives at—against Lippmann and against his return to the blind liberalism of slight variations—designating socialized intelligence and its efforts of control and planning in the matter of social action as the true subject of new liberalism and its self-government.

Dewey, like Lippmann and the neoliberals *The Good Society* will inspire, resolutely situates himself against the current of his era. While the 1930s are devoted to the crisis of liberalism and the rise in power of nationalized and centralized models, he quickly announces a "renascent liberalism" that is aligned in part with the original liberalism. In his new liberalism, what remains of classical liberalism is the ambition of liberating individualities, and with them, the creative emergence of the new by the self-government of society. But what is profoundly different in this new liberalism is that such a liberation of individualities occurs not through the retreat of the atomic individual into itself but through the political supports of processes of individuation—which involves a collective and democratic planning of social action that ensures the socialization of knowledge and the experimental methods of scientific inquiry. By proposing an entirely different theory of planning on the one hand and of democracy on the other, we are going to now see that Lippmann's "new liberalism," which will inspire the great postwar neoliberal movements, is going to be applied in contesting point by point the new liberalism promoted by Dewey since the 1929 crisis. Dewey will not leave this counteroffensive unanswered, virulently critiquing it in turn in his political texts at the end of the 1930s—and unknowingly making, while still in the name of "new liberalism," the first great philosophical critique of neoliberalism.

5

The Great Revolution

Switching Off Intelligence

After having hesitated for a long time between the Fabian model of a strong government centralized by experts and the liberal model of the self-government of society, Lippmann had finally clearly chosen in 1925 the path of a return to liberalism, which was in his eyes moreover compatible with a decentralized government of leaders and experts. But a few years later, and in the context created by the Great Depression, he will be obliged to take account, like all his contemporaries, of the profound crisis that liberalism is traversing. In his *Godkin Lectures* given at Harvard in 1934, he publicly recognizes that "laissez-faire is dead" and that the modern state is "responsible for the modern economy as a whole."[1] Government intervention is from now on inevitable. It is all only a question of degree. If the totalitarian states practice what he calls "absolute collectivism" in "directed" economies, the democratic alternative can only be that of a "free collectivism." Following the lessons of his friend John Maynard Keynes, he henceforth considers that salvation comes through a "compensated" economy in which the government counterbalances the vicissitudes of spending and private investment. While Dewey severely critiques the New Deal as insufficiently radical from the point of view of democracy and the critique of capitalism, Lippmann thus at first positions himself as an ardent defender of the Roosevelt presidency and as a partisan of the principles of Keynesian economics.

But starting from the second New Deal (1935–38), which lays the foundation of the welfare state, Lippmann will begin to judge that Roosevelt is going too far. In accordance with the model of intermittent democracy defended in *The Phantom Public*, the president must now surrender power—which had been conferred on him solely to resolve the crisis, now partly overcome—to private initiative, and he must not give in to the temptation of a planned economy.[2] Around 1935, Lippmann and Dewey are thus equally critical of the New Deal. Even if their opposition to Roosevelt is based on different reasons, both reject the temptation of a nationalization of the economy that is led from above by economists—who are viewed as the new social sciences experts—as well as by a strong and centralized power around the president. This context, which is also that of the rise of authoritarianism in the world, explains in great part the common demand for a liberal self-government of society. Added to this first convergence is another, inherited from their common reference to Graham Wallas's masterfully rendered problematic in *The Great Society*. Like Dewey, we have seen, Lippmann interprets the historical mission of liberalism as the readjustment of the human species and the Great Society. Also like Dewey, he notes the structural "lag" of our species and the unprecedented political problematic it finds itself henceforth confronting, torn between a flux in constant acceleration and the mental stases it inherits from its evolutionary history. Like him again, Lippmann henceforth advocates the crucial importance of education as the vector of a necessary "adaptability" or "flexibility" of the human species. Lastly like him, he founds this redefinition on a naturalism that breaks with that of the eighteenth-century liberals and is profoundly renewed by evolutionary theory. In light of all these convergences, one may ask whether Dewey played a crucial role in the genesis of neoliberalism to the extent that the thematic and lexical proximity of the analyses of Dewey and Lippmann about liberalism blurs the political meaning of contemporary pragmatism. Could the new liberalism defended by Dewey have inspired neoliberalism in one way or another in the end? In rereading *The Good Society*, which provided the theoretical matrix of the neoliberal movement as the last stage of the Lippmann-Dewey debate, we are going to quickly perceive that—as in the preceding phases of the debate—the clash between the political arguments of Lippmann and Dewey is clear and direct. While the new liberalism promoted by American pragmatism aims to establish the collective intelligence of publics as the only legitimate agent of political action, the great neoliberal revolution will seek to establish the opposite rupture: that of definitively switching off collective intelligence.

From the Great Revolution to Planning

It is not surprising, then, that the new stage of the Lippmann-Dewey debate crystallizes around planning. For Lippmann, planning is henceforth imposed as "the dominant dogma of the age."[3] By affirming that this dogma consists in the affirmation of a necessary "control" of human affairs, he deliberately adopts the term used by Dewey in 1935 which specifically pleaded for the control of consequences through planning. But this encompassing of the Deweyan notion of control within the "dominant dogma of the age" pointedly denies the specificity of liberal planning proposed by Dewey—regarding the nationalization of the economy practiced by the New Deal as much as the directed economy imposed in the Soviet Union and other totalitarian states. Scorning all the subtleties of Dewey's argumentation, Lippmann strictly reduces all forms of planning, including those intending to be "liberal," to an economy administered from above by the state—which would itself, like a "providential state," be a substitute for divine Providence.[4]

In his critique of planning, Lippmann follows the analyses of Ludwig von Mises and Friedrich Hayek, who will attend the Paris colloquium one year later.[5] But by reducing Dewey's new liberalism to the dominant models of planning, he makes a series of misinterpretations. He first forgets to say that liberal and social planning, as Dewey intends it, is not led from "on top" or "by the state" but by the publics themselves, and that this is one of the principal reasons for his critique of the New Deal. This is moreover what Dewey will object to in his review of Lippmann's book, very clearly distinguishing the socialist project from its authoritarian forms marked by nationalized interventionism and bureaucracy:

> [Lippmann] strangely identifies every form of socialism and collectivism with state or governmental socialism, and hence with overhead control of the activities of groups and individuals by a bureaucratic officialdom.[6]

Lippmann next suggests that planning standardizes ways of life from above, that it imposes a "coercive direction" of life,[7] while on the contrary Dewey insists on the liberation of the divergent potentialities that each newcomer bears. This second critique allows Lippmann to reproach all the planning models, including the one promoted by Dewey, for claiming to "direct the course of civilization" by providentially setting its *telos*. Yet if Dewey explicitly demands that the flux be controlled ("the flux . . . must be controlled"[8]), this is never by virtue of some set *telos* of evolution that, like divine Providence, "[would set] the shape of things to come." It is rather, as we have seen, precisely in the name of an evolutionary theory purged of the shadow of Providence and aimed toward liberating impulse—this creative and strictly unpredictable potential of individualities that is always threatened by the tendency of collective habits to stiffen.

Last, by reproaching all forms of planning for controlling economic activity, Lippmann implies that economic interactions automatically liberate individualities from the shackles of collective authority.[9] In doing so, he makes two other mistakes that had already been refuted by Dewey in his response to *The Phantom Public*. The first is that he does not see that economic association itself produces an interdependence that can turn into shackles. The second is that he continues to oppose the atomic individual, reduced to its economic behaviors, and the social and political life whose interactions should be limited, reviving the old dualism between individual and society that Dewey's liberalism intends for its part to overtake once and for all.

The centerpiece of the work—book 3, which is dedicated to the "reconstruction of liberalism"—sheds light on the underlying reasons for the divergence between Lippmann and Dewey on planning.[10] It shows that everything originates from their respective interpretations of what Lippmann names "the great revolution."[11] For Dewey, the great revolution began in the seventeenth century with the invention of the experimental sciences. From this ensued the technological revolution and the emergence of the industrial Great Society analyzed by Graham Wallas. But for Lippmann, the true revolution lies a century later, toward the middle of the eighteenth century. It is defined not by the scientific and technical revolution but by an upheaval of an economic nature: the appearance of "the world-wide division of labor."[12] Here is the "most revolutionary experience" in history:

> The transition from the relative self-sufficiency of individuals in local communities to their interdependence in a world-wide economy is the most revolutionary experience in recorded history.[13]

This explains why Lippmann places the whole of his thought under the aegis of Adam Smith, whose *Wealth of Nations* begins precisely with this discovery: "The greatest improvement in the productive powers of labor . . . seem[s] to have been the [effect] of the division of labor."[14] About which Lippmann comments:

> Adam Smith discerned the basic truth that the new industrial technic consists in the division of labor regulated in markets. For that reason, . . . he was a true [prophet]. He saw that the increasing division of labor was the essential revolution in modern times.[15]

Such was both the great discovery and the great revolution of the eighteenth century—that of the link between the wealth of nations, the division of labor, and its regulation by the market. While for Dewey this mode of production, which is none other than that of advanced capitalism, is at the same time secondary and contingent in regard to the true scientific revolution of modern times,[16] for Lippmann on the contrary it is the scientific and technological revolution that appears as secondary. The true revolution occurred in the eighteenth century, when humanity became aware that the division of labor should be ceaselessly increased and arbitrated by a market in expansion.

Yet far from being completed, this revolution continues to be fulfilled up to the present day by demanding, as Adam Smith already suggested,[17] an "increasing division of labor in ever-widening markets."[18] In Lippmann's view, this necessary globalization of the division of labor through the market entails the disappearance of all forms of stasis and local enclosure that still structured traditional societies. It is this heralded disappearance which explains that the great revolution necessarily destabilizes all societies with a more and more accelerated rhythm:

> [This revolution] has forced mankind into a radically new way of life and, consequently, it has unsettled custom, institutions, and traditions, transforming the whole human outlook. . . .
>
> . . . For more than a hundred and fifty years the revolution which converted these relatively independent and self-sufficing local communities into specialized members of a great economy has been proceeding at an accelerating tempo.[19]

Establishing the global division of labor as the *telos* of evolution, Lippmann encompasses all the great destabilizations of modernity and all the great political revolutions since the seventeenth century within his own economic definition of the industrial revolution:

> In the fullest sense of the term, the industrial revolution is a revolution. It is the general revolution of which the specific revolutions from Cromwell's onward have been incidents.[20]

This strictly economic interpretation of the great revolution leads him to an entirely different definition of liberalism. While Dewey defined his mission as the necessary collective "readjustment" of the old and the new in order to liberate the creative potentialities of individuals and again make possible the processes of individuation, Lippmann assigns himself the very different mission of readapting populations to this specific mode of production that can only be deployed at an "accelerated tempo":[21] to an always growing global division of labor entailing an exponential acceleration of all fluxes and a progressive disqualification of all stases inherited from the past.

This moral disqualification of all stases in the name of flux, in opposition to the tragic recognition of their dual necessity and their necessary tension, confirms Lippmann's entrenchment within a teleological conception of evolution. While at the beginning of the book he denounced planning and all forms of teleology, thereby "fix[ing] the shape of things to come," he henceforth no longer hesitates in setting the teleological endpoint of political and social evolution by incidentally adopting, as in many of his previous works, Herbert Spencer's evolutionism. Indeed, for Lippmann as for Spencer, all evolution must converge toward globalized capitalism, which they both interpret as a vast—and always better adjusted—global industrial cooperation:

> We must go back to the first principle of the economy in which we live, and fix clearly in our minds that its determining characteristic is the increase of wealth by a mode of production which destroys the self-sufficiency of nations, localities, and individuals, making them deeply and intricately interdependent. . . .
> . . . No Gandhi can withstand this tide in men's affairs. Nothing can prevent the whole of mankind from being drawn out of its ancestral isolation into the world-wide economy of interdependent specialists. For the new mode of production is incomparably more efficient in the struggle for survival.[22]

Combining Adam Smith's analyses of the wealth of nations and those of Herbert Spencer on the struggle for survival, Lippmann concentrates on the exponential growth that generates the global division of labor in the era of advanced capitalism. This *optimum* growth is what allows him to make it the first principle of his "good society," which he intends to "fix clearly in our minds"—with the value of the good society being removed from all collective or democratic discussion and transformed into an ultimate invariant end that is supposed to give evolution its meaning and goal. This designation of globalized capitalism as the transcendent end of the evolutionary process renders null and void all attempts, such as that embodied by Gandhi's resistance against the British industrial civilization, of recreating a form of local and stable independence in regard to the permanent mutations of globalized capitalism.

For Dewey, on the contrary, we remember that the irreducible tension between flux and stasis must be redoubled by that which is also entirely necessary between the global opening of the Great Society and the local scale of communities. Far from globalization and its accelerated rhythms being the *telos* ordering us to definitively destroy all forms of local and stable communities, the entire difficulty on the contrary, in *The Public and Its Problems*, is to articulate the two scales, global and local, of the collective problems—with such a rearticulation prolonging the heterochronies of evolutionary rhythm and pursuing the branching evolution of life and living beings, of which no one can predict the meaning and the goal.

Troubled by all forms of behavior control through political power, Lippmann no longer sees a problem in these very same behaviors being controlled by the transcendent ends of the globalized economy. Defending a global interdependence and a rigid collectivism when it concerns the economy, he advocates, exactly like Spencer, an atomized individualism as soon as it concerns everything else. Yet for Dewey, this paradoxical alliance of atomism and collectivism leads directly to the massive processes of deindividuation, producing the soft, docile, and passive "molluscan organization" of the masses required by advanced capitalism:

> We have now a kind of molluscan organization, soft individuals within and a hard constrictive shell without. . . .
> Persons acutely aware of the dangers of regimentation when it is imposed by government remain oblivious of the millions of persons whose behavior is regimented by an economic system through whose intervention alone they obtain a livelihood. . . . The kind of working-together which has resulted is too much like that of the parts of a machine to represent a cooperation which expresses freedom and also contributes to it.[23]

The "molluscan" character required for the masses, such as Lippmann understands them, comes from how it combines the rigid interdependence of economic relationships, comparable to those of the machine, and an empty and atomic interiority for all that pertains to moral, social, and political life. Because if Lippmann speaks ceaselessly about the "interdependence" created by the globalization of economic exchanges, it is the atomist postulates that continue to structure his analysis of regulation through the market:

> In the modern economy the personal motive of production is profit . . . ; goods are consigned . . . to a distant and impersonal market.
> The prices which a man's products fetch in those markets determine whether he will prosper or fail. . . . The market is, therefore, the sovereign regulator of the specialists in an economy which is based on a highly specialized division of labor. It does what the planning board is supposed to do in a planned economy.[24]

We find here the atomist postulate of the liberals in their analysis of work, which is criticized in detail by Dewey in *Human Nature and Conduct*.[25] Reducing work to a pure "labor," its meaning is restricted to only atomic profit that the individual calculates for himself. Instead of joining in a dynamic process where ends and means reciprocally form each other in collective and continuous interactions, labor divided by the "division of labor" is a simple means (having a cost, or causing a "pain") analytically separated from its end (having a benefit, or aiming toward "profit" and its "pleasures").

Returning again to the great dualist division between ends and means, the liberal conception of labor reduces the individual to a sum of atoms of pain and pleasure, or of costs and benefits. With work being disconnected from the collective aim of its meaning, and being degraded into a subjugated "labor" for survival or—in the best case—for profit, the challenge is henceforth knowing what authority can regulate these atomic interactions. For Lippmann, adopting here again the lesson that liberal tradition retained from Adam Smith, only the market can be the "sovereign regulator" of such an economy.[26] By putting the products of labor into competition in a great globalized market, the prices sort out the atomic choices of individuals by eliminating those that fail and selecting those that prosper. Thanks to this analysis, Lippmann can conclude that such a regulation, which occurs mechanically and without the intervention of human intelligence, disqualifies all ambitions for "control." The concern of all these analyses is ultimately—even while the 1930s are marked, including among liberals, by the return of social action and planning—to *switch off intelligence*.

The Liberal Switching-Off of Intelligence: Adam Smith versus Dewey

In his critique of planning through collective intelligence, Lippmann is thus first inspired by what the liberal tradition retained of Adam Smith and the Scottish Enlightenment thinkers, insisting on the disqualification of "human wisdom"—and with it, of all the projections and intentions aiming toward the widened horizon of an "extensive . . . utility." As Adam Smith wrote in *The Wealth of Nations*:

> This division of labor, from which so many advantages are derived, is not originally the effect of any human wisdom, which foresees and intends that general opulence to which it gives occasion. It is the necessary, though very slow and gradual consequence of a certain propensity in human nature which has in view no such extensive utility; the propensity to truck, barter, and exchange one thing for another.[27]

The liberal conception of capitalism, regulated in a blind and automatic manner by the market, is supposed to rest on this "propensity of human nature" to concentrate on a restrained and short-term utility—that of the atomic interest targeted by exchange, rather than the "extensive utility" targeted by human intelligence. Yet this conception of the division of labor cannot withstand the Deweyan critique of the atomist postulates of classical liberalism. With Adam Smith's famous sentence about the "benevolence of the butcher, brewer, and baker"—and on the condition that we arbitrarily exclude all input from *The Theory of Moral Sentiments*—*The Wealth of Nations* indeed seems to interpret the interdependence of the human species (the nearly constant need of "help from his fellow man") as beginning from individuals centered on themselves in "self-love."[28]

By "self-love," we must not understand here—as certain translations still sadly suggest—the moral vice of "selfishness," which would push for the excessive appropriation of wealth or social domination. Adam Smith means by this the natural inclination of members of the human species to pursue "their own advantage" or "their own interest," which is explained by the equally vital and natural inclination toward self-preservation. Yet in *Human Nature and Conduct*, Dewey intends to explicitly reject this conception of human nature and criticizes the Smithian notion of self-love as one of the first attempts to immobilize human nature and to establish the list of its instincts, which will not stop growing thereafter.[29] On the contrary, the whole effort of Dewey's naturalism consists, by countering it with the original tension between impulse and habit, in rejecting this atomic starting point of a living being preoccupied first with its own conservation and in denouncing the "mythology . . . of a *nisus* for self-preservation.[30] Rejecting this atomic starting point, Dewey's naturalism instead intends to show—against classical liberalism—that the tension between impulse and habit imposes the mediatory work of the collective intelligence and with it the collective aim of this "extended utility" that Adam Smith seeks to disqualify.

In *The Phantom Public*, Lippmann had already on his own account adopted the liberal disqualification of the collective intelligence and its aim toward an extended utility. It was one of the foundations of his devaluation of public opinion and its "general opinions," to which he countered the withdrawal of individuals into their "specific opinions"—their atomic choices, in other words, in the matter of consumption, production, and reproduction. The issue was thus to transform democracy, by refounding it on this liberal model of the blind and spontaneous regulation of interests by the market, in order to switch off the supposed wisdom of public opinion. But now, the role of Adam Smith's model and its interpretation of the great revolution is to disqualify the planning collective intelligence:

> The market is the only possible method by which labor that has been analyzed into separate specialties can be synthesized into useful work. . . . This bringing together . . . in accordance with the ability to produce and the desire to consume, cannot be organized and administered from above by any human power. It is an organic, not a

fabricated, synthesis which can be effected only by the continual matching of bids and offers.[31]

If we are witnessing both an atomic decomposition of labor that is more and more divided by the extension of the market and an atomization of economic activity into the "ability to produce" and the "desire to consume," the market is supposed to compensate for this division by producing the great "organic synthesis" of all these interactions—an organic synthesis that Dewey judges, on the contrary, in the passage from *Freedom and Culture* I cited above, to be mechanical. In the lineage of Adam Smith's naturalism and classical liberalism, and across this opposition between "organic synthesis" and "fabricated" synthesis, Lippmann here—against the artifices of human intelligence—opposes the natural movements of the market, themselves founded on the natural inclinations of man for exchange and self-conservation that are responsible for spontaneously producing the harmony of all these interactions.

This atomist interpretation of organic regulation allows Lippmann to switch off the role of human intelligence and its plans—not only in the economic field, but in all forms of regulation. Chapter 2 of *The Good Society*, which principally focuses on the techno-scientific revolution, shows that the Lippmannian disqualification of intelligence does not stop at the economic sphere. It is equally at the heart of his interpretation of scientific and technical experimentation, which contradicts Dewey's analyses point by point by opposing—against the "control" of consequences through the plans of the intelligence—the blind fumbling of the "trial and error" approach, itself imposed by competition:

> Technical progress, being in its essence experimental, calls for much trial and error. . . .
> . . . For these great centralized controls . . . are unsuited to a system of production which can profit by new invention only if it is flexible, experimental, adjustable, and competitive. The laboratories in which the technic is being developed cannot produce the inventions according to a centrally directed plan. The future technology cannot be predicted, organized, and administered.[32]

While Lippmann reduces the experimental method of the laboratory to a trial-and-error approach itself regulated by competition, we saw that Dewey promoted the emergence of experimental intelligence, with its capacities for control and planning, as a revolutionary improvement of the "genetic and experimental logic" of the evolution of the living, allowing it to precisely overcome the first blind fumblings of trial and error. Far from being the application of the competition between atomic and random slight variations to all fields of experimentation, it is the conscious coordination through collective intelligence and the control of consequences that, for Dewey, marks the true revolution— that which carries to fruition the experimental logic of evolution unveiled by Darwin. While the three great revolutions of modernity—the nineteenth-century Darwinian revolution, the eighteenth-century liberal revolution, and the seventeenth-century techno-scientific revolution—each allow Dewey to give collective intelligence a central function, Lippmann on the contrary relies on each of them to switch it off.

For Lippmann, this switching-off of intelligence seems to rest on the providential mechanism of competition. The competition between innovations for technical progress, between market agents for capitalism, and between organisms for the evolution of the living each time resembles a mechanism that, like Providence, automatically produces the *optimum*. Yet in looking closer we perceive that Lippmann does not completely subscribe to the providentialist tendencies of Adam Smith's naturalism.[33] If the latter was the "true prophet" of the great revolution, his prophecy was in great part incomplete and limited: "Adam Smith . . . was an incomplete and limited [prophet]."[34] Because the "organic regulation" of the division of labor by the market has not only been the source of improvement, growth, and the wealth of nations. It has also been a perpetual source of social sufferings and human destructions, justifying in part the trial of capitalism by the "Marxists":

> In the modern economy [of the world-wide division of labor] . . .
> there must be some power which induces or compels everyone to
> choose a specialty which fits in with the other specialties. The prices
> offered in the market do just that. They do it roughly and, because
> most markets are imperfect, they do it with great friction and human
> suffering. . . .
> . . . The progressive increase of wealth leaves behind it a trail of
> misery and failure and frustrated lives which has shocked the con-
> science of mankind. The statistics of improvement are not sufficiently
> impressive . . . to drown out the cries of the victims. . . . The market is,
> humanly speaking, a ruthless sovereign.[35]

If the picture of advanced capitalism described by Adam Smith remains the *telos* of evolution, Lippmann recognizes that the crisis of liberalism originates in great part from its naïve trust in the market's good nature—one capable of an automatic and providential regulation of economic and social interactions. In his eyes, we can no longer think that the accumulation of sufferings and miseries caused by capitalism will be progressively compensated by the "wealth of nations." The latter, we must concede to Marxism, is indeed incapable of "drown[ing] out the cries of the victims."

It is the observation of this failure that the Lippmann Colloquium will at first retain: "In the presence of the debacle of nineteenth-century liberalism, it would be vain . . . to believe that the mission [of liberals] consists in repeating the methods of last century."[36] It also will give its full weight to the critique of naturalism by German ordoliberalism—which was so well highlighted by Michel Foucault's lessons at the Collège de France:

> This is where the ordoliberals break with the tradition of eighteenth and nineteenth century liberalism. . . . When you deduce the principle of laissez-faire from the market economy, basically you are still in the grip of what could be called a "naive naturalism," that is to say, whether you define the market by exchange or by competition you are thinking of it as a sort of given of nature, something produced spontaneously which the state must respect precisely inasmuch as it is a natural datum.[37]

If the neoliberals distinguish themselves from the old liberals, it is precisely because they no longer believe that the market is a fact of nature that is itself governed by natural mechanisms providentially producing the best results. Yet it is also on the basis of this crisis or this "debacle," which was initially the defeat of the providentialist naturalism of the eighteenth century, that the temptation of planning and collectivisim is established almost everywhere in the world during the first half of the twentieth century. If nature does not do things well, must not a collective and artificial control of economic and social interactions through plans and collective intelligence be introduced?

Confronted with this temptation, Lippmann's whole undertaking will be not to break with naturalism but to reinforce the liberal switching-off of intelligence and its artifices by reconstructing liberal naturalism on entirely new bases that are evolutionary and no longer providentialist. It is precisely this point—in many ways decisive for the genesis of contemporary neoliberalism— that Foucault did not see. By interpreting all forms of neoliberalism as antinaturalism, he missed the evolutionary sources of new liberalism. Certainly, and like the German ordoliberals, Lippmann very much wants to purge new liberalism of Adam Smith's naturalist providentialism. But he does it not by excluding all reference to nature, but by integrating the contributions of evolutionary theory to the new liberal naturalism on completely different bases from those retained by Spencer.

In doing so, with *The Good Society*, Lippmann pursues a program that he has already been committed to for twenty-five years. Taking up again the project of *A Preface to Politics* (1913), which already placed him within the program initiated by his teacher Graham Wallas in *Human Nature and Politics* (1908), the issue remains opposing a realist naturalism based on the real evolution of the human species to the abstract naturalism of the first liberals (from Smith to Bentham). As we have seen, Lippmann shares with Dewey this ambition of refounding liberal naturalism on evolutionary theory and of proceeding with this rebuilding by breaking away from Herbert Spencer's mechanistic laissez-faire. Yet we are now going to see that the first of these contributions, for Lippmann and contrary to Dewey, is that evolutionary theory itself also switches off, like the naturalism of the first liberals, the plans and artifices of collective intelligence.

The Evolutionary Switching-Off of Intelligence: Bergson versus Dewey

In his attempt to switch off intelligence based on evolutionary theory, Lippmann adopts the Bergsonian critique of the primacy of intelligence. If Bergson's name is never cited in the 1937 book, his influence—which was already significant in Lippmann's first books—continues to persist in its analyses of planning. In *The Phantom Public*, we remember that the reference to Bergson's philosophy—which was highly influential in 1920s America—worked toward refuting the idea that we can complain of an objective "disorder" in the conflict of interests in the social and political field. At this time, Lippmann adopted from Bergson the idea that the concepts of order and disorder referred back only to the expectations (fulfilled or disappointed) of the intelligence, and that they thus had no meaning from the point of view of the infinite complexity of the real. In this text already, reality was carefully distinguished from the artificial projections of our intelligence—the originality of Lippmann's gesture consisting in transferring Bergson's analyses into the social, economic, and political field.

The first part of *The Good Society* will extend these intuitions and more systematically adopt the principal elements of *Creative Evolution*'s introduction. Thirty years after Bergson, Lippmann insists in turn on the fact that there exists an immeasurable gap between the fluid, oceanic, and open reality in which we are plunged and the necessarily limited and static character of our intelligence—which is turned toward solids and the fictive discontinuity of objects. Generalizing the fixity of "stereotypes" beyond the mass of public opinion, Lippmann then stretches his critique of stereotypy to all forms of human intelligence. In a section written against Dewey entitled "The Illusion of Control,"[38] he maintains with Bergson that the oceanic dimension of reality necessarily submerges the "little bottles of our intelligence":

The ocean of experience cannot be poured into the little bottles of our intelligence. The mind is an instrument evolved through the struggle for existence, and the strain of concentrating upon a chain of reasoning is like standing rigidly straight, a very fatiguing posture, which must soon give way to the primordial disposition to crouch or sit down.[39]

Lippmann paraphrases here the opening of *Creative Evolution*:

The history of the evolution of life . . . reveals to us how the intellect has been formed. . . . It shows us in the faculty of understanding an append-age of the faculty of acting, a more and more precise . . . adaptation of the consciousness of living beings to the conditions of existence that are made for them. . . .

But from this it must also follow that our thought, in its purely logical form, is incapable of presenting the true nature of life, the full meaning of the evolutionary movement.[40]

Thanks to evolutionary theory, we are in the process of realizing that our intelligence is only a tool, forged by evolution, to ensure our preservation in the struggle for existence. Like Bergson and against Dewey, Lippmann quickly centers the adaptive function of intelligence and the biological function of adaptation itself on simple preservation, which simultaneously allows him to switch it off when it is a matter of grasping the reality of the evolutionary move-ment itself:

Each species, each individual even, retains only a certain impetus from the universal vital impulsion and tends to use this energy in its own interest. In this consists *adaptation*. The species and the individ-ual thus think only of themselves.[41]

Centered on self-preservation like the atomic instinct criticized by Dewey, the exclusive role of Bergsonian intelligence is to "adapt" us to the physical surroundings in which we are plunged for our "own interest." For Lippmann as for Bergson, the adaptive function of intelligence proceeds through a fictive stabilization of the flux of reality that isolates, simplifies, and cuts out stereo-typed patterns in the oceanic complexity of the real: "out of the infinite com-plexity of the real world, the intelligence must cut patterns abstract, isolated, and artificially simplified."[42] This interpretation of intelligence as being re-stricted to creating fictive stases for self-preservation, and as being at the same time condemned to miss the oceanic flux of the evolution of life, takes up again the images from *Creative Evolution*. As with Bergson, the cut-outs of the Lipp-mannian intelligence hearken back to the solid bodies "cut out of the stuff of nature by our *perception*, and the scissors follow, in some way, the marking of lines along which *action*" is supposed to occur.[43]

While Dewey presents intelligence as the mediating function responsible for rearticulating the stases of habit and the flux of the new, Lippmann and Bergson enclose it within the exclusive order of stasis, that of self-interest and self-conservation, to better oppose it to the reality of flux:

> Our mind, which seeks for solid points of support, has for its main function in the ordinary course of life that of representing *states* and *things*. . . . It substitutes for the continuous the discontinuous; for mobility stability; for tendency in process of change, fixed points.[44]

As in *Creative Evolution*, it is biological evolutionism which is supposed to explain and justify the irreducible gap between the stases of intelligence and the flux of the real. When Lippmann declares against Dewey and against all forms of planning by collective intelligence that "it is, therefore, illusion, to imagine that there is a credible meaning in the idea that human evolution can be brought under conscious control,"[45] he is in his way extrapolating into the social and political field Bergson's argument according to which "intellectual tendencies . . . , which life must have created in the course of its evolution, are not at all meant to supply us with an explanation of life."[46]

Beyond Bergson's analyses, Lippmann draws from this first observation political consequences that will allow him to validate both classical liberalism's central argument concerning the limits of the government and the necessity of switching off the plans of collective intelligence:

> The essential limitation, therefore, of all policy, of all government, is that the human mind must take a partial and simplified view of existence.[47]

If limits to the government must be imposed and if planning must be contested, it is first because the intelligence of those who govern is, as much as that of public opinions and their stereotypes, necessarily overwhelmed by the infinite complexity of reality.

It is here that Lippmann stops reprising Bergsonian arguments. If he adopts — strategically and against Dewey — Bergson's evolutionary critique of the philosophical primacy of the intelligence, he no longer agrees with his positive and metaphysical intuition of the élan vital.[48] In his 1903 conference entitled "Introduction to Metaphysics," Bergson defended the idea that it was not only through the critique of our own intellectual tools, but also through the intuition of reality itself — grasped as pure duration — that we could "have contact with the continuity and mobility of the real."[49] The project of this new metaphysics was to recapitulate in an "integral experience" all of these intuitions, of these necessarily partial and occasional "soundings," already attempted in the immense and oceanic depth of duration.[50] With the adjective "integral," Bergson was comparing this undertaking to "the most powerful of the methods of investigation at the disposal of the human mind": "infinitesimal calculus," which made differential and integral calculus possible, and opened modern mathematics to the mobility of change and the analysis of its tendencies.[51] Yet Lippmann very clearly contests such a possibility:

> We do not possess the indispensable logical equipment—the knowledge of the grammar and the syntax of society as a whole—to understand the data available or to know what other data to look for.
>
> The ideal of a directed society requires, therefore, something much more than a proletarian revolution to fulfill it. It requires a revolutionary advance in the logical powers of men comparable with that which took place when they learned to use algebra or the differential calculus in the analysis of the physical world.[52]

Lippmann recalls that even an eminent expert like Vilfredo Pareto, who nonetheless went very far in the attempt to mathematize economic and social reality, recognizes it: this ideal "is almost never attained in the concrete."[53] Even if the elite of the metaphysicians, theoreticians, and scholars continue to fantasize about an integral grasp of the real through intuition, the limited reality of our intelligence makes us necessarily miss the unlimited social and political reality in which we are immersed. Since no intellectual device, even the most "revolutionary," can grasp the ocean of economic, social, and political reality, all government must thus recognize its own limitation. If Lippmann follows Bergson in his evolutionary critique of the tools of the intelligence, he no longer follows him when it becomes a matter of taking the great leap into the metaphysical and integral intuition of the real.

The divergence with Bergson on the role of intuition is confirmed in the rest of the text. In 1907, *Creative Evolution* will try to establish the possibility of intuition, which had been brought forward without justification in the 1903 conference, in evolutionary theory. If we can "have contact" with the reality of evolution, it is because our intelligence is biologically issued from a preintellectual and instinctive gangue, thanks to which we can sympathize from the inside, as a living being, with the totality of evolutionary movement. Intuition begins precisely at the point of contact between the intelligence and this instinctive nebula that encircles it, opening a possible access to the unity of the élan vital and of its multiple tendencies. For Lippmann, on the contrary, what "actually exists everywhere"[54] does not take us back to any original unity.

The reality of the evolutionary movement is none other than the "plurality of interests" that, instead of harmonically sympathizing, struggle against one another by taking the form of a relentless "competition" between individuals:

> All collectivist systems must . . . assume that plurality of interests, which actually exists everywhere, is evil and must be overcome. . . . Collectivists are profoundly monistic in their conception of life, because they regard variety and competition as evil.[55]

In light of this competition, all attempts to grasp the sympathetic and harmonic unity of the evolutionary movement must be denounced as monistic. It is clear that Lippmann here is countering what Bergson wanted to retain from Darwinian transformism—the unity of all the living in the same "tree of life"—with the other great lesson of Darwinism that *Creative Evolution* tried hard to downplay: evolution as the competitive struggle between separated individualities. If the path of intuition is for Lippmann impracticable, it is because unlike Bergson he conceives of evolutionary flux as a plurality in struggle or as an unsurpassable competition that no sympathetic unity between the living can either precede or overcome.

Through this model of the "organic" regulation of the conflict of interests through competition, which selects those who succeed and eliminates those who fail, we find again the liberal naturalism already promoted by *The Phantom Public*. This synthesis of the two models—one drawn from classical liberal economics, the other from the hypothesis of Darwinian selection—falls in line with the critique of Stephen Jay Gould, for whom Darwinian atomism betrays its dependence on Adam Smith:

> Darwin insisted upon a virtually exceptionless, single-level theory, with *organisms* acting as the locus of selection, and all "higher" order emerging, by the analog of Adam Smith's invisible hand, from the (unconscious) "struggles" of organisms for their own personal advantages.[56]

For Adam Smith as for Darwin, "improvement" occurs in a "slow and gradual" manner through the accumulation of blind slight atomic variations themselves selected by the competition of individual organisms each struggling for its own "advantage."[57] It is this atomic gradualism of favorable slight variations that Lippmann adopts—first in *The Phantom Public*, then, twelve years later, in *The Good Society*. If Bergson's evolutionism is useful for him in its critical aspect for disqualifying intelligence and its capacities for control, the positive core of Bergsonism, however—founded on the harmonic unity of the élan vital—is clearly rejected in the name of Darwinian atomism, which *Creative Evolution* had nonetheless done everything to disqualify.

Except that, since *The Phantom Public*, Lippmann's relationship with liberal naturalism had progressively become more complicated. If, in 1925, he still seemed to believe in an automatic adjustment of economic and social interactions, we have seen that in 1937 he considered the "debacle of liberalism" to be the primary issue before any "reconstruction" could take place.[58] How can Lippmann reconcile these two ambitions? Does he continue to subscribe to Adam Smith's naturalism, which believes in a natural and spontaneous optimization of the struggle of interests? Does he not on the contrary denounce, in the Smithian version of the regulation of the market and in the final avatars of laissez-faire, a form of providentialism overturned by evolutionary theory? It thus remains for us to see if the hybridization of Adam Smith's economic model with the biological hypothesis of natural selection moves toward a reinforcement, or on the contrary a deconstruction, of the belief in a nature that has been well organized by the providential action of an "invisible hand." In the second hypothesis, if Lippmann's new liberalism and the neoliberalism that he inspired no longer believe in the autoregulation of the market (Smith) nor the intervention of the state (Keynes, Roosevelt) nor collective intelligence (Dewey), the challenge is thus knowing what can be the artificial authority capable of readjusting the human species to its environment. The two chapters that follow will give a dual response to this question. Refusing both the providence of nature and the control of the future through the collective intelligence of the publics, the new liberalism theorized by Lippmann will decide to rely, on the one hand, on the artifices of law and, on the other, on the forced readaptation of populations to the demands of globalization—occurring through an invasive public policy responsible for actively transforming the dispositions and behaviors of the human species.

6

Reforming the Human Species through Law

Rejecting the liberal fiction of human good nature, the new liberalism seeking to rebuild itself at the time of the Lippmann Colloquium refuses to believe that the human species would be naturally gifted with the calculating capacities allowing it to exchange in an optimal manner on the market. For the organizer of the 1938 colloquium, the Frenchman Louis Rougier, one of Lippmann's great merits is precisely having demonstrated that such beliefs were economists' abstractions that corresponded with nothing in reality: "The pure economy reasons with theoretical models that involve simplifying hypotheses that are always removed from a reality that is complex and confusing."[1] For the new liberals, the debacle of classical liberalism and its fictions must encourage economic science to reconnect with the reality of the human species in its illogicality, confusion, and irrationality; and it is precisely this which seals the rupture of neoliberalism with classical liberalism, placing it light years away from the theoretical fictions of contemporary neoclassical economics with which we confuse it too often:

> Beginning with *homo economicus*, who acts in his best interests in a purely rational way, [science] must find the man of flesh, passion, and limited mind who is the subject of herd-like drives, obeys mystic beliefs and never knows how to calculate the impact of his acts.[2]

This confusion between neoliberalism and neoclassical economics, theorized by Léon Walras in the nineteenth century and becoming hegemonic in the following century, dominates for example Pierre Bourdieu's analyses:

> This theory . . . is a pure mathematical fiction founded on a formidable abstraction: that which . . . brackets the economic and social conditions of rational dispositions.[3]

Yet by attributing this theory to the neoliberals, Bourdieu is unaware that they are formulating exactly the same arguments against neoclassical economics, thereby leading him to miss his target. For Louis Rougier, one of the principal merits of Lippmann's book is precisely that it "reintegrates economic problems within their political, sociological, and psychological context by virtue of the interdependence of all aspects of social life."[4] Alexander Rüstow, the German ordoliberal who also attends the Lippmann Colloquium, retains exactly the same lesson:

> The economic point of view is insufficient for appreciating the vital situation. Man is a naturally social being, which means that social integration is decisive for his life and for the appreciation of life.[5]

There is nothing surprising, then, that—as Lippmann himself recognizes—the markets are largely failing and that their efficiency is entirely relative:

> Broadly speaking, the market does regulate the allocation of capital and labor with some efficiency. But there is a very large margin of error, which in human terms means personal misery . . . ; whereas the short-term fluctuations of prices are often misleading, and yet sufficiently violent to wreck many lives before men can readapt themselves.[6]

If they are not in agreement about the causes of failure, neoliberals share up to a certain point the Marxists' diagnosis of the market economy. For the former the problem comes from the deficiencies of the human species and its capacities for readaptation, while for the latter it is explained by the structural tendencies of capitalism itself, but they all agree in observing that far from spontaneously producing prosperity, the market economy achieved at the advanced stage of capitalism is a massive purveyor of "misery" and "violence." It is the admission of these failures, at the same time as the mourning for a good nature of humans and of the market, that will lead neoliberalism to give a leading role to the artifices of law and to their power of regulation.

But for this, it will be necessary to transform the law itself so that it no longer serves the stabilization of the old order but rather the liberation of new strengths. Yet such a mutation of its function first implies that we recognize the failures of the market and its agents. For it is the nonrecognition of the "misery" and "violence" produced by capitalism that, for Lippmann, finally produced this fatal reversal of liberalism, already described by Dewey, into a defense of the status quo—that is to say, of the vested interests of the dominant classes. A paradoxical reversal—since the economic and political revolution of liberalism in the beginning on the contrary must have entailed liberating the flux of the new from the domination of the scleroticized stases of the old world: "The . . . eulogists of the status quo . . . and latter-day liberals like Herbert Spencer became the apologists for miseries and injustices that were intolerable to the conscience."[7] This leads Lippmann to adopt Dewey's observation to the letter:

> A hundred years after Adam Smith published *The Wealth of Nations* the liberal philosophy was decadent. It had ceased to guide the progressives who sought to improve the social order. It had become a collection of querulous shibboleths invoked by property owners when they resisted encroachments on their vested interests.[8]

Ultimately, "liberal thinking was inhibited in the metaphysics of laissez-faire, and the effect was to make the political philosophy of liberalism . . . a complacent defense of the dominant classes."[9] With the defense of property and its enclosures, the law enmeshed liberalism in the defense of stases to the detriment of flux—a permutation of the signs that must now be reversed once again, putting the law back in the service of the liquidation of stases and the liberation of flux.

To explain this fatal reversal, Louis Rougier indeed adopts the second great lesson of Lippmann's book—that of having revealed the historic role that the law and its juridical instruments played throughout the nineteenth century in the defense of this status quo that it was precisely a question of denouncing. Behind the "metaphysical" fictions of laissez-faire, which postulate a natural world regulated by preestablished harmony, the history of advanced capitalism as Lippmann told it reveals that the liberals never stopped relying on the juridical interventionism of the state and on its enormous arsenal of regulatory artifices that enabled them to consolidate their vested interests:

> The second merit of Walter Lippmann's book is having shown that the liberal regime is not only the result of a spontaneous natural order, as numerous authors of the Laws of Nature declared in the eighteenth century; but that it is also the result of a legal order that supposes a juridical interventionism of the State. Economic life unfurls within a juridical framework, which sets in place the regime of property, contracts, patents, bankruptcy, the status of professional

associations and commercial companies, money and the bank—all the things that are not facts of nature, like the laws of economic equilibrium, but contingent creations of the legislator. From then on, there is no reason to suppose that legal institutions historically existent at the current time are the best suited for safeguarding the freedom of transactions in a definitive and permanent fashion. The question of the best suited legal framework for the most supple, effective, and fair functioning of the markets has been neglected by classical economists.[10]

In light of this quotation, we discover that neoliberalism refutes in a single gesture the fictions of natural law—and with them the long tradition of jusnaturalism—and the pretensions of economics in freeing the "natural laws" of the market. By breaking with these two metaphysical beliefs of the law and the economy—which moreover reinforce each other, the first by postulating a natural source of the juridical norm and the second by inventing the fiction of a good autoregulated nature of the market—new liberalism recognizes on the contrary that the market economy established itself on a group of juridical artifices themselves considered as fully contingent.

For the new liberals, this contingent nature of the instruments of law precisely allows for the consideration of their perpetual transformation. Far from being permanent or absolute, the rule of law, because it is never more than a fabricated instrument, a fiction that must be useful here and now, must be ceaselessly subjected to revision. It must ultimately work toward liberating what was in question from the beginning: the liberation of fluxes in an open world without enclosures. The whole juridical problematic of the new liberals will henceforth be the following: How can the stases invented by the law—essentially responsible for, as Louis Rougier's quotation reminds us, establishing frameworks, fixing stable regimes, and sustaining statutes—be reset to serve flux? How can they avoid continuing to contribute to rigidifying, as they have done up until now, the new status quo? Yet, by asking such a question, new liberalism connects once more with a fundamental preoccupation of pragmatism in general and juridical pragmatism in particular—which was upheld in the United States by the highly influential judge Oliver Wendell Holmes. By going back to the complex relationships between Lippmann, Dewey, and Holmes, we are going to see to what extent the juridical interventionism of the neoliberals joins with the program of juridical pragmatism. But we will also see in what sense it deviates from it, precisely in regard to the question of the *statu quo*—which is accused of blocking the liberation of the new. We will see how for the pragmatists the juridical interventionism of neoliberalism invents in turn a new modality of the status quo which, although draped in the defense of a world that is open, unpredictable, and in constant acceleration, in fact leads to fixing in advance the ends of evolution in one sole direction.

Law as "Rules of the Road": Neoliberalism or Juridical Pragmatism?

Before going into detail about the neoliberal conception of law, we must first recall an essential distinction to understand the emergence of neoliberalism: the central notion of *agenda*. By breaking with liberal laissez-faire, juridical interventionism is indeed established as the pivot of what Lippmann calls "the agenda" of new liberalism.[11] As Pierre Dardot and Christian Laval remind us, it was Keynes who first countered the late form of laissez-faire with the necessity of rethinking the distinction between non-agenda and agenda; that is to say between what the government should not do—or what it should "let happen" (*laissez-faire*)—and the list of everything it had *to do* (*agere, agenda*) itself, according to a distinction that Jeremy Bentham's highly interventionist liberalism already suggested in his *Manual of Political Economy*.[12]

Following Keynes, Lippmann wants to indeed register a whole series of measures in the agenda of liberal politics that themselves open into an immense "field of Reform."[13] But in opposition to Keynesian planning and its controlling ambitions, he hastens to clarify that liberal government must be not only juridical but strictly "judiciary."[14]

As Dewey has already seen, the neoliberal agenda calls here for a general judicialization of social relationships: "Mr. Lippmann's version of liberalism comes close . . . to government by continual litigation."[15] This judicialization is explained through a new art of governing which claims to abstain from imposing plans and a collective destination on society, limiting itself to regulating it through a regulatory framework that is perfected through litigations and jurisprudence. But for Lippmann, planning at its worst authorizes, as in totalitarian societies, the deciding of every minute detail of each individual's itinerary through an "intelligently planned direction"; and at its best imagines, as in the collectivist models of Dewey and Roosevelt, that one can impose a common "destination" on all citizens.[16] For Lippmann, this completely disregards the reality of a living and mobile entity like society.

Extending the metaphor of automobile traffic and accelerated transportation, Lippmann argues that the new liberal government of society must substitute—for this administrative interventionism on the one hand, and for simple laissez-faire on the other—the strict and precise definition of "rules of the road":

Officials can . . . regulate the traffic on the roads. . . . But if, instead of defining the rights of all the drivers, the officials seek to prescribe the destination of each driver, telling him when he must start, by what route he must go, and when he must arrive . . . many think they could direct not only the traffic on the highways but all the occupations of all the people.[17]

For Lippmann, regulation through the law runs directly counter to any prescription of a destination or an itinerary. Because contrary to what Dewey claims, no collective intelligence can agree "on what the destinations of all the drivers shall be."[18] The sole domain in which the rulers and the governed can agree is that of the improvement of the rules:

There is no way of agreeing on what the destinations of all the drivers shall be. But it is possible to agree on traffic regulations which offer the same rights and the same obligations to all the drivers. . . . That kind of government officials and motorists can understand. Its problems are problems which they can study and debate, and the solutions can be perfected progressively.

This metaphor of the rules of the road will be adopted and amplified by the Lippmann Colloquium during the opening address of its organizer, Louis Rougier:

To be liberal does not mean, like a member of the Manchester School, allowing cars to circulate where they like and however they please, which would result in congestion and incessant accidents; it does not mean, like the "planner," fixing a time of departure and itinerary for each car; it is imposing the Rules of the Road, while admitting that these are not the same in the time of accelerated transport as those in that of the stagecoach.[19]

The progressive acceleration of all fluxes involves, as in the transition from the time of stagecoaches to the world of accelerated transportation, more and more rules to avoid collisions and accidents from multiplying. From this point of view, laissez-faire belongs to the time of stagecoaches. The Great Society asks complex questions that no longer spontaneously resolve through the simple play of economic and social interactions. This is what the birth of a new liberalism imposes: the objective can no longer be of letting fluxes "happen" (*laissez-faire*), but of regulating them in the most precise and subtle manner— not by an itinerary or by a "plan" that would decide the destination of each person, but through more and more improved rules of the road.

This metaphor of the rules of the road, which takes on its whole meaning only in the context of accelerated transportation, is particularly enlightening for understanding the neoliberal conception of law. For Louis Rougier, the law's sole function is to readapt the social order to the accelerated transformations of the contemporary world:

> To be liberal . . . [is to] be essentially progressive, in the sense of a perpetual adaptation of the legal order to scientific discoveries, to the progress of economic organization and technique, to the changes in the structure of society, to the demands of the contemporary conscience.[20]

Yet this conception of the law seems at first glance to fit in quite well with what was called "legal pragmatism"—which was embodied in the United States by the judge Oliver Wendell Holmes. In his redefinition of the law as an instrument of adaptation to the environment and its changes, Holmes strove to draw legal consequences from the pragmatism of William James. Holmes's pragmatist reinterpretation of the law inspired in turn Dewey's legal conceptions. Dewey paid explicit homage to Holmes in *Experience and Nature*, where he presents him as "one of the great American philosophers."[21] In *The Public and Its Problems*, Dewey himself already interprets the law, before Lippmann and Rougier, with this same metaphor of the rules of the road.[22] And Lippmann, for his part, regularly pays homage to the pragmatism of Holmes.[23] All these convergences allow us to here identify again an underlying problem. Does not the Lippmann-Dewey debate about liberal planning conceal a more fundamental agreement on the place of law and rules in the political and social field? Does not the disagreement ultimately come from a simple misunderstanding over words? When Lippmann imagines an improvement of rules and the common law through a collective and decentralized intelligence that would serve the equality of opportunities, does he not precisely align with what Dewey calls for his part the "self-government" of society—which must constantly be planned? In the end, is not the neoliberal conception of law as the "rules of the road" faithful in every point to legal pragmatism?

Behind the Rules of the Road: Status Quo on the Destination of the Human Species

Behind this superficial convergence about the definition of the law and their common admiration for Justice Holmes, we find in reality—here as elsewhere—a string of fundamental disagreements. The first of them bears on the possibility of collectively discussing a common destination. For Lippmann, in 1937 as in 1925, the discussion can only be procedural. This is what he calls the "improvement" of the rules and what allows him to reduce the political field to the judiciary. For Dewey, on the contrary, discussion and collective inquiry must bear on the substance of values, which must be collectively debated and experimentally put to the test.[24] That, very precisely, is what Dewey retains from Holmes's work:

> There is every reason . . . for trying to make our desires intelligent. The trouble is that our ideals for the most part are inarticulate, and that even if we have made them definite we have very little experimental knowledge of the way to bring them about.[25]

Dewey comments on this as a double justification of inquiry and philosophy, with their common aim being that of a collective and extended utility:

> And this effort to make our desires, our strivings and our ideals . . . articulate, to define them (not in themselves which is impossible) in terms of inquiry into conditions and consequences is what I have called criticism; and when carried on in the grand manner, philosophy.[26]

The directions taken by the evolution of the human species occur, for Lippmann, through the sum of the atomized behaviors of each individual—with each tied to their own advantages and preferences, and each regulated simply by a form of "rules of the road" that is progressively improved by the local application of the rule of law. It is these atomist postulates that Lippmann believes he has found in the legal pragmatism of Holmes. Dewey considers on the contrary that with the human species the vital logic of experimentation takes a new turn in which the conditions and consequences of its acts can be collectively reflected upon. Far from disqualifying the philosophy of extended utility and its wider perspective, the legal pragmatism of Holmes entirely restores, according to Dewey, its place in the political and social inquiry on values and ideas—that is to say, on the destinations that societies must choose together.

This underlying divergence also sheds light on their disagreement about the central notion of adaptation. For Lippmann, as for Spencer, the environment of the Great Society, which is reduced to the mode of capitalist and globalized production, is imposed on the human species, which must adapt to it without resisting if it wants to survive. This is what Lippmann calls "the inexorable law of the Industrial Revolution":[27]

Those who do not practise this new economy, the so-called backward nations, will become the prey of those who do; they must enter the new economy if they are to survive.[28]

For Dewey, on the contrary, the social environment is defined by a multiplicity of possible interactions, of which economic exchanges are only one aspect among many others. Reducing the environment, as Lippmann does, to just one of its dimensions goes back to transforming it into shackles that inhibit all the other creative potentialities of individuals and reactivate the impasses of the status quo that it was precisely a matter of denouncing. To absolutize the dominant economic environment of capitalism in the process of globalization as the unique and definitive framework to which it would be necessary for the human species to adapt—and to make the law the exclusive tool of this readaptation—is to deny the reality of the evolutionary process itself, in which all living species adapt not by passively submitting to the demands of their environment but by actively transforming it in turn.

Ultimately, by absolutizing capitalism as the definitive environment to which the human species must adapt, and by assigning it its destination from above, Lippmann contradicts himself. While he does everything to disqualify the functional role of collective intelligence in the determination of ends, and while he contests all possibility of agreeing on a destination chosen in common—even local and provisional—he does not hesitate in considering that the final destination of the whole human species is already fixed. His displayed disagreement with Spencer masks in reality an underlying convergence. If he critiques the means of laissez-faire, if he counters its providentialist naturalism with the necessity of legal artifices, he adopts its determination of ends to the letter. Adhering without distance to the teleology that underlies Spencerian evolutionism, he does not hesitate to present, against Marx, the new economy as "the really inexorable law [of history]."[29]

By thus fixing the *telos* of evolution, new liberalism imposes a new philosophy of history, rivaling that of Marxism, which seeks to systematically separate what Lippmann continues to call "the masses" from all discussion about its destination. This explains why, in his homage to Justice Holmes, he interprets the common law as alone being capable of seeing "the supreme law" of history—while also entirely bypassing the incompetence of the masses and their representatives:

> Since the beginning of the American experiment there has existed always a feeling that the will of the people could not be refined successfully enough. . . . For after all the mass itself might become so

thoroughly indoctrinated with false ideas that it would, despite all the safeguards of debate, will the destruction of its own vital interests. . . .

. . . American jurisprudence and political theory adopted the idea of a supreme law more absolute than the Constitution itself. This super-law was never enacted. It was customary law which judges, lawyers, lawmakers, and publicists developed and imposed. . . . This was the beginning of that supreme, yet unenacted, law above the Constitution itself which caused Mr. Justice Holmes to protest that the Fourteenth Amendment did not enact Herbert Spencer's *Social Statics*.[30]

Lippmann faithfully recalls here what American history would retain of Holmes and his role at the time in the famous Supreme Court ruling *Lochner v. New York* (1905). While his colleagues on the Supreme Court read the Fourteenth Amendment, which concerns individual freedom, as the legitimation of Spencerian laissez-faire in social matters, and thought that it could not consequently relate to limiting the working hours of bakers in the State of New York to sixty hours per week, Holmes tried to counter that they were confusing the law with their personal convictions regarding economics. But at the same time, the historical legacy of Holmes is in large part distorted by this quotation. Indeed, the generalized judicialization of the social relationships that Lippmann promotes has not only the disqualification of laissez-faire and its belief in a nature without laws at stake. It has above all as a dual objective, on the one hand, to withdraw the law from the incompetent hands of the masses and their political representatives, and, on the other, to thereby remove the capitalist mode of production from all public deliberation:

Present-day men can reform the social order by changing the laws. But by political means they cannot revolutionize the mode of production. Until invention, which is as yet not even within the speculative possibilities, creates a more efficient and radically different method of producing wealth, mankind is committed to the division of labor in a market economy.[31]

Political deliberation must be limited to "reform[ing] the social order" to adapt it to the new environment of the human species, which is itself defined by the mode of production of globalized capitalism. Erected as the *telos* of evolution, this mode of production itself is not destined to change. Without further rational justification, Lippmann decrees that a transformation of the mode of production is "not even within the speculative possibilities," placing the law in turn back in the service of the fixing of a status quo that conserves the current order instead of critiquing it. While for Dewey, the human species must always remain in an active relationship of interaction and transformation with its environment, which is as much economic as social, Lippmann fixes in advance the economic ends of evolution, which imposes reforming the social order in an already fixed direction:

> In the end [the] peoples must return to the division of labor in an ex-
> change economy as surely as the farmer must return to his land if he
> would harvest a crop. It is the social order that has to be reformed.[32]

This social order itself must serve a transcendent goal that no political or philosophical speculation can counter with an alternative.

With Dewey and the tools of legal pragmatism, we can thus turn Lippmann's critique against him. His procedural democracy conceals an authoritarian fixing of the destination of the human species which claims to be able to escape all democratic and collective discussion. The law, interpreted as a collection of procedural rules that enables the human species to readapt to the demands of capitalism, must submit to what Lippmann calls both "the superior law" and the "common law"—which he perceives very precisely as a universal and transcendent law in spite of all the lessons of pragmatism:

> In the end no nation can fail to enter this system where common law
> prevails: if it is backward, unable or unwilling to make its portion of
> the earth secure for the new economy of the division of labor, its cer-
> tain destiny is to be conquered. Unless it is as remote as Tibet, in one
> way or another it will be brought within the necessary jurisdiction of
> the Great Society. Nor can any portion of the earth permanently secede
> from the society of common law: in the end the rebellion will be over-
> come. For the necessity of common laws throughout the world econ-
> omy is the necessity of all the multitudes of mankind in all their daily
> transactions, and its cumulative force is invincible.[33]

Justifying in passing the conquest of "backward" nations by more advanced nations on the road toward a globalized market economy, Lippmann like Spencer prefers that all nations fully enter the capitalist system of production, which is henceforth responsible for dispensing the common law, to these brutal forms of colonial war.

Through a first misinterpretation, the Great Society finds itself reduced to the mode of capitalist production, and even becomes through this reduction the source of a "necessary jurisdiction." Wallas's entire reflection on the dual necessity not only of adapting to the Great Society but also of readapting it to the dispositions of our species through collective deliberation is brutally pushed aside. Through a second misinterpretation of the same type, Lippmann empties common law of the meaning that Holmes's legal pragmatism sought to give it. Its new content is the globalized becoming of capitalism—which was also predicted by Marxism, but is this time transformed into the ultimate *telos* of evolution:

> It is perfectly true, as Marxian socialists contend, that the capitalist system had to expand all over the world; it is true that it has accomplished its expansion by imperialism. But the socialists are demonstrably wrong in thinking that what capitalism needed was closed colonies to be exploited for huge profit by capitalists with excess savings. That is merely what some capitalists hoped. What capitalism as a whole has needed was security and equal opportunity for the division of labor.[34]

As Spencer said before him, the *telos* of evolution is not the degraded capitalism of colonial war and predation. Capitalism only fully realizes itself, and only fully accomplishes evolution's ends, if it gives to each individual and to each nation equal opportunities to succeed in global competition. Such is, for Lippmann, the supreme law or the common law that must give its meaning to all other laws. If Lippmann, following pragmatists like Holmes and Dewey, conceives of the law as a tool of readjustment between the human species and its environment, it is to immediately—breaking away from them—absolutize one aspect among others of this environment as a "supreme law" that is responsible for giving the evolution of the living as a whole its goal and meaning in advance.

It is this resort to a transcendent law that explains the final return to metaphysics and the resumption of the Bergsonian lexicon in the last book of *The Good Society*, which invokes a "profound and universal intuition of the human destiny":[35]

> The conviction that there is a higher law, higher than statutes, ordinances, and usages, is to be found among all civilized peoples. . . . The belief in a higher law is in effect a prayer invoking against the material powers of an actual ruler some immaterial power which he can be compelled to respect; it imputes to the nature of things universal principles of order to which humans can be held accountable.[36]

Commenting on this passage, Dewey concedes to Lippmann that it is necessary to believe in a law higher than positive law: "I, too, believe there is a law higher than that of any positive legal system, and that the latter should be its instrument."[37] But it is to give it an entirely different content:

This "higher" law is that of supremacy of ties, relations and interdependences among human beings over the desires, activities and institutions which foster and support activities for purely individual profits. The problem of translating this moral supremacy into concrete economic and legal terms is the ultimate problem of politics.[38]

If he himself adheres to the higher law of liberalism, which demands that the dominant powers be limited so that the emancipation of individuals is possible, it is to support the necessity of the collective processes of individuation—involving a group of "ties," "relations," and "interdependences" that invalidate the atomist postulates of classical liberalism. Yet *Human Nature and Conduct* shows that this "higher" law is in no way transcendent in regard to the immanent conditions of evolution. It instead expresses the experimental logic of Darwinian evolution by improving it. In light of the formidable laboratory of evolution, as well as its creativity decoupled by human experimentation, to reduce interdependence to an individual lone search for profit is to lose sight of the multiplicity of possible and real interactions between individuals. The intensification and variation of interdependencies require on the contrary submitting the mode of capitalist production to public discussion and the tests of collective experimentation. For Dewey, all this shows that Lippmann "misses the essential core of socialist thought: that only by overthrow of a profit-economic system can the freedom of production and exchange he postulates be brought about."[39]

If for Dewey, Lippmann "postulates" freedom, it is in the sense that he totally disregards the real economic conditions from which emerge individuation at the same time as the freedom of producing and exchanging. This placing into parentheses of economic and social reality reinstates, according to Dewey, the metaphysical dualism that separates the end from the means. If the free individual is established as the supreme end, Lippmann claims to have arrived at this conclusion, following Bergson, through a pure metaphysical intuition that is separated from the instrumental intelligence concerning the material means that condition its emergence:

> But its conditions lie in the actual functioning of human beings in their actual relations with one another, not in "intuition" or in the "spiritual" segment of a divided human nature. Anything that can be justly termed "spiritual" in any intelligible sense of that word is the fruit, not the source, of the continual bettering of culture and civilization. Economic, legal and political institutions are the instruments of either forwarding or retarding and distorting the human relationships by which individuals are civilized. The separation of the individual

from the social milieu in which he lives, moves and has his being is the straight road to social philosophy *in vacuo*.[40]

This placing into parentheses of economic and social reality leads for Dewey to an abstract liberalism that reasons "in a vacuum" (*in vacuo*) and that sinks into a "conception . . . of the vague metaphysical sort."[41]

But when looking at it closer, it is not so clear that the higher law invoked by Lippmann is so abstract and disconnected from the means of its realization. When Dewey reproaches him for glossing over capitalism, and in this sense for isolating the naked individual invoked by classical liberalism, he bowdlerizes Lippmann's words in part. Far from whitewashing capitalism, the object of this passage, and of the whole final part of *The Good Society*, is on the contrary to fuse in one sole "common law" three fundamental laws, in order to submit them all to the fulfillment of capitalism. The higher law demanding the respect of the fundamental rights of the individual—which Lippmann traces back sometimes to the Stoics, sometimes to the Christian Gospels[42]— must fuse at the same time with the "necessary jurisdiction of the Great Society," imposing the cooperation of each individual in a globalized capitalist economy regarding the objectives, and involving the legal regulation of this cooperation through fair and honest competition regarding the means. Rather than functioning "in a vacuum," Lippmann's liberalism is filled on the contrary with the full and entire economic purpose that Spencer had already assigned to it, all while enriching itself with a completely new reflection—as we will soon see—about the means that need to be implemented to reform the social order and, with it, the human species itself.

The Law as "Rules of the Game": From the Law That Orders to Reform That Adapts

Rather than postulating an abstract individual, two naturalisms now enter into conflict. While Spencerian naturalism, in the degraded form that was popularized in the United States by William Graham Sumner, believes that the "laws of nature" impose lawless competition and that "we must . . . resign ourselves to an interminable struggle for existence in a war of all against all,"[43] Lippmann counters with another "higher law" that is itself founded on "the nature of things." This higher law denounces the savage competition celebrated by the decadent form of liberalism:

> The liberal, as distinguished from the anarchist, holds that mere unrestraint does not give the freedom of a voluntary society, that

unrestraint merely inaugurates a competitive struggle in which the ruthless will exploit the rest.[44]

Against this destructive and distorted competition, the higher law invoked by Lippmann suggests a true competition civilized by just rules and framed by a fair arbitration. Based on "the nature of things," this civilized form of competition allows for a natural hierarchy to emerge where inequalities are no longer based on arbitrary artifices but on the "intrinsic superiorities"[45] of each individual:

> A free society is one in which inequalities in the condition of men, in their rewards, and in their social status do not arise out of extrinsic and artificial causes.[46]

We must understand that a free society is one in which social inequalities are due to *intrinsic* and *natural* causes. Lippmann's new liberalism, under the guise of equal opportunities, leads to the justification of inequalities through their naturalization.

Yet the whole paradox brought to light by this new liberalism is that this natural inequality cannot emerge spontaneously or without rules. Because the whole arsenal of law precisely always tends to be requisitioned by the dominant classes, and because it was requisitioned throughout the nineteenth century by state capitalism to favor the privileged and to cheat at the natural game of competition, it is necessary to regain control of the law and to reorient it in a good direction. This direction is that of a fair and nondistorted competition arbitrated by equitable "rules of the game"[47] and the fundamental principles of fair play that prevail in sports competitions:

> The libertarian does not demand that all the runners in the race must keep in step and finish together; he asks that they start from scratch and none shall be permitted to elbow his rival off the track. Then the winner will be the best runner. The winner will not be the competi-tor who wangled a handicap from the judges, or obtained an advan-tage which had nothing to do with his ability to run the race. Manifestly, the liberal conception of equality does not promise to make all men equal in riches, influence, honor, and wisdom. On the contrary, its promise is that as the extrinsic inequalities imposed by prerogative and privilege are reduced, the intrinsic superiorities will assert themselves.[48]

By associating the *telos* of the global market economy with a fair and non-distorted competition, Lippmann seeks to establish that the concentration of profits is not part of the essence of capitalism. Far from being the work of the global division of labor arbitrated by the market, it is the product of a determined legal system that cheats the rules of the game by favoring certain of its actors to the detriment of all the others. In this sense, the enemy denounced by Marx and the socialists and the God adored by Spencer and the partisans of laissez-faire is not capitalism itself. It is state capitalism—made iniquitous by an arsenal of unjust laws. This analysis allows Lippmann to impose two central arguments. The first exonerates capitalism of all responsibility for the growth of misery and inequality throughout the nineteenth century, as it exonerates it of all responsibility for the crisis of the 1930s. The second orients capitalism toward a questioning of large corporations and the struggle between monopolies in favor of competition between small individual units, of which the individual participating in the sporting race or the driver contributing to the regulated acceleration of traffic provides the emblematic figures. Instead of forming immense monopolies and conglomerates, a capitalism that is freed from the stranglehold of the state will at last be able to organize a fair competition between "the more gifted"[49] individuals—who are recognized from now on as the basic unit of innovation, enterprise, and risk-taking. For all these reasons, Foucault was certainly correct to see in the new liberalism of the Lippmann Colloquium the launching of a new anthropology: that of the "entrepreneur of the self," of which the theory of human capital is the inheritor in certain aspects.[50]

The recurrent metaphor of the "rules of the game," to which the set of laws and rules of law is henceforth reduced, gives to the Lippmannian conception of the "equality of opportunities" a very different meaning than the one that Dewey attributes to it. But the difference is not, contrary to what his critique suggests in "Liberalism in a Vacuum," between a concrete equality and an "in the vacuum" abstract reality. It is between two incompatible conceptions—one just as concrete as the other—of nature and evolution. In *Human Nature and Conduct*, the "equality of opportunities" designates the social and collective conditions in which all individuals have the possibility of liberating the "impulse" which they bear, and with it, the creative capacity of each to transform the social environment by compelling collective habits to reorganize themselves. In the later texts, it is still a matter of freeing the creative and transformative "potentialities" of individuals that are never conceived of as realities that are "ready-made" or already there. Yet in Lippmann's texts, the "equality of opportunities" is used within the incomparably more restrained framework of a competition that is responsible for unleashing a hierarchy between "the most gifted" and the less gifted—a competition in which "the winner will be the best runner." "Opportunity" here does not signify potentiality in its creative dimension, but a game in which the resources are scarce and where it is a question of selecting the best and eliminating the less good.

By conceiving of this game as a competition that would have to be fairly arbitrated in order to liberate an "intrinsic" hierarchy, Lippmann produces a dual justification of liberal atomism. In place of a common destination, only competition and the complementarity of interests remain—where each individual retreats into their own preservation, advantages, and competence in the division of labor: "in order to be effective . . . [the system] would have to represent . . . collaborating and competing interests."[51] This cooperative competition, or this competitive cooperation, is itself entirely arbitrated by the atomist liberal postulate according to which—in a context of resource scarcity—the superiorities that emerge are "intrinsic," that is to say native or natural. As individuals, superiorities are considered as ready-made realities or as the facts of nature—expressed in the vocabulary of "talents," "aptitudes," and "gifts"—that the artifices of the law paradoxically have as their mission to reveal.

With this reconstruction of liberal atomism, Lippmann thinks he is very closely following Darwin's logic:

> There is no plan of the future: there is, on the contrary, the conviction that the future must have the shape that human energies, purged in so far as possible of arbitrariness, will give it. Compared with the elegant and harmonious schemes which are propounded by the theoretical advocates of capitalism, communism, fascism, it must seem intellectually unsatisfying, and I can well imagine that many will feel about the liberal society as Emma Darwin felt when she wrote about the *Descent of Man*, "I think it will be very interesting, but that I shall dislike it very much as again putting God further off.[52]

By abstaining from believing that society regulates itself through intelligence, by showing that it governs itself through the competition between the intrinsic aptitudes of agents, but while adding that, in the human species, this competition can only remain effective through the reorientation of the rules of law, Lippmann thinks he is drawing—better than Spencer on the one hand and Dewey on the other—the conclusions that are imposed by the Darwinian revolution and its definitive challenging of Providence.

This profound transformation of liberalism allows us to better understand how Lippmann can both criticize the empty abstraction of classical liberalism and place his entire book under the authority of Adam Smith. As the social misery of the nineteenth century and the dramatic historical events of the twentieth century showed, the liberal economists were largely mistaken. The human species produced by evolutionary history is neither as rational as classical economics demands, nor as reasonable as the liberal method of common law demands. But the mistake of classical liberalism was not so complete. It was only that of confusing the end with reality, or of not having recognized the normative character of what it was presenting as descriptive:

> [The classical economists] assumed that there were no legal privileges, no natural monopolies, no conspiracies in restraint of trade, but only perfect and fair competition among equally intelligent, equally in-formed, equally placed and universally adaptable men.
>
> In such a society all values would be "natural" values. . . . In such a society the perfect competition of men with absolutely equal opportu-nities, infallible foresight, complete adaptability, and no prejudices about what they wished to do or where they wished to live would pro-duce perfect justice.[53]

This fundamental text has a double meaning. In terms of social and anthro-pological realism, classical economics was entirely wrong. Claiming to describe reality, it postulated a falsely natural world in which the artifices of law and the possibility of their arbitrary utilization did not exist. Forgetting the biases produced by legal artifices, it supposed that the equality of opportunities be-tween agents was already ensured and that the competition was loyal and fair play. Forgetting as well the anthropological reality produced by the evolutionary history of the human species, it supposed that humanity was totally adaptable. It overlooked the inertia of stases, habits, and attachments, which entangle the preferences of humans in prejudices and which ruin all rational calculation of costs and benefits in advance. In short, it preferred the abstraction of theory to the real content of the human species—ballasted by the artifices of law and stuck in the stases of its evolutionary history.

But the text does not, on the contrary, boil down to this critical observation. If the reality of the human species has been missed, the norm erected by clas-sical economics was on the other hand correct. This norm is very much that of a "perfect and fair competition" involving at the same time "equal opportu-nities" and the "complete adaptability" of individuals to the accelerated muta-tions of the new economy. If reality met with this norm, we would thus arrive at a "perfect justice" in which all inequalities would be intrinsic and based on a natural hierarchy between the more and the less gifted: "In such a society all values would be 'natural.'"

Once the fundamental defect of classical economics has been corrected, once the normative nature of economic science has been recognized and assumed, all classical liberalism can thus be adopted again—but on the con-dition that the new liberalism assumes the normative dimension of the supreme law at the same time that it assumes the teleological character of its evolutionary theory:

> The classical economics, properly understood, [is] not an apologetic description of the status quo; it [is] a normative science which criticize[s] the status quo, disclosing the points at which reform [is] necessary, and indicating the kind of reform that [is] desirable.[54]

Because it is in reality normative, classical economics cannot avoid speaking out concerning reforms. Because it sets the norm, it also specifies the content of the reforms and determines what is desirable for societies. After having removed from the people and its representatives the determination of the law through common law, Lippmann dispossesses them of the elaboration of reforms though a normative economic science authorized to set the norm itself for all social evolution to come. Yet according to him, such normative thought can in no way spare itself of the legal, social, and anthropological conditions of its fulfillment. It is precisely because it sets fair competition in an open and globalized market not as a reality but as the ideal norm to come that the priority of new liberalism becomes the reform of everything that the species inherited from its past evolution:

> The best of the classical economists knew that they had constructed an hypothetical order. . . .
> So what the political economists had conceived in their science was not a picture of the world as it is but a picture of the world as it needs to be remade. . . . What they overlooked was that in order to imagine how the division of labor would work with perfect justice, it had been necessary to assume a reformed society of reformed individuals. It should have followed, then, that, in order to achieve the result in practice, it is necessary to make the reforms in practice.[55]

Instead of concentrating on economic theory, of postulating abstract rational agents, and of abandoning the problems of adjustment between this ideal norm and social reality, the first mission of new liberalism intends to be on the contrary political, social, and even anthropological.

This explains on the one hand why the almost exclusive content of neoliberalism would become the *reform of society*, and how it succeeded at the same time in progressively dispossessing the whole camp of progressives of the vocabulary of reform as well as of revolution. And this explains on the other hand why this reform is based not on the creative and transformative potentialities of the human species, but on the general postulate of an anthropological deficiency according to which all the old dispositions which it has inherited from its past evolution are judged as "lagging" or "maladapted" in regard to what the "great revolution" demands:

> Had the liberal economists realized this [critical] implication of their own hypothesis, they would have embarked at once upon the task of exploring the legal, psychological, and social circumstances which obstructed and perverted the actual society. They would not have left the criticism and the reform of society to those who did not understand, or were determined to abolish, the new mode of production. They would have seen that the mission of liberalism was to develop the principles by which mankind could readapt its habits and institutions to the industrial revolution.[56]

By accusing him of proposing "a legalist conception of human relations" that operates "in a social *vacuum*,"[57] Dewey focuses on the Lippmannian reinterpretation of common law and tends to attenuate the radicality of the social and anthropological reform demanded by the neoliberal agenda. Instead of postulating an abstract liberty disconnected from economic and social conditions in the manner of classical liberalism, it is rather a question of not only "reforming the social order" but of *readapting the human species* itself, notably in its "habits" and its "psychological" dispositions, through ambitious policies concerning education, health, and environment that are at the elevated level of the demands of the "great revolution."

7

The Neoliberal Agenda

Toward a New Age of Biopolitics

While classical liberalism promotes laissez-faire and that set of domains where one must know *to not act* (the *"non-agenda"*), new liberalism distinguishes itself, we have seen, through the definition of an *agenda*, of a set of voluntarist political measures that mark the return of the government in the life of populations.[1] What legitimizes the rupture and what inspires the agenda of new liberalism is based on the diagnosis of a "cultural lag"[2] in the human species— one which calls for a "readjustment" between the stases of habit and the flux of the new, and for thus increasing a "adaptability" or "flexibility" that has been established as the new content of educative action. But by designating educative policies as a priority for reforms and as the principal tool of the re-adaptation of the human species to its own evolution, does not Lippmann agree with Dewey's positions? By placing the public policies of education and more widely the social actions surrounding care (the health of populations, the conservation of natural resources) at the heart of new liberalism, do they not struggle together and in the same direction against the debacle of liberalism and the excesses of laissez-faire?

Before further exploring the neoliberal agenda, and to be able to fully respond to this question, the Foucauldian genealogy of liberalism must push us to question the radicalness of the rupture that these new liberalisms and their social action display. By going back to the sources of what he calls "biopolitics," Foucault indeed shows that classical liberalism progressively took the form of a public action for the human species, the health of populations, and the quality of their natural and urban environments.[3] From this point of view, the biopolitical dimensions of the neoliberal agenda attest to a profound continuity rather than to any rupture with classical liberalism. But by exhuming the evolutionary sources of new liberalism, I intend to advance a new argument here. The new liberalism theorized by Lippmann opens *a new age of biopolitics*—one that is no longer based on trusting in a good nature but on the observation of a radical deficiency of the human species linked to the inertia of its evolutionary history.

In his courses on the *Birth of Biopolitics*, the hypothesis of neoliberalism's essential antinaturalism led Foucault to lose sight of what should have been his subject from the beginning—biopolitics—and ultimately to leave the question of a properly neoliberal biopolitics unresolved:

> I would like to assure you that, in spite of everything, I really did intend to talk about biopolitics, and then, things being what they are, I have ended up talking at length, and maybe for too long, about neoliberalism, and neo-liberalism in its German form.[4]

In Foucault, neoliberalism in general, and German ordoliberalism in particular, because they were supposed to be based on a radical critique of classical naturalism, progressively obscured the question of the posterities of biopolitics. However, a precise analysis of the Lippmannian agenda shows that it is indeed by starting with a certain interpretation of the nature of the human species and of the meaning of its evolution—and that it is indeed from policies for life, health, and the quality of populations—that the neoliberal reform takes all its meaning. The rupture is neither in the affirmation of an ambitious public policy in the matter of public health or the environment, nor in the objective to improve the productive force of the human species by transforming it, already at the heart of all liberal biopolitics since the second half of the eighteenth century. If there is a rupture, it is rather in the conception of human nature. While the biopolitics of the first liberals bases itself, more and more clearly for Foucault, on trusting in the good nature of the human species, we are going to see that the neoliberal agenda inspired by Lippmann is based on the opposite conviction of a *defectiveness of human material*.

This interpretation, if confirmed, would be a first point of reference for measuring all that separates the new liberalisms of Lippmann and Dewey. If the politics of evolution defended by pragmatism renews the trust of the first liberals in the potentialities of the human species, we will see that the neoliberal version of biopolitics, which is based on the opposite diagnosis, sanctions the return in force of the apparatuses of surveillance and punishment that Foucault named, in *Discipline and Punish*, the "disciplines."[5] Yet it is precisely on these two points—that of the nature of the human species and that of the meaning of evolution—that the new liberalisms of Lippmann and Dewey collide head-on. While evolutionary sources nourish Lippmann's argument concerning a defect in human material, which thereby repaves the path to a government of experts, Dewey relies on both evolutionary theory and the great scientific and technical revolution to nourish his faith in democracy, and with it, his trust in the always renewed creative potentialities of the human species: "Democracy is a way of life controlled by a working faith in the possibilities of human nature."[6] While the Lippmannian conception of human nature involves a coercive and disciplinary reeducation imposed from above, one of the last great books by Dewey, *Freedom and Culture* (1939), counters with the intimate connection of democracy and "the faith in the potentialities" of our species:

> Democracy has always been allied . . . with faith in the potentialities of human nature. . . . Belief in the "common man" has no significance save as an expression of belief in the intimate and vital connection of democracy and human nature.[7]

This "faith" gives an entirely different color to the "force of lag" and to the question of heterochronies. It involves a radically divergent response about the tense relationship between stases and flux—one that is disqualifying for Lippmann, and necessary and creative for Dewey. In the same way, within the liberal field of biopolitics and its diversity, it also opens a true alternative to the neoliberal interpretation of the government of the living, whose force of resistance remains to be measured today.

A Disciplinary Biopolitics

Advocating a disciplinary biopolitics, as Lippmann does, subverts the subtle distinctions proposed by Foucault. Concerning the complementarity or on the contrary the tension between biopolitics and the disciplines, Foucault's thought rapidly evolved.[8] If the Rio conferences do not yet clearly distinguish "biopowers" from the disciplines that came out of convents and monasteries to be imposed on all bodies by state capitalism from the seventeenth century onward,[9] the course entitled "Society Must Be Defended" already distinguishes them more clearly.[10] The disciplines train individual bodies, while biopowers target populations and the human species in general. But in this course, these two technologies of power nevertheless continue to complement one another in the framework of the demands of advanced capitalism. If there is distinction, there is not yet opposition. We must wait for the course entitled "Security, Territory, Population" for a new idea to arrive that will allow Foucault to associate biopolitics no longer only with the development of capitalism but with the birth of liberalism as a new mode of government. Here, it is no longer the complicity between biopolitics and disciplines but their tension that Foucault is going to highlight. Because while the disciplines optimize the workforce by regulating, preventing, and *not allowing* "*things to happen*" (laissez-faire), biopolitics breaks away from the disciplines by understanding that a counterweight must be set against this invasive government of behaviors and that on the contrary letting the fluxes circulate, "letting things happen," is something that must be taught.[11] "Laissez-faire" does not precisely mean here, as it will in the degraded form it will take with Spencerian liberalism and contemporary ultraliberalism, *abandoning* public policies regarding health and environmental protection. Laissez-faire does not mean deregulating, but much to the contrary means *regulating the fluxes and circulations*—which involves taking control of the health of populations and the quality of their environments. But regulating does not mean controlling or regimenting everything either; and it is in the space of this nuance that liberalism and its critical distancing from the disciplines are born. "Laissez-faire," in its well-understood biopolitical sense, means moving from a state that directly overexploits the workforce—one which regiments it and plans it hour by hour (mercantilism, state capitalism)—to a government that on the contrary liberates the fluxes and circulations all while ensuring their relative security.

If the last lesson of "Society Must Be Defended" still insisted on the complementarity of the disciplines and biopolitics, the first lessons of "Security, Territory, Population" insist on the contrary on their tension, which opens a breach in the meshes of power:

> Discipline works in a sphere that is, as it were, complementary to reality. Man is wicked, bad, and has evil thoughts and inclinations, etcetera. . . . Security, unlike . . . discipline that works in a sphere complementary to reality, tries to work within reality, by getting the components of reality to work in relation to each other. . . .
>
> The game of liberalism—not interfering, allowing free movement, letting things follow their course; *laisser faire, passer et aller*—basically and fundamentally means acting so that reality develops, goes its way, and follows its own course according to the laws, principles, and mechanisms of reality itself.[12]

While discipline assumes a deficient human nature that must be entirely redressed ("man is wicked, bad, and has evil thoughts and inclinations"), biopolitics oppositely assumes a trust in nature and wants to liberate—while regulating—the game of interactions between the human species and its environment. We now understand why the birth of biopolitics is also that of liberalism, defined both as resistance to the disciplines and as criticism of government excess.[13]

If there is for Foucault a dark version of biopolitics—which will flourish in the twentieth century in the totalitarian states and their racial politics but also, to a lesser extent, in the democratic states controlling the "publics" through propaganda[14]—its first version is not only liberal but potentially liberating because it is less on the side of reining in the productive force of capitalism and more on the side of a general liberation of fluxes, circulations, and movements, necessarily opening, according to Foucault, unforeseeable breaches in the meshes of power. Yet this critical counterweight that biopolitics sets against the painstaking regulations of the disciplines and their constant pressure for optimization supposes a trust in the good nature of spontaneous processes. Biopolitics is a government of men who think first and fundamentally of the nature of things and no longer of the bad nature of men. Everything is based on the good nature of the human species and its desires:

> This desire is such that, if one gives it free play, and on condition that it is given free play, all things considered, within a certain limit and thanks to a number of relationships and connections, it will produce the general interest of the population. . . . The spontaneous, or at any rate both spontaneous and regulated play of desire . . . is what distinguishes both the naturalness of the population and the possible artificiality of the means one adopts to manage it.
> . . . The problem of those who govern must absolutely not be how they can say no. . . . The problem is how they can say yes; it is how to say yes to this desire.[15]

In his famous analysis of common law as the rules of the road, Lippmann seems at first glance to adopt on his own account this liberal model of a regulated liberation of the fluxes of circulation. On the condition that they are framed by general rules regulating risks, it is necessary to trust the desires of the drivers in the choice of their destination. The newness of Lippmannian biopolitics is thus not on the side of this regulation of risks through the law. It is rather in the theme of the reform of the human species itself, which indicates the limits of the common law's field of action. For, if we look at it more closely, we perceive that the trust Lippmann's new liberalism has in the natural preferences of the drivers is not so clear. Scrupulously respected when their control through planning is criticized, the desires of the human species are the rest of the time presented as defective, maladjusted, or ill-adapted to the new environment, which opens up a new age of biopolitics.

It is this poor quality of the population and the poor orientation of its preferences which indeed make up all the newness of Lippmannian biopolitics. Yet the theme is not new for him. From his first books, good government must start from the desires of the population, but on the condition of reorienting them in the right direction thanks to a sublimation ensured by experts. In *Public Opinion*, everything was based on the cognitive defectiveness of the masses, or their stereotypy—of which it was a matter of "manufacturing" consent. *The Phantom Public* provisionally readopted the liberal trust in a self-government of society ensured by the desires and atomized preferences of individuals occupied with their own conservation. But this trust was short-lived. In the context of the Great Depression and of the debacle of liberalism, *The Good Society* again took up the previous theme of a deficiency in the human species based on evolutionary arguments and amplified it to the point of redefining the mission of liberalism as the reeducation of the human species.

This rupture with liberal naturalism's trust in the penchants of human nature reactivates the anthropological foundation of the disciplines, which are based on the contrary on the observation of a bad nature that must be constantly redressed or corrected. If Lippmann's new liberalism expands the objectives of liberal biopolitics by taking charge of the quality of life of populations and of the securing of their environments, it also inscribes at the center of its agenda the program of a permanent correction of the behaviors through the disciplines—which follow to the letter their objective of reining in the workforce under the demands of globalized capitalism. By expanding public health policies through educative and cultural policies that redress the human species and orient it in the right direction, Lippmannian biopolitics thus reinforces the disciplinary project instead of offsetting it.[16] From this point of view, it can be doubted that new liberalism continues, like classical liberalism, to open breaches in the relationships of power; and one can wonder if, on the contrary, it does not contribute to tightening its meshes.[17] But if the potentially emancipatory aspect of liberalism is seriously threatened in the neoliberal version, must not we see there in exchange the welcome return of a protecting state undertaking a legitimate and necessary social policy? Once again, does not Lippmann agree with Dewey in maintaining that new liberalism will necessarily have to translate into a "social action"?

Neoliberalism as Social Action or Social Market Economy?

We have seen that Dewey wanted to overcome the dichotomy between individual and society by rethinking new liberalism no longer as the emancipation of the individual in relation to society but as the planning of a social action. The title of his 1935 book, *Liberalism and Social Action*, means that new liberalism *must be* a social action. Chapter 11 of *The Good Society*, which presents in detail the agenda of new liberalism, seems at first glance not to say otherwise.

New liberalism must devote all its strength "to the study of social readjustment" and take the measure of "the crying need for reform."[18] Instead of ignoring, like the classical economists, the reality of social suffering, this must become "the primary concern of the liberals" and "the constant care of their politics."[19] Here, we are very far from a spontaneous readjustment through common law—which is itself reinterpreted as a process of judicializing society for the improvement of the rules of the market. Alongside this judicialization of social relationships, the agenda of neoliberalism demands something else, which occurs through the return of ambitious public policies regarding education, health, and environment.

In his presentation of the "agenda" of new liberalism, Lippmann indeed announces a very interventionist social policy and a large-scale fiscal policy. "The correction of the conditions involves . . . large social expenditure," he warns.[20] The list of public intervention priority sectors that follows on this warning greatly exceeds the domains traditionally designated by liberalism, which are classically confined to the security of goods and people.[21] In a burst, Lippmann lists enormous expenses in the domain of health, education, conservation of natural resources, equipment, improvement of the markets, insurance, and even leisure activities and culture. Yet an equally ambitious public policy imposes an important fiscal reform involving the redistribution of income:

> These public investments and social services are, of course, expensive, and the process of financing them is a redistribution of income. . . . [Their] cost . . . can be properly charged in a graduated scale against the larger incomes.[22]

This new liberalism *as social action* could make certain participants at the Lippmann Colloquium—Jacques Rueff, for example, but also certain contemporary commentators—say that they were witnessing the emergence of a "liberal policy of the left."[23]

Is this judgment pertinent? Let's begin by remarking that Lippmann's argumentation marks a true turning point here in regard to the preceding chapters. The liberal (Smith) then evolutionist (Bergson) switching-off of intelligence sought to disqualify the aim toward an extensive utility—and that this aim would emanate from planning, popular will, collective intelligence, or the government. Under the jurisdiction of common law, the experts themselves with all their experimental intelligence were cast aside.[24] This switching-off of broader aims had the result of promoting a self-government of society through the atomic withdrawal of individuals into their rights (in competition) and their duties (in cooperation). But in chapter 11, Lippmann is obliged to recognize that the market—even when regulated by fair rules and even when achieving its maximum point of improvement—will always have a too narrow view of utility. Contradicting all his preceding analyses, he suddenly begins pleading for an aim toward extensive utility, which only public action would be capable of achieving:

> Values created by the schools in educating the next generation, by public works to preserve the fertility of the soil, do not have a market price and would, therefore, not be undertaken by ordinary private enterprise. This is the realm of investment by public authority which does not have to pay its way and show returns measured in money within a short span of time. For the most farsighted private investment cannot look much beyond one generation; only the exceptionally prudent plant trees for their children. But a society, as Burke so eloquently said, comprehends the dead, the living, and the unborn. And as the living inherited the national estate from their ancestors so they must transmit it to their posterity. This carries with it the obligation to plough some portion of the current income into the foundations of the social economy.[25]

Two fields of public action are put forward here. Of course there are other domains of public policy (health, equipment, control of the markets, social insurance, leisure activities, and culture); but we are going to see why the domains of education on the one hand and what we could call today environmental protection on the other are intended to appear as being emblematic of the rupture of new liberalism with laissez-faire.

For Lippmann indeed, education and the conservation of natural resources produce "values" that are not themselves assessable on the market. Does he want to indicate by this an order of value that would escape the sole economic logic of the market? Is he not drawing closer to Dewey's liberalism, for which economic interdependence must be completed and made more complex by other forms of interaction—beginning with those of education and culture? This would be a misreading of the text. Education and the conservation of natural resources are on the contrary presented as "the foundations of the social economy." The rupture with classical liberalism comes from the fact that by apprehending the social reality of the economy, and by taking account of the real quality of the human species and its natural environment, we finally grasp their "foundations." This alone justifies that the wealth created by the market is "reinvested" in these two domains. There are thus "returns on investments" that are just as real even if they are "imponderable and deferred," and even if they exceed for this same reason the too narrow perspectives of the market.

If the perspective of the market agents is considered too narrow here, it is not because "utility" would cover, as with James and Dewey, a much wider field than the economy. It is because the agents, when they are inside the market, cannot see what underpins or what constitutes the market itself. It is the theme—which will prove fundamental in German ordoliberalism—of an a priori set of conditions of possibility, in the Kantian sense of the word, required so that the order (*ordo-*) of the market can be constructed in its ideal normative or even "eidetic"[26] functioning. The values produced through education and environmental protection are thus by no means aneconomic. They are rather the transcendental conditions of possibility of the market economy itself and, for this same reason, not assessable by the market.

In relation to classical liberalism, this transcendental conception of the market gives a central role to "public authority," since it will be henceforth responsible for establishing its conditions of possibility. From this point of view, it has exactly the same role as that assigned to common law: making the ideal functioning of the market possible. Except that this efficiency is no longer gained only by improving the rules of law, but by improving the moral, cognitive, and competitive quality of its agents. This is the precise meaning of the "reform of the social order" targeted by the agenda of new liberalism. Behind the new theme of a properly liberal reform of society, the issue is more profoundly that of *reforming the human species* in order to readapt it to the needs of the globalized market economy. Yet for Lippmann, it is clear that common law cannot produce this reeducation itself. As is shown by the behaviors of excessive predation and exploitation that are endorsed by laissez-faire liberalism, economic agents are neither spontaneously rational nor even spontaneously reasonable:

> That anyone who thought he was preserving the system of free enterprise should have persuaded himself to believe that the law must leave men free to destroy the patrimony of their children is one of the curiosities of human unreason.[27]

The role of public power is thus not only that of protecting goods and people. It is also that of compensating for this unreason—that of a system whose partisans themselves destroy the conditions of possibility through a dual policy of education and conservation of natural resources:

> But there is required no less, and again the classical economics takes this for granted, the conservation of the land and of all natural resources, and their progressive improvement by clearing, reclamation, and

fertilization. The land and what is under it, the seas and the highways, are the patrimony of all the generations to come, and all rights of private property in this patrimony must, therefore, be subject to the condition that this natural inheritance will not be wasted or destroyed, that it will, on the contrary, be enriched. Since it would be . . . impossible for the new economy to produce wealth in an exhausted land . . . , the conclusion is undeniable that conservation . . . is a paramount obligation of a liberal state.[28]

This text particularly stands out in the American context of the confrontation between the partisans of "preservation"—who, with John Muir, insist on the intrinsic value of the wilderness—and those of "conservation" who, with Gifford Pinchot and Theodore Roosevelt, see instead a source of wealth and profit for the human species itself. From his first book in 1913, Lippmann clearly takes the side of conservation, which was already at the heart of Theodore Roosevelt's Republican program. It is thus a matter of becoming aware of the finite character of natural resources, of guaranteeing the equality of opportunities to all agents in their access to natural resources, of favoring their optimization in order to avoid losses and wastes, but also and especially of recognizing the natural environment's status of patrimonial value as the foundation of the wealth of nations for future generations. Against laissez-faire, the relationships of predation, and the unlimited exploitation of natural resources by large corporations and industrial monopolies, the idea is to impose a usage of resources that is regulated by the equality of opportunities within a context of scarcity. In 1937, exactly the same approach dominates. Natural environments are presented as "resources" for whose "progressive improvement" humans are responsible. Reduced to the status of "patrimony" or "heritage," entirely collective and not limited to the rules that govern private property, they are at the same time conceived of as a form of wealth among others that must not be "wasted" but rather "enriched" and as the very condition of all the wealth that is past, present, and still to come: "it would be impossible for the new economy to produce wealth in an exhausted land." If the services that nature provides for the economy are not quantifiable by the market, it is these services provided for the market economy that nevertheless make up all its value.[29]

The public authority's extensive vision of the conditions of the market is revealed in all its breadth here. Instead of being fastened to the short-term monetary value of whatever form of merchandise, "the correction of the conditions" of the new economy involves not only regulating the exploitation of natural resources but also regulating the exploitation of the workforce and its environment:

> The correction of the conditions involves . . . many other things, such
> as providing the opportunities for recreation which would not other-
> wise exist in specialized and congested communities.[30]

Here clearly appears the unique source of legitimization of the cultural politics
promoted by new liberalism, whether it is a question of financing natural spaces,
"playgrounds," or "museums."[31] Reducing culture to *leisure*, all public intervention in the matter has as its sole justification the recreation of the productive
force spent by work, itself interpreted as effort or as "labor," and the reoxygen-
ation of the industrial and urban environments—which are themselves degraded
by the necessary division of tasks, and by the saturation of the fluxes of exchange
and circulation.

It is therefore not surprising that the set of measures taken by the "public
authority" in regard to natural resources must be applied to health in exactly
the same way. Lippmann begins by criticizing the excesses of Spencerian
laissez-faire in this domain.[32] Convinced that the laws of evolution apply mechanically provided that the state abstains from disturbing them, Spencer
advocates not only for the abandonment of all public health policies but also
for the absence of all legislative intervention in the domain of health.[33] For
Lippmann, in the first place, this does not recognize the vulnerability of patients vis-à-vis the potential abuses of medical power—relationships of power
that involve regulation by law. This furthermore overlooks how refusing to
protect the rights of the sick automatically amounts to reinforcing the status
quo by protecting the dominant power of doctors. Contrary to what Spencer
believes, there are no relationships in economic and social matters that "escape"
the law. But this also allows the short-sighted private initiatives of individuals
to "let things happen" in a domain that is just as patrimonial as those of education and natural resources and that must also, as such, be recognized as one
of the conditions of possibility for the economy.

What public health is based on—like all other public policies regarding education, conservation, or social insurance—is not a simple program of social
aid but the recognition of health as one of the "foundations of the economy":

> The taxes levied on the rich must be spent not on doles to the poor but
> on the reform of the conditions which made the poor. The dole, by
> which I mean cash given by the government directly to the poor, is a
> relief of, but not a remedy for, their poverty, whereas money spent on
> public health, education, conservation, public works, insurance, and
> indemnification is both a relief and a remedy. It improves the produc-
> tive capacity both of the individual and of the national patrimony. . . .

By improving the marginal productivity of labor, it raises the minimum wage of all labor out of an increased national dividend.[34]

Public policies thus must not above all be reduced to a simple redistribution
of income, which would maintain poverty. They must rather aim to redistribute
the equality of opportunities in competition while themselves ensuring the a
priori conditions of possibility of such a competition, or of what Lippmann
calls the "foundations of social economy." If liberalism is indeed a social action,
it is thus an action that tends to reduce all social interactions—beginning with
those of education, care, culture, or work—to the economic relationships of
cooperation and competition governed by a globalized market to which they
must be readjusted.

Yet in Lippmann's model, as in the neoliberal trend that inspired it, this
reduction and this readjustment are never the object of any kind of democratic
discussion. Decreed from above, starting from a transcendent and normative
conception of the final destination of life and the living, the concrete modalities of readjustment must be implemented by a "public authority" that—after
having disqualified collective intelligence and after having made that of individuals retreat into their own atomic short-term interests—alone is capable of
having a sufficiently extensive vision to reconstruct the transcendental conditions of the social order. It is the announced return of the centralized government of experts, with leadership now granted to the economists. Dewey does
not hesitate in highlighting this paradox, enjoying how Lippmann finally begins
to advocate the same overhanging state interventionism as President
Roosevelt:

> [Lippmann] suggests a number of needed reforms to correct these
> maladjustments—reforms suspiciously similar to the theory, if not the
> practice, of the New Deal which he criticizes as gradual collectivism,
> sharing with revolutionary collectivism the radical error of control by
> overhead coercive officialdom.[35]

Once the true concern of social action in Lippmann's sense of the term has
been unveiled, that of a competition that makes it possible to establish intrinsic
and legitimate inequalities between individuals, and once it has been reiterated
that this reconstruction of the social order must be led from above by an overhanging authority that avoids all democratic control, one can only be surprised
by the opinion of Jacques Rueff that Lippmann's agenda can be placed within
a "liberal politics of the left." Indeed, to continue now to argue that neoliberalism consists of "the democratic promotion of a *real equality of opportunities*"

and that it must at last be recognized as fully belonging to the "patrimony of the left" is simply delusionary.[36]

The "Stupendous Readaptation of the Human Race"

Beginning with the observation of what he calls its "cultural lag," Lippmann thus calls for, as we have seen, a "stupendous readaptation of the human race."[37] His conviction is that this readaptation involves a large-scale public policy opening out into an immense field of future reforms. These reforms are not limited to extending the biopolitical regulation of risks regarding health and environmental security. They are not confined to liberating the fluxes of circulation and exchange while regulating them. They aim more deeply at transforming an ill-adapted human species into a group of flexible individuals who are more and more adaptable to the acceleration of changes. This argument constitutes the most innovative theoretical core of Lippmann's new liberalism while at the same time providing the political, sociological, and anthropological matrix for neoliberalism. It is crystallized in two principal texts that each deserve a very detailed reading and in which we are going to see how biopolitics and the disciplines reciprocally reinforce each other, announcing a model of society where the meshes of power are constantly tightened.

The first of these texts is found in chapter 9, which focuses on the Great Revolution and the Great Society, and it precedes the section entitled "The Cultural Lag." We will see that Dewey, who will adopt exactly the same expression in *Freedom and Culture*, will strive to give it an entirely different content—making in this 1939 text his response to Lippmann about the question of the reform of the human species that was still missing from his 1937 report. The second text is found in chapter 11, which focuses on the agenda of liberalism, and opens the section entitled "The Field of Reform." It is here that Lippmann proposes redefining education and health starting from the central notion of "adaptability." This time, it is Lippmann who adopts this expression from Dewey, but only to precisely invert its meaning.

The first text, which focuses on "cultural lag," opens with a return to the theme of the "Great Society":

> For it was in the nineteenth century that the self-sufficiency of nations, of local communities, and of individuals, gave way to a deep and intricate interdependence. Men found themselves living in a Great Society. . . .
>
> It is no exaggeration to say that the transition from the relative self-sufficiency of individuals in local communities to their interdependence

in a world-wide economy is the most revolutionary experience in recorded history.[38]

As we have seen regarding the "great revolution," Lippmann's misinterpretation consists in shrinking the "Great Society" that was theorized by Wallas and adopted by Dewey down to the "world-wide economy." By identifying the Great Society and the great revolution with globalized capitalism, Lippmann makes a reduction that his teacher Wallas, who had died five years earlier, would have certainly denounced. The "profound and complex interdependence" created by the industrial revolution finds itself diminished and arbitrarily simplified. It comes down, on the one hand, to a cooperation that demands the division of tasks; and on the other, to the fairest competition of competencies possible. For Lippmann, interdependence is not primarily due to collective intelligence and its techno-scientific inventions, as Dewey thinks. Nor is it essentially moral and affective, as the latter argues in *Freedom and Culture*. It is purely and simply economical, which Dewey explicitly contests:

> Physical interdependence has increased beyond anything that could have been foreseen. Division of labor in industry was anticipated and was looked forward to with satisfaction. But it is relatively the least weighty phase of the present situation. . . .
> . . . The kind of working-together which has resulted is too much like that of the parts of a machine to represent a cooperation which expresses freedom and also contributes to it.[39]

For Dewey, the real question that the Great Society asks lies elsewhere. In any case, it is certainly not that of knowing how to fully realize the mechanization of cooperation and the equality of opportunities in competition.

On the contrary, this is the new "way of life" for Lippmann:

> [This revolution] has forced mankind into a radically new way of life and, consequently, it has unsettled custom, institutions, and traditions, transforming the whole human outlook.[40]

The expression is not chosen at random. Like all those who from this era onward invoke "an American way of life,"[41] the determination of the new way of life, far from being purely descriptive, is clearly normative. For Lippmann, the new "way of life" is that which begins to establish itself at the beginning of the "great revolution"—that of a division of labor intensified and regulated by a more and more expansive market that must inexorably expand everywhere in the world. But for Dewey, the content of the new "way of life" is entirely different. It is a matter of democracy understood not as an institutional regime ("this external way of thinking") but precisely as a "personal way of individual life"—that is to say, as a set of attitudes and habits forming the stable character of a person, denoting at the same time the desire and the goal that orient their way of living:

> We can escape from this external way of thinking only as we realize in thought and act that democracy is a *personal* way of individual life; that it signifies the possession and continual use of certain attitudes, forming personal character and determining desire and purpose in all the relations of life.[42]

These habits are those that favor the intensification and diversification of social interactions, allowing for both the detection of conflicts and their resolution through collective intelligence—that is to say, through experimentation. Yet such an experimentation excludes knowing in advance how things end. Ends and means always remain to be collectively redefined and discovered in a continuous relationship of retroaction or of co-constitution: "Democracy as compared with other ways of life is the sole way of living which believes whole-heartedly in the process of experience as end and as means."[43] By refusing to block the end of the process in advance, and by refusing for this same reason all obedience in principle to the argument of authority, the challenge is to liberate the creative potentialities which all individuals bear, and which can at any moment bifurcate and reorient the direction of the experience:

> Democracy is the faith that the process of experience is more important than any special result attained, so that special results achieved are of ultimate value only as they are used to enrich and order the ongoing process. . . . All ends and values that are cut off from the ongoing process become arrests, fixations. They strive to fixate what has been gained instead of using it to open the road and point the way to new and better experiences.[44]

This interpretation of the new "way of life" is a systematic critique of the one Lippmann gives. The new mode of life described by *The Good Society* consists on the contrary of setting in advance the endpoint of evolution—with the globalized economy as *telos*—to which all means precisely contribute by switching off collective intelligence to prevent the pursuit of what Dewey calls "experience"; and with that the functioning of democracy, in the broadest sense of the word, in the government of societies. For according to Lippmann, the first determination of the new "way of life" is indeed the division of labor as hyperspecialization, whose beginnings date back to Adam Smith's England and his description of the pin factory in 1776:

For more than a hundred and fifty years the revolution which con-
verted these relatively independent and self-sufficing local communities into specialized members of a great economy has been proceeding
at an accelerating tempo.[45]

The two distinctive elements of this new "way of life" head in a strictly opposite
direction from the one Dewey advocates. The acceleration of tempo initially
suggests an irreversible movement toward an already given endpoint, which
straightaway excludes its collective discussion and testing. As we have repeatedly seen, it is precisely here that Lippmann adopts the metaphysical separation
between the ends and the means. Everything happens as if the endpoint of the
process were already established independently of the means, which only then
have to be applied secondarily. Instead of favoring the interactions of collective
intelligence and the continuous retroactions between the determination of
both the ends and the means, the intensification of the specialization at an
accelerated tempo makes each individual withdraw even more into their own
labor and their own narrow skill set instead of favoring the common aim of an
extensive utility. The following sentence adds the hardening of competition
to this acceleration and hyperspecialization:

In the struggle for survival the less productive economy of self-
sufficiency has not been able to withstand the superior effectiveness of
a mode of production which specializes in labor and natural resources,
and thereby promotes the use of machinery and mechanical power.[46]

While for Dewey, the scientific and technical revolution of the seventeenth
century intensified the experimental logic of the living by creating the conditions of a still more open collective experimentation, Lippmann interprets
technoscience as a required means for a higher end: the growth of economic
productivity through globalized capitalism. Yet instead of an open experimentation—where the "equality of opportunities" as understood by Dewey would
allow for each individual to liberate their creative potentialities so that they
reorient the course of the collective experimentation—this end demands an
entirely different interpretation of the "equality of opportunities": that of an
intensification of competition allowing for a fairer selection of the fittest and
a more just elimination of the less fit. Let us remember here that if in the expression "equality of opportunities," "opportunity" refers, in Dewey's thought,
to the possible or to potentiality in its most creative sense—assuming the acceptance of some deviation, conflictuality, and rupture—with Lippmann it
refers rather to luck, understood here as access to a rare resource that must be
equitably distributed at the beginning in order for the best to win the game.

For Lippmann, it is this new way of life that gives the process its entire meaning in advance. A *contrario*, everything that has sought to resist it has only "retarded the process."[47] Sliding from the neutral description of "process" to the normative evaluation of "progress," Lippmann quickly draws from this end the transcendent criterion that allows for distinguishing what is truly "progressive" from the false social progress that seeks to resist progress. It is in "recognizing the primacy of the division of labor in the modern economy" that we will be able to "successfully distinguish between truly progressive and counterfeit progressive phenomena."[48] By setting the endpoint of the process in a static form of economic organization, new liberalism no longer fundamentally seeks, like the liberalism of the eighteenth century as Foucault presents it, to liberate circulations, movements, and fluxes without ever anticipating the endpoint or meaning of history. By fixing in advance the meaning of evolution, by delivering in turn a great teleological narrative of historical processes, Lippmann's new liberalism intends to dispossess all the "progressive" adversaries of capitalism of the rhetoric of progress, condemning all forms of resistance to the side of reaction, conservatism, and decline.

It is because it already knows the endpoint of history that neoliberalism can tell the difference between those who are "ahead" and those who are "lagging." And it is from the summit of this endpoint that Lippmann can declare the lag of the human species and what he begins to call in chapter 9 its "cultural lag." As he himself explains, he borrows the idea from contemporary American sociology—and very probably from William Fielding Ogburn, a sociologist at the University of Chicago who had begun using the expression in 1922.[49] Yet Dewey himself also adopts Ogburn's expression in *Freedom and Culture* and was already advancing this theme in *Liberalism and Social Action*, evoking the "lag in mental and moral patterns" that "stand in the way of accomplishing this great transformation."[50] But how can Dewey talk of "lag" and "advance" if evolution as experimentation signifies that—like the always local and provisional perspectives of living organisms—the endpoints of the process are not transcendent but inherent to the process itself? The response to this question involves a detailed comparison of the texts of Lippmann and Dewey on this "cultural lag."

The Cultural Lag of the Human Species

When Ogburn talks about "cultural lag," it is to observe that technical changes occur more rapidly than social changes—with this difference in tempo having incompressible effects of disorganization. But for him, the observation of such a heterochrony does not in any way anticipate the meaning of evolution. Nothing allows for declaring a priori that social changes should "catch up" with technical changes; or that on the contrary, technical changes should slow down to readjust themselves to social rhythms. But when Dewey talks about the "lag in mental and moral patterns" in *Liberalism and Social Action*, it is in a much more normative sense:

> Since the legal institutions and the patterns of mind characteristic of ages of civilizations still endure, there exists the conflict that brings confusion into every phase of present life. The problem of bringing into being a new social orientation and organization is . . . the problem of using the new resources of production, made possible by the advance of physical science, for social ends, for what Bentham called the greatest good of the greatest number. Institutional relationships fixed in the pre-scientific age stand in the way of accomplishing this great transformation. Lag in mental and moral patterns provides the bulwark of the older institutions; in expressing the past they still express present beliefs, outlooks and purposes. Here is the place where the problem of liberalism centers today.[51]

The "lag" is here that of the group of stases of the human species—institutions, moral and mental patterns, habits—behind the advance of the "new forces generated by science and technology."[52] Even while having liberated unheard-of possibilities of social innovation with the scientific revolution, which arise from the extension of experimentation and its democratic "logic" into all fields of action, the human species somewhat lags behind its own evolution owing to a heterochrony between its future potentialities and the lasting and fixed stases it has inherited from its past evolution. It is this difference in rhythm between the lasting inertia of the past and the creative mobility demanded by the future that explains the conflicts and troubles of the present era, and that constitutes the "central problem of liberalism." The challenge of new liberalism for Dewey, as we have said, is thus to readjust the old and the new, to rearticulate the stases of habit and the flux of the new, which are now in conflict. Quite close to Lippmann on this point, *Liberalism and Social Action* tends to present all institutional, mental, and moral stases as necessarily hindering the possibilities of experimentation. The lag of the human species is here the lag of *all* stases inherited from the past behind the flux of technical, scientific, and social innovation. Yet *Freedom and Culture* gives a noticeably different analysis of the question of "cultural lag." Adopting this time to the letter the expression that Lippmann himself adopted from Ogburn by speaking of "cultural lag," Dewey complicates his analysis by showing that the problem is not that of the lag of stases behind the flux of the new; or of the inertia of a human species whose rhythms must be accelerated by making it more flexible. Rather than this particular lag, the true problem comes from what he calls a "gap" or "split" between new habits and old beliefs, which creates "intellectual and emotional divisions":[53]

> [These divisions] exist on a wide scale when there has been a period of rapid change in environment accompanied by change in . . . overt habits, but without corresponding readjustment of the basic emotional and moral attitudes formed in the period prior to change of environment. This "cultural lag" is everywhere in evidence at the present time. The rate of change in conditions has been so much greater than anything the world has known before that it is estimated that the last century has seen more changes in the conditions under which people live and associate than occurred in thousands of previous years.[54]

The new habits created by the globalized Great Society and its accelerated tempo have changed incomparably faster than the values, faith, and emotions inherited from the past. Here, the opposition is no longer between the stases of habit and the flux of innovation, but between the new stases—the exterior habits created by the environment—and the old stases—the ways of thinking, of believing, or of being affected—that produce profoundly divided personalities. For more and more individuals, the real acts and attitudes, those demanded by the accelerated rhythms of the Great Society, permanently contradict the values and beliefs they profess:

> The pace has been so swift that it was practically impossible for underlying traditions and beliefs to keep step. Not merely individuals here and there but large numbers of people habitually respond to conditions about them by means of actions having no connection with their familiar verbal responses. And yet the latter express dispositions saturated with emotions that find an outlet in words but not in acts.[55]

It is this gap between the change in habits of action demanded by the accelerated tempo of industrial society and the survival of habits of thought and emotional dispositions inherited from the past which explains that the cultural world always seems to be "delayed" compared to the new world created by the Great Society. Yet Dewey in no way draws from this the conclusion that new habits are "in advance" of old beliefs and still less that the latter must be liquidated as obsolete relics of the past. The example that he chooses—exposing the gap between the moral attachment still professed today for the democratic values of Jefferson's America[56] and the new habits that, in a country that is still

called democratic, tend to reinforce discipline, uniformity, and submission to
"The Leader"—takes precisely the opposite view of such a conclusion:

> Splits, divisions, between attitudes emotionally and congenially at-
> tuned to the past and habits that are forced into existence because of
> the necessity of dealing with present conditions are a chief cause of
> continued profession of devotion to democracy by those who do not
> think nor act day by day in accord with the moral demands of the pro-
> fession. . . . The serious threat to our democracy is not the existence of
> foreign totalitarian states. It is the existence within our own personal
> attitudes and within our own institutions of conditions similar to those
> which have given a victory to external authority, discipline, uniformity
> and dependence upon The Leader.[57]

This entire passage must be read as a close critique of Lippmann's political
arguments. The danger that threatens democracy comes less from totalitarian
collectivism—and from these seeds supposedly already sown in liberal collectivism—than from the pathological split between the old Jeffersonian ideal of
democracy and the new habits produced by advanced capitalism, which con-
strain individuals to always betray in action what they say in words. While the
environment of the Great Society—by producing an atomization of meaning
and a division of tasks—increases interior splitting, it cannot be hoped that the
new because it is new will disqualify the old because it is old, nor that the flux
of innovation and the acceleration of rhythms will produce a general liquidation of the stases, values, and beliefs inherited from the past. The struggle
against division will instead come to pass through the "intellectual and moral
integration"[58] of the old and the new, which itself involves a collective debate
about the question of ends, beliefs, and values—"incorporating" in culture the
methods of experimental science.[59] Like the biological adaptation of the organism and its environment, this integration must be understood in a dual
sense: as the capacity of beliefs, values, and ends to be modified by the new
conditions of the environment; and as their capacity to modify in return these
conditions themselves. In this sense, the observation of heterochrony shows
adjustments whose outcome remains, like all interaction, radically open and
unpredictable.

If there is a "lag," it is thus not that of the human species in general, which
would be too inert, too stable, or too closed in regard to the new, mobile, accelerated and open conditions demanded by the globalized Great Society.
When Dewey uses the normative term "lag," it is on the contrary to observe
the lagging of certain of these conditions—which have become dominant in
the Great Society—behind the nature of the human species itself. The role of

collective experimentation is precisely not to catch up to these conditions or to passively adapt to them but to submit them to discussion, to evaluate the "cultural conditions, conditions of science, art, morals, religion, education and industry, so as to discover which of them in actuality promote and which retard the development of the native constituents of human nature."[60] Here, a major difference with Lippmann is affirmed. Far from being inert or defective, human nature holds, for Dewey, an inexhaustible reserve of creative potentialities— something already theorized in *Human Nature and Conduct* with the idea that every individual carries within them a native impulse toward newness. This trust in human nature is the fundamental legacy of liberalism to which Dewey lays claim—on the condition of course that it dispenses with its atomist understanding of the individual and its native dispositions.

By insisting on the potentialities of human nature rather than its insufficiencies, Dewey intends very precisely to refute the interpretation that Lippmann gives of "cultural lag" in *The Good Society*. Relying on the observation of a deficiency in the human species linked to its past evolutionary history, Lippmann judges the whole of humanity—with its dispositions, habits, ideas and values, and particularly with its intelligence—as being "delayed" in regard to what the transcendental conditions of the globalized economy demand of it: "Our social intelligence has been shaped to a mode of life which was organized on a small scale, and, in respect to the duration of any particular generation, was static."[61] As in his Bergsonian critique, intelligence is limited here to an approach to reality that encloses and immobilizes it in stases. While the direction of evolution opens toward a globalized Great Society in which the fluxes of innovation are urged to accelerate, the intelligence inherited from its long evolutionary history has adapted the human species to stable and closed environments. In light of the final destination of evolution, the principal organ of adaptation for the human species has brutally become that of its maladaptation, maladjustment, and structural lag.

This lag, ceaselessly aggravated by the acceleration of the pace of change, explains the entire negative burden of the "great revolution" that is so well described by the great philosophies of the nineteenth century—which rightly insisted on the negative (Hegel), social misery (Marx), and the crisis of culture (Nietzsche):

> men have brought to the solution of present issues ideas and habits appropriate to a situation that no longer exists. Like passengers looking backward from the end of a swiftly moving train, they have seen only the landscape which they have already passed by. Multitudes of men have had to readapt themselves not merely to a new mode of existence

but to one in which the newest situation has soon been transformed into a still newer one. It has not been easy, and the sense of spiritual confusion, frustration, and insecurity which has pervaded all of modern culture has truly reflected the misery and the difficulty of the readaptation.[62]

While the eighteenth century still believed, with Adam Smith, in a providential regulation of the division of labor that was itself based on a preestablished harmony between the nature of the market and the natural penchants of the human species, the nineteenth century made the discovery—which had already been announced by Malthus at the very end of the preceding century—of the dyschrony and structural maladjustment between evolutionary rhythms, and in particular, between the pace of the global economy and that of the human species. It is this discovery that for Lippmann involves rebuilding liberalism from top to bottom by taking seriously the lag of the species and the suffering linked to its inertia.

Globalized capitalism resembles a train running at high speed in which the perceptive and cognitive capacities of the travelers are structurally overwhelmed. This dyschrony in no way appeared in Adam Smith's analyses, which described a pin factory where each worker remained riveted their entire life to perfecting the same task:

> The division of labour, by reducing every man's business to some one simple operation, and by making this operation the sole employment of his life, necessarily increases very much the dexterity of the workman.[63]

But this was a description of the early stages of the great revolution. From the following century onward, it demanded that individuals not only be specialized, but that they would be capable of regularly changing their specialty. Not only that they would adapt to a new situation, but that they would be capable of readapting to a newer situation again and again. In short, it demanded "adaptability" to a "new mode of existence [...] in which the newest situation has soon been transformed into a still newer one."[64] The whole problem comes from how instead of a preestablished harmony there is a seemingly insoluble contradiction between the inertia of the human species and the adaptability required for the great revolution. Such is for Lippmann the unique source of the negative and of the crisis that was rightly diagnosed—against the naïve naturalism of the first liberals—by the nineteenth century.

In *The Phantom Public*, the nature of a "problem" was already defined by dyschrony. In *The Good Society*, it becomes the source of the negative that tears history apart and provokes the crisis of the present time. In 1925, Lippmann still believed in the ability of procedural democracy to readjust the rhythms. In 1937, neither procedural democracy nor the judicialization of social relationships—required otherwise for the improvement of the rules of the market—are able to produce the "stupendous readaptation of the human race"[65] that the great revolution demands of it. In parallel to judicialization through common law, a true public policy of culture, education, and knowledge that will transform the "most intimate" dispositions of the human species is thus needed in order to fight against its inertia:

> The whole experience of the epoch since the revolution began, from the diplomacy of the Great Powers to the subtlest and most intimate issues of religion and taste and personal relationship, has been radically affected by this transformation of the way men live.[66]

This completely unprecedented situation will lead Lippmann to transform his conception of government and to return to the Fabian model of a high power in which experts and leaders readapt the populations to the demands of the Great Society. Abandoning the 1925 model—that of a purely procedural democracy that claims to refrain from all interference in the sphere of values, beliefs, and affectivity by returning them to the inner selves or intimate lives of individuals—the new liberalism endorsed by Lippmann relies on his faith in the revolution to call for a government strengthened by ways of feeling, thinking, or believing that readapts humanity to its new condition.

Toward a Neoliberal Redefinition of Education and Health

This is what the second text, entitled "The Field of Reform," shows as it is principally concerned with redefining the meaning of health and education.[67] Adopting the Spencerian vocabulary of the survival of the fittest in the selective context of competition, the text opens with the observation of an "unfit" human species, or one whose aptitudes are "badly fitted": "This malaise of the spirit reflects, like the discomfort of a badly fitted shoe, the maladjustment of men to the way they must obtain a living."[68] What Foucault discovers as the anthropological foundation of the disciplines—this bad nature of the human body and its penchants that justify its redress—is renewed here through the categories of Spencerian evolutionism. Evil is no longer, as in the ascetic disciplines that perfected themselves over the course of centuries in monasteries, that of the flesh but that of the "bad" adaptation or the "bad" adjustment of the human species to the demands of its environment. While Spencer believed that it was enough to allow the evolutionary mechanisms to "let things happen" so that the fittest would be selected and the unfit eliminated, Lippmann considers that all competition is flawed from the beginning through the defectiveness of human material. It is this observation that legitimizes, in his eyes, both an ambitious policy of public health and large public policies of education that Spencerian laissez-faire believed on the contrary it was necessary to abolish.

The first objective of all public health policy must initially consist in fighting against disabilities: "There are those who are born handicapped; by the deterioration of the stock from which they spring they are without the capacity to make their way."[69] For Lippmann, the quality of "stock" must be clearly understood here in a genetic sense; and this is what justifies in his eyes that public health assumes an ambitious policy in the matter of eugenics: "The economy of the division of labor requires . . . a population in which these eugenic . . . problems are effectively dealt with."[70] But genetic improvement must not limit itself to aiming toward the elimination of hereditary anomalies, which skew the equality of opportunities. It must not only return all individuals to equality at the same starting line in order to combat the inequalities linked to heritage, whether it be biological or social, for the purpose of unleashing the intrinsic inequalities that individuals would owe only to themselves.[71] It must also correct the bad quality of human stock in general and try to contribute to the continuous improvement of the human species:

> The economy requires not only that the quality of the human stock,
> the equipment of men for life, shall be maintained at some minimum
> of efficiency, but that the quality should be progressively improved.[72]

For those who are born differently abled, the agenda of new liberalism has nothing very clear to propose. It is steadfast in announcing their inevitable failure in competition. But for the rest of the population, it is partly a matter of protecting the genetic patrimony from all anomalies, but also of constantly improving its quality to readapt it to the needs of the economy. Here are outlined the first political justifications of an unlimited "enhancement" in the performance of the human species.[73]

This new conception of health in general and public health in particular falls perfectly in line with the emergence in the 1930s of a new form of eugenics, "a loose coalition of what one might call 'reform eugenicists.'"[74] For this new eugenics, the prejudices of class and race hardened through classical eugenics were serious misinterpretations. There are talents, gifts, and capacities that can be sought in all classes of the population. This is exactly the meaning of the Lippmannian metaphor of sporting competition. So that the race is as fair as possible, it is necessary to combat all forms of disability that are handed down through biological or social heritage as they bias the competition and prevent the detection of the "instrinsic superiorities" that are hidden in the underprivileged classes. But these new eugenics equally contest biological reductionism and classical eugenics—to which they oppose the essential role of social environment, which must ensure an equality of opportunities for all individuals. Daniel Kevles insists in this respect on the important role that Lippmann played in the 1920s in the criticism of IQ tests.[75] Presenting intelligence, like the pragmatists, as the complex result of interactions between natural dispositions and the environment, he rejected its reduction to an innate aptitude, as I have noted. But between 1920 and 1930, eugenics became considerably more refined, which henceforth allowed Lippmann to subscribe to it while maintaining the importance of social factors, in addition to genetic factors, in the appearance of handicaps:

> Others grow up handicapped by disease in childhood, by malnutrition and neglect. . . . They do not adapt themselves easily. Then there are those who have been broken by the poverty and squalor of their youth, and who never do obtain an equal opportunity to develop their faculties.[76]

"The faculties" whose development is in question here designate the necessary key skills for social survival—enhanced by the intrinsic superiorities that competition unleashes—which itself involves an ever greater adaptability to the transformations of the social order.

The endpoint of evolution remains, we see, defined by Spencer's terms. It is when it concerns the question of the means that there is a rupture and that the idea of an *agenda* emerges—a list of all there is to do against laissez-faire. Just as the markets cannot spontaneously improve without the legal artifices of common law, the naturally deficient human species cannot spontaneously produce these faculties without the artifice of a large public health policy. Readapting the human species to the demands of the globalized economy involves not only continually improving its defective genetic patrimony through the elimination of anomalies and the enhancement of performance, but also assuming ambitious social policies in the matters of prevention, care, and health—which promote at the same time the equality of opportunities and adaptability.

If the agenda of new liberalism redefines health as the increase of performance in competition, it redefines education as the production and constant improvement of the "adaptability" of populations—itself understood from the demands of the global division of labor:

> There is the whole unresolved task of educating great populations, of equipping men for a life in which they must specialize, yet be capable

of changing their specialty. The economy of the division of labor requires, and the classical economics assumes, a population in which
these eugenic and educational problems are effectively dealt with.[77]

As I have recalled, in the unfinished state of capitalism described by Adam
Smith, the worker could limit himself to specializing in and being identified
by a "peculiar trade" for his entire life—allowing at the same time for optimiz-
ing work hours and improving working conditions.[78] But with the acceleration
of competition, each worker must then be capable of regularly changing jobs
throughout his life, at the same time as he must be sufficiently "versatile" to
constantly move from one task to another within a single job.[79] Versatility and
adaptability allow for the hyperspecialization of tasks and the mobility of markets to be combined. For the agenda of the new liberalism, such will now have
to be the true content of educational public policies and the new meaning of
education itself: "It should be the aim of educational policy to make most men
versatile and adaptable in the place where they were born."[80]

Before returning in the conclusion of this chapter to this strange final precision ("to make most men adaptable *in the place where they were born*"), further
reflection is needed on Lippmann's resumption of this concept of adaptability—already central in the Deweyan theory of education, and which blurs the
clear distinction between the neoliberal agenda and the political philosophy
of pragmatism. A parallel reading of the texts shows that although Lippmann
adopts the term "adaptability" and its central place in the pragmatist redefinition of education from Dewey, he completely subverts its meaning.[81] This point
is essential because our contemporary world—in the field of education in
particular—could be permeated with these ambiguities.

In *Democracy and Education*, Dewey is entirely conscious of the ambivalences of the term, which are also those of the biological concept of adaptation
and of its multiple ambiguities in the field of evolutionary theory. According
to him, Spencer's mechanistic conceptions and the strictly experimental logic
promoted by Darwin are brought into opposition around these notions of adaptation and adaptability. To highlight the specificity of his own concepts of
adaptation and adaptability, which he reckons to be much more faithful to
Darwinian logic, Dewey proposes a very clear distinction between two meanings of adaptability that are currently confused: adaptability as "plasticity" and
adaptability as malleability—which he associates sometimes with docility,
sometimes with passive submission to circumstances. Like adaptability, plasticity is incidentally itself also full of the same ambivalences:[82]

> The specific adaptability of an immature creature for growth consti-
> tutes his *plasticity*. This is something quite different from the plasticity

of putty or wax. It is not a capacity to take on change of form in accord with external pressure. . . . It is essentially the ability to learn from experience. . . . This means power to modify actions on the basis of the results of prior experiences.[83]

While adaptability as Spencer theorized it in his conception of "industrial society" is at the same time mechanical and passive, adaptability—which for Dewey constitutes the very meaning of the educative act—is on the contrary active and indissolubly linked to the "experimental logic" of evolution:

> Education is not infrequently defined as consisting in the acquisition of those habits that effect an adjustment of an individual and his environment. . . . But it is essential that adjustment be understood in its active sense of *control* of means for achieving ends.[84]

If adaptability and readjustment are indeed the focus of all true education—distinguished from training or conditioning—it is necessary to thus understand them, as we are repeatedly reminded, not as a docile submission to the demands of the Great Society but as the capacity of the human species to resume experimental control of its own evolution within the context of industrial society by redefining its ends and means in a collective and continuous manner.

This is the whole meaning of the title of the 1916 work, which announces an organic link between education and democracy. By severing individuals and populations from any capacity for collectively transforming their environment and redefining their own ends together, "adaptability" as Lippmann interprets it misses the meaning of education, adaptation, evolution, and democracy all at the same time:

> If we think of a habit simply as a change wrought in the organism, ignoring the fact that this change consists in ability to effect subsequent changes in the environment, we shall be led to think of "adjustment" as a conformity to environment as wax conforms to the seal which impresses it. The environment is thought of as something fixed, providing in its fixity the end and standard of changes taking place in the organism; adjustment is just fitting ourselves to this fixity of external conditions.[85]

Lippmann certainly agrees that the current environment has harmful qualities that social policies must correct. But it is through an exterior environment that is idealized and interpreted as the *telos* or ultimate endpoint of evolution—the final form of global division of labor as Spencer theorized it—that the organism will be transformed into a putty that immediately obeys the injunctions of the global economy to come. The paradox, which is that of all teleological approaches to becoming, is that the evolutionary character of evolution, in spite of the injunction for mobility, is entirely lost from view—to the benefit of a transcendent law and an already fixed endpoint.

As in Watson's behaviorist psychology, which Dewey critiques in the preceding chapter, everything for Lippmann is thus still based on a "negative conception"[86] of the immaturity of the human species, which is deemed unfinished and deficient in regard to the new demands of its environment. For Dewey, it is precisely this immaturity—more marked in the human animal than in all other mammals—which obliges a constant experimentation with new possibilities and which is on the contrary the inexhaustible source of its "growth."[87] This exceptional slowness in developing, which biologists today would call its "neoteny," is one of the most precious and most creative aspects of the lag of the human species. Inversely, negative conceptions of human nature and its lag open the path to strictly disciplinary biopolitics—where population quality is optimized through the constant pressure of disciplines that are at the same time sanitary, educational, and professional, responsible for always correcting and reeducating the somatic and psychological dispositions of individuals. The democratic faith of Dewey and American pragmatism in the experimental potentialities of the human species calls for an entirely different government of life and the living—a truly liberal self-government in which the government of the living is tested and readjusted collectively. If this new form of biopolitics intends to establish a powerful counterweight to all the forms of disciplinary control and to all the requisitions of the workforce through the demands of globalized capitalism, the neoliberal biopolitics announced by Lippmann foresees an unprecedented reinforcement of the disciplines, which jeopardizes the tension between these two technologies of power that Foucault was still theorizing at the end of the 1970s.

The text by Lippmann that is perhaps the most explicit in this regard is that in which he affirms the superiority of capital over work, and which sheds light on the enigmatic formula that I cited above: to make "*most* men adaptable...*in the place where they were born.*" As Lippmann explains, the mobility of human labor produced by adaptability will never be able to rise to the level of the hypermobility of capital. To imagine that the human species could catch up by becoming hypermobile itself is an abstract utopia that he deems already lost. Because they are inexorably ballasted by the stases of habit and by the shackles of attachment, it is necessary to reimplant the populations in fixed places where they will remain attached to their roots and under house arrest:

A civilized life is impossible for nomads who settle nowhere and do not put down roots in a particular place. For men who have just arrived and will soon depart tend to be crudely acquisitive. They are transients who have no permanent stake in any community. . . .

It follows that if the necessities of a civilized life are to be accommodated with the new economy, the stipulation of the classical economics, that labor and capital must both be perfectly mobile, has to be modified. Capital has to be more mobile than labor, sufficiently more mobile to compensate for the inevitable and desirable human resistance to a migratory existence.[88]

At first glance, Lippmann may seem to admit here, following Dewey, the tragic necessary tension between stasis and flux. If it is necessary that the fluxes of the circulation of capital accelerate, he concedes that it is also necessary that the stases of attachment, habit, and community consolidate themselves. Yet far from understanding this duality in the tragic fashion of a necessary tension, Lippmann transforms it into a hierarchical distinction that hardens the opposition between the leaders and the masses. If the leaders and the experts remain associated to the end with mobility and globalization, it is the mass of populations—"most men," he clarifies—for whom it is a question of establishing residence to better ward off the risks of an uncontrolled mobility; while the best among them, those who are exceptions from most men, seem to escape this coercion in principle:

> The tides of population must move slowly if old communities are not
> to be devitalized by emigration and new communities overwhelmed
> by inassimilable immigration. It should, therefore, be the aim of policy
> to mitigate this human evil by using social controls to induce inanimate capital, rather than living men to achieve high mobility. It should
> be the aim of educational policy to make most men versatile and
> adaptable in the place where they were born, and of economic policy
> to make capital mobile.[89]

Based on the contradictory dual constraint of making the masses more mobile by immobilizing them, Lippmann draws the conclusion of a necessary "social control" that on the one hand fixes populations in space while avoiding the "evil" of immigration; and on the other hand, makes the mass of individuals more and more malleable, docile, and polyvalent "in the place where they were born." In doing so, it is the meaning and the very "aim" of all "educational policy" that finds itself radically transformed, being moved outside of all collective deliberation about its ends. While classical liberalism thought of education in terms of emancipation, Lippmann's new liberalism makes it authoritatively work toward flexibility, declaring through its many traits what the jargon of contemporary educational policies will later call "employability."[90]

A restrictive migratory policy, an employability-based educational policy, and an economic policy grounded in the deterritorialization of capital: some of the main features of the globalized capitalism that prevails today are announced here. Yet for Dewey, this new liberalism denies the liberty of the individuals that it is supposed to liberate. When he denounces "a kind of molluscan organization, soft individuals within and a hard constrictive shell without,"[91] he is taking aim at the already prevailing model of society that Lippmann intends to further reinforce. With the growth of the coercive character of social control, it is ultimately a question of tightening the hierarchy between a population under house arrest ("most men") and its leaders, who are themselves associated with the mobility of capital—a hierarchic separation of those who govern and those who are governed that breaches the very principle of self-government.

Instead of a biopolitics which, like that described by Foucault, liberates exchanges, fluxes, and circulations, and in which freedom and security constantly remain in tension, Lippmann thus calls for a tightening of the disciplines and social control; and with them, for an authoritarian liberalism that damages the circulation of people in the name of a better circulation of goods. It is not surprising then that he henceforth revives in the following chapter his Hamiltonian and vertical conception of power—in which only the leaders are capable of perceiving the transcendent principles of a "good society": "The fundamental question is how the formless power of the masses shall be organized, represented, and led."[92] Which primarily supposes, as in the Hamiltonian model that Lippmann opposes to Dewey's constant referencing of Jefferson, that the representatives of the masses protect them from themselves by manufacturing their consent from above:

> Since it was obvious that no mass of men can as a mass make more
> than the simplest decisions of yes and no, and is physically incapable
> of administering its affairs, the practical question was how a govern-
> ment could be made to represent the people.[93]

Thus, a confrontation is taking shape between two clearly political versions of the government of the living: between a disciplinary biopolitics that takes place in the realm of work, education, and health through an increasingly coercive social control and, in terms of a democracy, through the manufacturing of consent of the masses; and another possible version of the government of the living that is centered both on the liberation of the capacities of participation of all individuals in social experimentation and on the determination through collective intelligence of the ends and means of evolution.

But the challenge that remains for us now is ultimately that of knowing if, beyond Lippmann, it is indeed his agenda that, since the end of the 1930s, has reigned supreme over new liberalism and in so-called liberal societies. The diversity of neoliberalisms initially resists such a hypothesis in advance. Neither German ordoliberalism, nor Friedrich Hayek's spontaneous order, nor the Chicago School theory of human capital are entirely soluble in Lippmann's new liberalism. A whole series of tensions and fractures that would merit being reexamined in regard to this genealogy makes the relationship between neoliberalism and the government of life and the living still more complex. The diversity of biopolitics then complicates the theory of a hegemonic domination of neoliberalism itself. Can our era be reduced to the sole hegemony of neoliberalism and its disciplines? Are not the different ages of biopolitics, that described by Foucault at the end of the eighteenth century and that of the diverse agendas of neoliberalism in the second half of the twentieth century, regularly in tension with each other? And is not Dewey's new liberalism—another biopolitical vision of the human species and its environment—also taking shape, and perhaps increasingly profoundly, in the new power relations that are being invented within the contentious fields of labor, as well as those of education, health, and the environment?

Conclusion: Governing Life and the Living
Toward New Conflicts

Like all genealogies—in the precise meaning of the term given to it by Nietzsche and then Foucault—this book was born from both a situated and an embodied need: that of understanding the origins of this widespread feeling of a *generalized lag* that is more and more oppressive and increasingly shared. It was this long interrogation on the sources and strength of this new feeling, which few among us still seem to resist and whose pathological effects are nevertheless more and more clearly felt, that first led me to the evolutionary sources of neoliberalism.

But one could legitimately object that this feeling of *lag* when confronted with the ineluctable evolution of the course of things—which in many ways has taken over, in bodies as in consciences, from sin—actually has much older sources. One can indeed suppose that it is one of the late outcomes of the generalized acceleration of rhythms and fluxes, which was already noticeable in eighteenth-century ways of feeling, and which Marx would impute in the nineteenth century to the development of capitalism. And it is true that the current feeling we have of lagging behind the demands of the future was without a doubt already emerging from these new ways of living, feeling, and thinking generated by the development of capitalism and the atmosphere of permanent revolution that it imposed on all social rhythms from the beginning of modern times up until the industrial revolution.[1] Like us, the people of the past two centuries were already hurried. Like us, they were already subjected to the sufferings and exultations of acceleration, lag, and rush. They also imagined traveling around the world in just a few days and hoped to resolutely participate—"like the traveller who gets to know a land and its people from a railway carriage"— in what Nietzsche called "the tremendous acceleration of life" (*die ungeheure*

Beschleunigung des Lebens).[2] One could fundamentally object that the feeling of our lagging behind is maybe quite simply the fundamental affective tonality of modernity, which is itself determined by the revolutionary tendencies of capitalism. Neoliberalism and the "lag of the human species" are just business as usual.

To this strong objection, I will begin by responding that this pathological feeling of lag actually has entirely unprecedented aspects that the history of capitalism and modernity cannot manage to explain on its own. Following another lesson of Nietzsche and Foucault about genealogy, it is moreover necessary to definitively renounce establishing one sole cause for its emergence.[3] Nietzsche shows how the grammar of European languages motivates us to seek a unique and stable subject behind each event to be understood as its originary cause—a sort of "original thing" (*Ursache*), the German word for "cause." When the event displeases us, we quickly make this original "cause" the guilty party and fantasize about its removal. Thus, explains Nietzsche, the logic of *ressentiment* can be nourished from metaphysical grammatical illusions. Contesting this grammatical logic of *ressentiment*, genealogy begins on the contrary by accepting that there is no clearly identifiable authority, no underlying subject of the action, no culprit to slay whom one could blame for the situation and be rid of like a scapegoat. To understand the "surging" or the "emergence" (*Ursprung*) of this new feeling like any other new phenomenon, it is thus necessary to instead admit a body of interactions that forces us to plunge into the nooks and crannies of our archives and the gray of documents. No more than the development of capitalism, the completion of the industrial revolution, or the explosion of new technologies, there can thus be no question of designating neoliberalism as *the* unique and exclusive cause of this new way of feeling time that is both unprecedented and inherited from the long term.

Nevertheless, as we have seen throughout this journey, one of the great strengths of neoliberalism is how it reinterprets in its own way the modern feeling of lag by imposing on it an entirely new meaning inspired by the contributions of the Darwinian revolution. For how can we not imagine a secret and intimate link between this interpretive coup of neoliberalism—that of establishing an evolutionary meaning for the modern feeling of lag—and the currently dominant biologizing vocabulary in which the theme of lag is now expressed while saturating everything around us? "Evolution," they say, demands "mutations" that allow for "survival" and "adaptation" to our new "environment"—that of increased "competition" in a context of "scarce resources." How can we explain this progressive colonization of all the domains of human life in general—and of the political field in particular—by this biological or, if one prefers, biologizing vocabulary of evolution?[4]

In this constant deploring of "lag" and in this permanent injunction for "adaptation" in the service of "competition," should we only see simple economist metaphors that have no impactful substance and that certainly would in no way call into question the hermetically sealed boundary supposed to protect the field of politics from biological assaults since the trauma of World War II? Must we not see on the contrary the dull persistence in our contemporary world of social Darwinism and its sinister residues whose legacy the postwar years, at least in Europe, had hoped to expunge?

All the usual statements are thus loaded with ambivalence. These injunctions to adapt in order to better evolve can be understood sometimes as simple metaphors popularized by economics experts, and sometimes as betraying a latent social Darwinism that our societies have never truly overcome. Content with neither of these responses, the genealogical course that I have proposed here has consisted in defending an entirely different thesis. The unprecedented turn that the feeling of our own lag has taken and the evolutionary vocabulary with which it has begun to dominate our minds can probably be reduced neither to simple metaphors without gravity or significant substance nor, conversely, to the harmful vagrancies of social Darwinism. It can also be explained, and in a much more assured way, by *the evolutionary sources of new liberalism*—which notably involve fascinating relationships of hybridization and conflict between the history of neoliberalism and American pragmatism that have remained far too rarely studied up until now.

Yet in the course of this inquiry, the sudden entrance of John Dewey profoundly disturbs the terms of the question. Through the study of his complex exchanges with Lippmann and with everything that the Lippmann-Dewey debate added—from the 1990s onward—to their debate, it appears that Dewey himself advanced his own interpretation of the *lag of the human species* that was largely incompatible with Lippmann's and explicitly directed against him. In doing so, American pragmatism has come to complicate the question of lag. It has given it new meanings and revealed its profound ambivalence. What is lagging? Must we or must we not lag? Is lag always the sign of defectiveness in human material? Such are the new questions that Dewey's political thought raises against Lippmann's unilateral understanding of lag.

But it remains to be seen, and I will return to it to finish, if the pragmatist interpretation of lag plays an equally structuring role in the current feeling of our lag and in the permanent injunction for adaptation. What about, for example, the ambivalences regarding the question of lag, adaptation, and adaptability in the field of education and new pedagogies? Is our feeling of lag nourished not just by the sources of capitalist modernity and its reinterpretation by neoliberalism, but also by the evolutionary dimensions of American pragmatism? If such is the case, there would then be, at the heart of the contemporary motif of the lag of the human species, an entire field of new conflicts to explore that would profoundly transform the political polarities inherited from the past.

And it is true that the essence of the political conflict will henceforth focus on the question of knowing *who is lagging* and *who is ahead*. This reconfiguration of the traditional polarities may explain why all political signs seem to currently be repositioning and reversing with a rapidity that disorients even the most politically well-armed minds. Deprived of the engines of both reform and revolution, the supposedly progressive parties have been disarmed everywhere, stunned as they watch this troubling disturbance of signs that seems to condemn them either to a passive adherence to the neoliberal "revolution" or to the reactive struggle against its "reforms" and for the defense of the status quo. Former conservatives transform into progressives, while former progressives are denounced as conservatives. The fact that neoliberalism—through its powerful reinterpretation of the Darwinian revolution and the meaning of evolution for life and the living—has monopolized the question of lag and advance explains this current situation to a large extent.

Yet this situation itself brings new perils. On the side of the former "progressives," there is a great danger of becoming embroiled in the defense of deceleration, stability, and all stases in general *against* the injunction to advance, evolve, and adapt. How can one resist the neoliberal disqualification of all stases without yielding to reaction against flux and its accelerations? How can one not succumb to the logic of *ressentiment*—which Nietzsche precisely defines as the hate of the flux of becoming and the reactive embedding of stases that are supposed to oppose it?[5] Such is the particularly difficult question, particularly on the economic and social front, that is facing most of the "left" everywhere in the world. How can the tragic tension between flux and stases be maintained? This becomes a central political question, as Dewey so masterfully foresaw in his otherwise more subtle analysis of the multiple modalities of the lag and the advance of the human species.

All of this opens both new and illuminating perspectives on the situation of political confusion in which we are plunged today. Yet it is now time to say that throughout this genealogy, one doubt has never left me. Even if it was both fascinating and unquestionably central in America between the two wars, what *real* impact did the Lippmann-Dewey debate concerning the lag of the human species have on the much vaster history of neoliberalisms? And beyond the texts of the neoliberals themselves, does it have any real relevance in the neoliberal government of our societies and their feeling of perpetually needing to catch up?

The challenge, which moreover torments all genealogical endeavors, is ultimately of knowing how texts and archives, which are exclusively bookish and which Nietzsche and Foucault call the "gray of documents," become a living and embodied reality of relationships of power—"archives" in the much wider sense of the term that also comprise the marks and signs that relationships of power imprint on both psychic and somatic bodies in addition to the texts.[6] How can one ward off the risk of genealogy becoming vain erudition, of it being confined within the texts of minor figures ("Lippmann? . . . A simple American journalist," someone recently said to me, not without reason) that say nothing about the real relationships of power, of it even hazarding the risk that the exorbitant and almost supernatural power of having opened a new era might be attributed to some lone second-rate author? To the risk of vain erudition, which neglects true crises out of fear of confronting them, could also be added the still more harmful temptation of conspiracy: that of seeing in Lippmann and in his posterity on Mont Pèlerin the cause of all our woes— which follows a line of thinking that is widely shared today by partisans from all sides, illustrating the logic of *ressentiment* and its causal imputations in all their purity.

The avoidance of this dual pitfall, at the same time as the establishment of the centrality of the Lippmann-Dewey debate in contemporary forms of neoliberal governmentality, involves in reality two complementary tasks that I have not had the time to complete within the framework of this book. The first is that of reevaluating the centrality of Lippmann himself—celebrated by the Lippmann Colloquium and highlighted by Foucault, but only in passing—in the different doctrinarian currents that make up neoliberalism. The second is that of studying the impact of these neoliberalisms within the reality of the relationships of power by notably examining the role of the Lippmannian element and of the complicated relationship that it has ceaselessly built with the American pragmatist tradition in the real governing of life and the living— particularly in the domain of education, health, and the environment.

The first of these tasks will begin with Lippmann's role and his debate with Dewey during the Lippmann Colloquium—which took place almost exactly one year after the publication of *The Good Society* (1937) and one year before that of *Freedom and Culture* (1939). It will involve a close comparison with Friedrich Hayek's theses, which were widely hybridized with those of Lippmann and which also gave a central role to life and evolution while maintaining a very different treatment of evolutionism and evolutionary theory. A systematic inquiry will next need to be pursued, following and going beyond that of Foucault, about Lippmann's relationships with German ordoliberalism as well as the meaning—whether real or supposed—of his antinaturalism and his native hostility to biology. It is still Foucault's genealogy that will ultimately need to be adopted and extended concerning the links between the Lippmann Colloquium, the diversity of the neoliberalisms that it illustrates, and the theory of human capital championed by the Chicago School two decades later—particularly in the domain of education, which was already defended as a priority by new liberalism at the end of the 1930s.

This last aspect of the genealogy of neoliberalisms leads me straight to the second large and much vaster task for which this book calls. How did the diversity of neoliberalisms transform the government of life and the living in the domains of education, health, and the environment; and were the concrete practices in these domains inscribed and archived in the texts of the neoliberals themselves?

In the domain of education, the great texts of the European institutions could provide the ideal material for such a genealogy. Drawing from both the ordoliberal definition of European construction and the adoption of the ideal of emancipation that animated the founding fathers of Europe, all the shades of gray that the documents deploy are dream material for a genealogist working toward detecting the still active conflicts at work in our own archives. For these texts are not just marked by the double, and potentially contradictory, seal of the Enlightenment and German ordoliberalism. It could be that they also inherit multiple tensions from neoliberalisms themselves concerning the question of education, by hybridizing, for example, Hayek's analyses on the one hand and those of Theodore Schultz and Gary Becker on the other. Or maybe also by drawing from—and this is the real question—the long debate between Lippmann and Dewey over the meaning of education.

Extending into public policies of education that elicit new relationships of power, the question is that of knowing whether these texts do not concern the dual and profoundly ambivalent mark of the Lippmannian redefinition of education as adaptability and employability on the one hand and of the influence of new pedagogies on the other, which could have been in part inspired by Dewey's pragmatism and the unprecedented role that he granted evolution and adaptation in his redefinition of education. How, for example, does the both dominant and profoundly ambivalent notion of the "equality of opportunities" draw from the tension between Lippmann and Dewey, and does it transform the relationships of power that structure the field of education?

The same type of questions criss-cross the domain—which is increasingly contentious today—of health care. In the field of chronic disease, for example, the emergence of what American diabetologists call "therapeutic patient education" has taken on a profoundly ambivalent meaning.[7] While therapeutic education programs are now being established almost everywhere in the world as a public health priority, at least two models are in conflict over its meaning—and with it, that of health and education.

Very close to the neoliberal conception of democracy, liberalism, and education, a first model sees in therapeutic education a means for public health experts to better govern populations, defining disciplinary programs from above that produce the auto-control of individuals who are called on to become integral agents of public health by interiorizing the performance and optimization objectives of the health system. Here, Foucault's analyses in the fields of medicine, disciplines, and biopolitics provide a particularly illuminating gateway for better ascertaining the ethical and political challenges of therapeutic education. If for obvious historical reasons Foucault had not been able to produce his own critical analysis of therapeutic education—as it was only beginning to be established at the time of his death in the mid-1980s—it is clear that the topic would have fascinated him and that he has left us the necessary tools to construct a critical genealogy.

Yet it turns out that—like all good subjects calling for a genealogy—therapeutic education is traversed by another set of forces that have launched an unprecedented battle with this democratic, educative, and sanitary model. It was precisely in the 1980s, and notably with the appearance of HIV and the transformation that it induced in the relationships of power between doctors and patients, that therapeutic education and sanitary democracy became the terrain of new struggles. Led by Foucault's ideas, the partisans of this new model rejected the government of experts and the vertical conception of education regarding health.[8] One of the questions that the inquiry will need to determine is the role of Dewey's model in this battle. If their echoes and resemblance are striking and incontestable, is there a real genealogical link between on the one hand the current struggles around sanitary democracy and the role of experts in public health policy and, on the other, the long conflict between Lippmann and Dewey concerning democracy, liberalism, and education? If this debate has widely structured American political thought, has it equally reconfigured our own conception—in Europe in general, and in France in particular—of the relationships of power?

The recent evolutions of the health system under the influence of what is now called "big data"—the explosion of digital data and its automation—are creating echo effects that are even more striking regarding the conflict of Lippmann and Dewey. Between a democracy of experts, which tends to automate decision trees, and the participation of the publics in the inquiry, opening the path toward an assumed and unpredictable political conflict in the health field that redefines the relationships between science and democracy, the conflict that has never ceased to oppose Lippmann and Dewey on the meaning of the Darwinian revolution may be found in all its freshness.[9]

Two relationships to time and the evolution of life and the living also confront each other here. On the one hand, the automation of data seems to reinforce both the gradualist conception of living—which is also interpreted here as a homogeneous, isotropic, and predictable material—and the strictly procedural approach of democracy in which the ends are defined exclusively by the technical knowledge of experts who favor the automation and judicialization of all decision processes. On the other, the new demands regarding public health and sanitary democracy evoke what Dewey countered against Lippmann precisely in the name of the Darwinian revolution and its new lessons about the evolution of life and the living. As in Dewey's political model, they are based on the conflict and diversity of evolutionary rhythms, the always possible deviancies of "impulse" which all individuals possess, and the multiple lags of heterochrony.

It would be necessary lastly to show that the same conflicts are at play again in the fields of the environment and political ecology between, on the one hand, a government of experts that defines the automated processes of optimization from above, and, on the other, a rebuilding of democracy through the active participation of the publics. In this last model, it is a question on the contrary of noting the tragic dimension of the heterochrony of evolutionary rhythms—against which all living beings, both human and nonhuman, must succeed in surviving together by enduring the conflictual plurality of their perspectives.

Only such an inquiry—in the precise sense that Dewey gave to this word and which exceeds by definition the capabilities of one isolated individual—in the triple field of public policies of education, health, and the environment could truly accomplish the project of this book by putting its central argument to the test. It alone would ultimately allow us to know if the confrontation between the neoliberalism inspired by Lippmann and the democracy reshaped by Dewey sheds light on the new conflicts concerning the government of life and the living that are active today more than ever.

If the argument that inspired this genealogy from the outset were confirmed, we would better understand why political conflicts are now structured around "advance," "lag," and "evolution"; and why the government of the living is henceforth made the central issue of confrontations to come. And it would thus be necessary to acknowledge that most of our contemporaries, in expelling the biological from the field of politics while actually reshaping it as "biopolitics," saw nothing of these new conflicts coming. By becoming enmeshed in a constructivism that is hostile to all naturalism, contemporary thought has on the contrary widely contributed to abandoning the government of the living to the most reductionist tendencies of the life sciences.[10] Such could essentially very well be the ultimate challenge of this critical genealogy of the evolutionary sources of neoliberalism: that of reconstructing *a new philosophical and political conception of the meaning of life and evolution* that overtakes the sterile face-off between constructivism and biologism. Philosophy could thus fully play its role in the arena of the political battles to come, shedding light on history and the meaning of the politics of evolution, and contributing to a collective, democratic, and enlightened takeover of the government of life and the living.

Notes

Introduction: The Lag of the Human Species

1. For a republication with commentary on this colloquium see Serge Audier, ed., *Le Colloque Lippmann: Aux origines du néo-libéralisme* (Lormont: Le Bord de l'eau, 2008).

2. Michel Foucault, *Naissance de la biopolitique: Cours au Collège de France, 1978–79* (Paris/Seuil: Gallimard, 2004; trans. Graham Burchell as *The Birth of Biopolitics: Lectures at the Collège de France, 1978–1979*, ed. Michel Senellart [New York: Palgrave Macmillan, 2008]), as well as my commentary: "Qu'y a-t-il de nouveau dans le *néo*-libéralisme? Vers un nouveau gouvernement du travail, de l'éducation et de la santé," in *Le nouvel esprit du libéralisme*, ed. Fabienne Brugère and Guillaume le Blanc (Lormont: Le Bord de l'eau, 2011), 106–48.

3. I am thinking particularly of Nietzsche and Bergson, who moreover had a decisive influence on Lippmann's thought. On the importance of this tension in the work of Nietzsche, see my *Nietzsche et la critique de la chair: Dionysos, Ariane, le Christ* (Paris: Puf, 2005) and *Nietzsche et la vie: Une nouvelle histoire de la philosophie* (Paris: Gallimard, 2021). On the proximity of Nietzsche and Bergson on these questions, see *Nietzsche et la vie*, chap. 10.

1. Readapting the Human Species to the Great Society

1. Walter Lippmann, *A Preface to Politics* (New York: Mitchell Kennerley, 1913).

2. Herbert Spencer, *The Principles of Biology* (1864; London: Chapman and Hall, 1899).

3. This belief would come under attack in the 1890s by August Weismann. Let us remember that Darwin himself—by adopting the Spencerian expression "survival of the fittest" for the fifth edition of *On the Origin of Species*—would contribute to the

confusion between his own arguments and those of Spencer; and with this, to the emergence of the inappropriate expression "social Darwinism."

4. Herbert Spencer, *The Principles of Psychology* (London: Longman, Brown, Green, and Longmans, 1855), 620.

5. Herbert Spencer, *The Man versus the State* (London: Williams and Norgate, 1884).

6. William Graham Sumner, *The Challenge of Facts and Other Essays*, ed. Albert Galloway Keller (New Haven, CT: Yale University Press, 1914), 90.

7. Graham Wallas, *Human Nature in Politics* (London: Archibald Constable, 1908).

8. Wallas.

9. Lippmann, *Preface to Politics*, 13.

10. See Ronald Steel, *Walter Lippmann and the American Century* (1980; New Brunswick, NJ: Transaction, 1999, 2008), 17.

11. Lippmann, *Preface to Politics*, 225, 233ff.

12. John Dewey, "The Influence of Darwinism in Philosophy" (1910), in *The Middle Works, 1899–1924*, vol. 4 (Carbondale: Southern Illinois University Press, 1977), 3.

13. Concerning the critique of Spencer's *Principles of Psychology* (1855) by William James in *The Principles of Psychology* (1890), see Stéphane Madelrieux, *William James: L'attitude empiriste* (Paris: Puf, 2008), 134–35.

14. Lippmann, *Preface to Politics*, 12.

15. Lippmann, 38.

16. Lippmann, 34ff.

17. Lippmann, 50–51.

18. Lippmann, 83.

19. See John Dewey, *The Public and Its Problems* (1927), in *The Later Works, 1925–1953*, vol. 2 (Carbondale: Southern Illinois University Press, 1984, 2008).

20. A tension that is notably explained by the rivalry, in young Lippmann's mind, between the two large influences of his Harvard years: on the one hand, that of William James's pragmatism; and on the other, that of his other great teacher George Santayana. On this point, look in particular at Steel, *Walter Lippmann*, 21.

21. John Dewey, *Human Nature and Conduct: An Introduction to Social Psychology* (1922), in *The Middle Works, 1899–1924*, vol. 14 (Carbondale: Southern Illinois University Press, 1983, 2008), 6, 108.

22. Dewey, 67. On the critique of social psychology that perceives impulses as instincts fixed by evolutionary history, also see pp. 66 and 75.

23. Dewey, 5, 70.

24. Dewey, 47.

25. Lippmann, *Preface to Politics*, 98.

26. Lippmann, 46.

27. Lippmann, 47.

28. Steel, *Walter Lippmann*, 23–24.

29. Steel, 40.

30. The emblematic text in this regard is that of the Fabian Society's founding couple, Beatrice and Sidney Webb, entitled *Industrial Democracy* (1897)—which Lippmann closely read during his years of study at Harvard (see Steel, *Walter Lippmann*, 24).

31. Lippmann, *Preface to Politics*, 314–15.

32. Graham Wallas, *The Great Society: A Psychological Analysis* (1914; New York: Macmillan, 1916), v.

33. Wallas, x.

34. Wallas, 8.

35. Wallas, 138.

36. Wallas, 8.

37. Wallas, x.

38. See Wallas, xi, for the synopsis of chap. 10.

39. Wallas, 271, 282–85.

40. Walter Lippmann, *Drift and Mastery: An Attempt to Diagnose the Current Unrest* (1914; Madison: University of Wisconsin Press, 2015).

41. Lippmann, 59–60.

42. Lippmann, 99.

43. Lippmann, 100.

44. Lippmann, 175.

45. Lippmann, 151.

46. Lippmann, 82ff.

47. On the close links between Lippmann, Herbert Croly, and Theodore Roosevelt, see Steel, *Walter Lippmann*, 58–59, 65–66, 78–79.

48. Lippmann, *Drift and Mastery*, 80.

49. Lippmann, 86.

2. A Darwinian Democracy

1. For a precise history of this debate, see chap. 3 of this book.

2. Ronald Steel, *Walter Lippmann and the American Century* (1980; New Brunswick, NJ: Transaction, 1999, 2008), 128ff.

3. Steel, 141ff.

4. Steel, 129.

5. Walter Lippmann, *Public Opinion* (1922; New York: Classic Books America, 2009), 185; the expression is analyzed later in this chapter.

6. Steel, *Walter Lippmann*, 142.

7. Steel, 158.

8. Lippmann, *Public Opinion*, 1.

9. Plato, *The Republic* VII, 514 a, in *Plato in Twelve Volumes*, vols. 5–6, trans. Paul Shorey (Cambridge, MA: Harvard University Press, 1969).

10. On the notion of "stereotype," see part 3 of *Public Opinion*.

11. See the English translation of the Plato quotation in *Public Opinion*, 1.

12. Lippmann, *Public Opinion*, 14.

13. Lippmann, 62. Lippmann cites here the description of the perceptive world of the newborn made by William James in the *Principles of Psychology*, which he will moreover adopt much later in *The Good Society*.

14. Lippmann, *Public Opinion*, 69.

15. See chap. 3 of this book.

16. Lippmann, *Public Opinion*, 24–25.

17. Lippmann, 185.

18. Lippmann, 289. For Aristotle's famous maxim, see *Politics*, trans. Peter L. Phillips Simpson (Chapel Hill: University of North Carolina Press, 1997), VII, 1326 b 20–25, p. 124: "So it is clear that the best limit for the city is this: the furthest that the excess of numbers for securing a self-sufficient life can go and still be easy to survey."

19. Lippmann, *Public Opinion*, 198.

20. Lippmann, 199.

21. Lippmann, 198.

22. Lippmann, 188.

23. Lippmann, 25.

24. Here, Lippmann follows to the letter the Hamiltonian model that inspired the American republic. See Denis Lacorne, *L'invention de la République américaine* (Paris: Hachette Littératures, 1991), as well as Bernard Manin, *Principe du gouvernement représentatif* (Paris: Flammarion, 2012).

25. See chap. 3 of this book, and the very critical reading of *Public Opinion* by the followers of the Lippmann-Dewey debate.

26. Lippmann, *Public Opinion*, 168–69.

27. Lippmann, 85.

28. Lippmann, 93.

29. Lippmann, 230.

30. Lippmann, 232.

31. Lippmann, 231.

32. Michel Foucault, *Sécurité, Territoire, Population: Cours au Collège de France, 1977–1978* (Paris: Seuil/Gallimard, 2004); trans. Graham Burchell as *Security, Territory, Population: Lectures at the Collège de France, 1977–1978*, ed. Michel Senellart (New York: Palgrave Macmillan, 2007).

33. Immanuel Kant, *"An Answer to the Question: What Is Enlightenment?"* (London: Penguin UK, 2009).

34. Lippmann, *Public Opinion*, 171 and 166, respectively.

35. Lippmann, 167.

36. Lippmann, 145.

37. Lippmann, 163.

38. Lippmann, 155.

39. Lippmann, 164.

40. Lippmann, 21.

41. Lippmann, 171.

42. Lippmann, 183.

43. Lippmann, 185.

44. Lippmann, 185.

45. Lippmann, 185.

46. Steel, *Walter Lippmann*, 215.

47. Lippmann, *The Phantom Public* (1925; New Brunswick, NJ: Transaction, 1993, 2015), 37, 63.

48. Plato, *Republic* VII, 515 b.

49. Lippmann, *Phantom Public*, 3.

50. Lippmann, 27.

51. Lippmann, 47–48.

52. Lippmann, vii.

53. Lippmann, 3.

54. Lippmann, 14–15.

55. Lippmann, 32–34.

56. Lippmann, 68. See Aristotle, *Politics* VII, already commented on earlier in the chapter.

57. Lippmann, 69.

58. This expression gives chapter 6 of *The Phantom Public* its title (Lippmann, *Phantom Public*, 67–70).

59. Lippmann, *Public Opinion*, 69, cited and commented on earlier in the chapter.

60. Lippmann, *Phantom Public*, 10–11.

61. Lippmann, 12.

62. See Steel, *Walter Lippmann*, 207.

63. Lippmann, *Phantom Public*, 24–25.

64. It will remain to be seen why Lippmann ultimately favors a eugenicist policy in *The Good Society*. See chap. 7 of this book.

65. Lippmann, *Phantom Public*, 12ff.

66. Lippmann, 16.

67. Lippmann, 17.

68. Lippmann, 15.

69. Lippmann, 1.

70. Lippmann, 75.

71. This is noticeably different in one sense from that which paleontology has imposed on the theory of evolution, which very precisely designates the modifications of evolutionary rhythms in ontogeny—meaning the development of organisms. The most well-known example of heterochrony is neoteny, a situation in which somatic development—persisting in the larval state instead of developing "normally"—lags behind sexual maturity. Paleontologists, as we will see, find this phenomenon interesting because it allows one to understand evolutionary change in a nongradualist way. Regarding the link and the differences between these two usages of the term "heterochrony," see chap. 3 of this book.

72. Lippmann, *Phantom Public*, 21.

73. Lippmann, 22.

74. Lippmann, 22.

75. John Dewey, "The Influence of Darwinism in Philosophy" (1910), in *The Middle Works, 1899–1924*, vol. 4 (Carbondale: Southern Illinois University Press, 1977).

76. Lippmann, *Phantom Public*, 22–23. Lippmann here cites Bergson, *L'évolution créatrice* (1907; Paris: Puf, 2008), 223: "Suppose that there are two species of order. . . . The idea of disorder . . . would objectify, for the convenience of language, the disappointment of a mind that finds before it an order different from that which it needs."

77. Lippmann, *Phantom Public*, 37.

78. Lippmann, 21.

79. Lippmann, 17.

80. Lippmann, 35.

81. Lippmann, 35.

82. Lippmann, 158–59.

83. Lippmann, 36. Concerning the importance of this distinction, see Claude Gautier, "*Le public et ses problèmes*: Le problème social de la connaissance," *Philosophical Enquiries: Revue des philosophies Anglophones*, no. 5 (December 2015): 45–77.

84. Lippmann, *Phantom Public*, 37.

85. Lippmann, 56.

86. Lippmann, 37–38.

87. Lippmann, 60.

88. Lippmann, 47, 51.

89. Lippmann, 48–50.

90. Lippmann, 73.

91. Lippmann, 73.

92. Lippmann, 73–74.

93. Lippmann, 117.

94. Lippmann, 117.

95. Lippmann, 117–18.

96. Lippmann, 151.

97. Lippmann, 117.

3. The Biological Sources of the Conflict

1. Dewey, "Practical Democracy: *The Phantom Public* by Walter Lippmann" (1925), in *The Later Works, 1925–1953*, vol. 2 (Carbondale: Southern Illinois University Press, 1984, 2008), 213.

2. Dewey, 219.

3. James W. Carey, *Communication as Culture* (1989; New York: Routledge, 2009).

4. Carey, 57.

5. Carey, 63–64.

6. Noam Chomsky and Edward Herman, *Manufacturing Consent: The Political Economy of the Mass Media* (1988; New York: Pantheon Books, 2002).

7. Christopher Lasch, *The Revolt of the Elites and the Betrayal of Democracy* (New York: Norton, 1995).

8. See in particular Michaël Schudson, "The 'Lippmann-Dewey Debate' and the Invention of Walter Lippmann as an Anti-democrat, 1986–1996," *International Journal of Communication* 2 (2008): 1–20, for whom Lippmann's elitism does not make him an antidemocrat, but "a subtle thinker concerned with how to integrate expertise into a functioning democracy." For Schudson, this "invention of Walter Lippmann as an Anti-Democrat" is in fact based on a fallacious interpretation of democracy which does not account for the clearly elitist and representative republican origins of our political model—so rightly recalled, according to him, by Bernard Manin in his analyses of representative government (B. Manin, *Principes du gouvernement représentatif* [Paris: Flammarion, 2012]). Along the same lines, also see Sue Curry Jansen, "Walter Lippmann, Straw Man of Communication Research," in *The History of Media and Communication Research: Contested Memories* (New York: Peter Lang, 2008); as well as S. C. Jansen, "Phantom Conflict: Lippmann, Dewey, and the Fate of the Public in Modern Society," *Communication and Critical/Cultural Studies* 6, no. 3 (2009): 221–45; and S. C. Jansen, *Walter Lippmann: A Critical Introduction to Media and Communication Theory* (New York: Peter Lang, 2012).

9. On the side of those who defend an opposition between Lippmann and the pragmatist tradition, see notably the already mentioned positions of James Carey and Christopher Lasch, as well as those of Joëlle Zask (*L'opinion publique et son double: John Dewey, philosophe du public* [Paris: L'Harmattan, 1999]) and of Dominique Trudel ("Quelle nouvelle histoire pour la recherche en communication? Le cas de Walter Lippmann," *Communication* 29, no. 2 [2012]). It is in this very polemical context that Bruno Latour hammers out, in his presentation of *The Phantom Public*, that Lippmann is both a "true Democrat" and a true pragmatist (Bruno Latour, "Le fantôme de l'esprit public: Des illusions de la démocratie aux réalités de ses apparitions," in W. Lippmann, *Le Public fantôme*, trans. Laurence Decréau [Paris: Démopolis, 2008], 12, 16). If Bruno Latour does not deny that there is a "Lippmann-Dewey debate" in which Dewey rejects the solutions proposed by Lippmann, it remains for him an internal debate within pragmatism, which I contest in the pages that follow.

10. John Dewey, *The Quest for Certainty: A Study of the Relation of Knowledge and Action* (1929), in *The Later Works, 1925–1953*, vol. 4 (Carbondale: Southern Illinois University Press, 1984, 2008), 157.

11. Walter Lippmann, *Public Opinion* (1922; New York: Classic Books America, 2009), 230.

12. John Dewey, *German Philosophy and Politics* (New York: Henry Holt, 1915), 127.

13. John Dewey, "The Influence of Darwinism on Philosophy" (1910), in *The Middle Works, 1899–1924*, vol. 4 (Carbondale: Southern Illinois University Press, 1977), 13.

14. In chap. 7 of *Democracy and Education* (1916), in *The Middle Works, 1899–1924*, vol. 9 (Carbondale: Southern Illinois University Press, 1980, 2008).

15. See Walter Lippmann, *Drift and Mastery: An Attempt to Diagnose the Current Unrest* (1914; Madison: University of Wisconsin Press, 2015), 144: "I have to follow the orders of my physician. We all of us have to follow the lead of specialists. . . . We cannot be absolute pragmatists."

16. In this regard, the world of health care seems to be torn—with the institutional concept of "sanitary democracy," a very influential concept in France—between two incompatible conceptions of democracy in which one recognizes the respective political models of Lippmann and Dewey. The first, conforming to the Lippmannian model of the government of experts, reinforces the dichotomy between an experimentation led from above by experts and the target of the experimentation: a population reduced to "consent" and the "social acceptability of innovations." The other, much closer to the participatory democracy theorized by Dewey, intends to reinterpret "sanitary democracy" as the occasion for an active participation of the publics in experimentation, the production of knowledge, and the choice of collective aims regarding public health. See the conclusion to this volume, where I return more in detail to the extensions of the inquiry about the Lippmann-Dewey debate into the educational and sanitary domains.

17. John Dewey, *Reconstruction in Philosophy* (1920), in *The Middle Works, 1899–1924*, vol. 12 (Carbondale: Southern Illinois University Press, 1982, 2008), 86–87.

18. Stéphane Madelrieux, *La philosophie de John Dewey* (Paris: Vrin, 2016), 68.

19. Dewey, *Reconstruction in Philosophy*, 128–29.

20. Dewey, *Democracy and Education*, 146.

21. Madelrieux, *La philosophie de John Dewey*, 62, 71. The end of the quotation comments on the famous description of a child burning himself, in the same passage of *Reconstruction in Philosophy*, 129: "The doing and undergoing, the reaching and the burn, are connected. One comes to suggest and mean the other. Then there is experience in a vital and significant sense." On experience as a connection of "passive and active phases," also see Joëlle Zask, *L'opinion publique et son double*, 2:17ff., as well as *Introduction à John Dewey* (Paris: La Découverte, 2015), 50ff.

22. Dewey, *Democracy and Education*, 15.

23. Dewey, "Influence of Darwinism on Philosophy," 3.

24. Dewey, 7.

25. On this point, see Mathias Girel, "James critique de Spencer: D'une autre source de la maxime pragmatiste," *Philosophie*, no. 64 (1999): 69–90. On the link (or the gap) between the psychology of James with Darwinism, see also Stéphane Madelrieux, *William James: L'attitude empiriste* (Paris: Puf, 2008), 97ff.

26. Dewey, *Democracy and Education*, 347.

27. Dewey, "Experience and the Empirical" (1911), in "Contributions to *Cyclopedia of Education*," in *The Middle Works, 1899–1924*, vol. 6 (Carbondale: Southern Illinois University Press, 1978), 448.

28. Dewey, "Influence of Darwinism on Philosophy," 11.

29. Dewey, "Experience and the Empirical," 448.

30. Dewey, "Influence of Darwinism on Philosophy," 3.

31. On the complex relationships between Darwinian functionalism and teleology, see Jean Gayon and Armand de Ricqlès, "Fonction," in *Les mondes darwiniens: L'évolution de l'évolution*, vol. 1 (Paris: Éditions Matériologiques, 2009, 2013), 137–61. On the pragmatist usage of the term "teleology," as opposed to its Spencerian and metaphysical usage, see Madelrieux, *William James: L'attitude empiriste*, 140ff. Also see Claude Gautier, "*Le public et ses problèmes*: Le problème social de la connaissance," *Philosophical Enquiries: Revue des philosophies anglophones*, no. 5 (December 2015): 57.

32. Dewey, "Influence of Darwinism on Philosophy," 11.

33. Dewey, 10.

34. Dewey, "Experience and the Empirical," 448.

35. Charles Darwin, *On the Origin of Species by Means of Natural Selection* (1859; London: Penguin Classics, 1985), 133.

36. See Julian Huxley, *Evolution: The Modern Synthesis* (London: Allen and Unwin, 1942).

37. John Dewey, *Human Nature and Conduct: An Introduction to Social Psychology* (1922), in *The Middle Works, 1899–1924*, vol. 14 (Carbondale: Southern Illinois University Press, 1983, 2008), 66.

38. In "The Influence of Darwinism on Philosophy" the expression repeats almost a dozen times ("the logic of knowledge"; "the modern world became self-conscious of the logic that was henceforth to control it, the logic of which Darwin's 'Origin of Species' is the latest scientific achievement"; "new logical outlook"; "new logic"; "Darwinian logic"; "Darwinian genetic and experimental logic").

39. Dewey, *Democracy and Education*, 5.

40. John Dewey, *The Public and Its Problems* (1927), in *The Later Works, 1925–1953*, vol. 2 (Carbondale: Southern Illinois University Press, 1984, 2008), 364–65.

41. Remember that the expression "free and enlightened consent of the patient" structures contemporary medical ethics.

42. Dewey, *Public and Its Problems*, 364.

43. Dewey, 365.

44. Dewey, *Democracy and Education*, 3.

45. Dewey, *Human Nature and Conduct*, 92.

46. Dewey, 77.

47. Niles Eldredge and Stephen Jay Gould, "Punctuated Equilibrium: An Alternative to Phyletic Gradualism," in *Models in Paleobiology*, ed. T. J. M. Schopf (San Francisco: Freeman, Cooper, 1972).

48. Dewey, *Public and Its Problems*, 245–46.

49. Dewey, 314: "the indirect, extensive, enduring and serious consequences of conjoint and interacting behavior call a public into existence having a common interest in controlling these consequences."

50. Dewey, 250: "Reproduction . . . is dependent upon the activities of insects which bring about fertilization."

51. Dewey, 250.

52. Dewey, 255.

53. Dewey, 290.

54. Dewey, 318–19. On the "return" of Dewey himself to liberalism in the 1930s and on this new stage in the Lippmann-Dewey debate, see chap. 4 in this book.

55. See Dewey, *Democracy and Education*, 158: "Yet a thoughtful survey of conditions is so careful, and the guessing at results so controlled, that we have a right to mark off the reflective experience from the grosser trial and error forms of action."

56. And which Bruno Latour's commentary endorses later on. See "Le fantôme de l'esprit public," 8: "Nobody knows, nobody sees, nobody foresees. Everyone blindly fumbles according to the circumstances." By attributing the noble adjectives of an "ecological," "Darwinian," and "pluralist" conception to the Lippmannian theory of democracy, Bruno Latour obscures the core disagreement between Lippmann and Dewey, which is precisely connected—as we have just seen—to the posterity of Darwinism.

57. Dewey, *Public and Its Problems*, 346.

58. In terms of phylogenetics (that of the evolution of the species), the controversy comes, as I mentioned above, from Stephen Jay Gould and Niles Eldredge—with their theory of "punctuated equilibrium" calling Darwinian gradualism profoundly into question. In terms of ontogenetics (that of the development of organisms), it can also be based on "heterochronies," in the technical sense of the term: on those modifications of the rhythms of development studied by developmental biology. See Charles Devillers and Henri Tintant, *Questions sur la théorie de l'évolution* (Paris: Puf, 1996), 156–57: "The evolutionary interest of heterochronies is the realization of organizational changes that are more or less important without passing through intermediary steps. As a result, they hold the attention of paleontologists who see, in the intervention of such processes, the possibility of transformations that would not have to be confronted with the too-often frustrating research of intermediary forms demanded by excessive gradualism."

59. Dewey, *Public and Its Problems*, 254–55.

60. Dewey, *Human Nature and Conduct*, 77.

61. Dewey, *Public and Its Problems*, 367–68.

62. On the indissoluble link between common, community, and communication, see *Democracy and Education*, 7: "There is more than a verbal tie between the words common, community, and communication."

63. Dewey, *Public and Its Problems*, 350.

64. Gautier, "*Le public et ses problèmes*: Le problème social de la connaissance," 69, which rightly contests this misinterpretation that is often made about these pages by Dewey.

65. Dewey, *Public and Its Problems*, 370: "Unless local communal life can be restored, the public cannot adequately resolve its most urgent problem: to find and

identify itself. But if it be reestablished, it will manifest a fullness, variety and freedom of possession and enjoyment of meanings and goods unknown in the contiguous associations of the past. For it will be alive and flexible as well as stable, responsive to the complex and world-wide scene in which it is enmeshed. While local, it will not be isolated. . . . Territorial states and political boundaries will persist; but they will not be barriers which impoverish experience by cutting man off from his fellows."

66. Dewey, *Public and Its Problems*, 368–69.

67. Dewey, 330.

68. Dewey, 331: "But when phases of the process are represented by signs, a new medium is interposed. As symbols are related to one another, the important relations of a course of events are recorded and are preserved as meanings. Recollection and foresight are possible; the new medium facilitates calculation, planning, and a new kind of action which intervenes in what happens to direct its course in the interest of what is foreseen and desired."

69. Dewey, 369: "The psychological tendency can, however, manifest itself only when it is in harmonious conjunction with the objective course of events. Analysis finds itself in troubled waters if it attempts to discover whether the tide of events is turning away from . . . [the] acceleration of motion."

70. Dewey, 369.

71. "Tragic" thought in the sense that Nietzsche intended in *The Birth of Tragedy*, which interprets Greek tragic thought as the capacity to affirm—against all forms of dualism or oppositional thought—that there is a dangerous and necessary insoluble tension between two adverse tendencies that are constrained to both struggle *and* mate. On this point, and also for a rereading of the entirety of Nietzsche's work on the basis of the tragic tension between flux and stases, see my work *Nietzsche et la critique de la chair: Dionysos, Ariane, le Christ* (Paris: Puf, 2005).

72. Dewey, *Quest for Certainty*, 194.

73. Daniel Dennett, *Darwin's Dangerous Idea: Evolution and Meanings of Life* (New York: Simon and Schuster, 199), 203.

74. See Stephen Jay Gould, *The Structure of Evolutionary Theory* (Cambridge, MA: Harvard University Press, 2002).

75. For these "radical differences" that Lippmann's political model intends precisely to eliminate, see *The Phantom Public* (1925; New Brunswick, NJ: Transaction, 1993, 2015), 117.

4. Toward a New Liberalism

1. John Dewey, *Individualism Old and New* (1930), in *The Later Works, 1925–1953*, vol. 5 (Carbondale: Southern Illinois University Press, 1984, 2008).

2. John Dewey, *Liberalism and Social Action* (1935), in *The Later Works, 1925–1953*, vol. 5 (Carbondale: Southern Illinois University Press, 1987, 2008).

3. See the already cited Dewey passage in *The Public and Its Problems* (1927), in *The Later Works, 1925–1953*, vol. 2 (Carbondale: Southern Illinois University Press, 1984, 2008), 318–19.

4. This is the famous theme of the "lost individual" that Dewey will develop in *Individualism Old and New*, 66ff.; and that he is already sketching out in *The Public and Its Problems*, 295.

5. Dewey, *Public and Its Problems*, 300.

6. Dewey, 299.

7. See chap. 1 in this book.

8. Nietzsche and then Stephen Jay Gould reproach Darwin for having reinitiated this atomism by postulating readymade individual organisms (see my contribution "L'hommage de Stephen Jay Gould a l'évolutionnisme de Nietzsche," *Dialogue: Revue canadienne de philosophie* 54, no. 3 [2015]: 409–53). From his viewpoint, Dewey prefers to retain the inverse lesson from Darwinism, which is itself also present—as Gould himself moreover concedes—in *Origin of the Species*: that of highlighting multilinear chains of interactions and making obsolete all understanding of life in terms of atomic elements—which would themselves be submitted, within the model of a misunderstood classical physics, to the universal laws of nature.

9. Dewey, *Human Nature and Conduct*, 60.

10. Dewey, 38.

11. Dewey, 73.

12. Dewey, 75.

13. Dewey, 88.

14. Dewey, *Public and Its Problems*, 243.

15. Dewey, *Human Nature and Conduct*, 46.

16. Dewey, *Public and Its Problems*, 355–56.

17. See Dewey, *Human Nature and Conduct*, 79 ff.

18. See Dewey, *Individualism Old and New*, chap. 1.

19. Dewey, 56.

20. Dewey, 86.

21. Dewey, 122–23.

22. Dewey, *Liberalism and Social Action*, 23.

23. Dewey, 31–32.

24. Only up to a certain point, though, as Dewey elsewhere adopts Heisenberg's uncertainty principle; and with it, a conception of physical nature that itself also deconstructs the fiction of the atom. See Dewey, *The Quest for Certainty: A Study of the Relation of Knowledge and Action* (1929), in *The Later Works, 1925–1953*, vol. 4 (Carbondale: Southern Illinois University Press, 1984, 2008), 161ff.

25. Dewey, *Liberalism and Social Action*, 32.

26. Dewey, 32: "The conception of experimental method in science demands a control by comprehensive ideas, projected in possibilities to be realized by action."

27. Arnaud Milanese, "Dewey et le radicalisme politique dans les années 30: Entre critique et réappropriation," *Philosophical Enquiries: Revue des philosophies*

anglophones 5 (2015): 91. On the Deweyan critique of the New Deal as "state capitalism," also see Guillaume Garetta's "Presentation" of John Dewey, *Après le libéralisme? Ses impasses, son avenir*, trans. Nathalie Ferron (Paris: Flammarion, 2014), 16–17, which itself goes back to Robert B. Westbrook, *John Dewey and American Democracy* (Ithaca, NY: Cornell University Press, 1991), 440–41.

28. Dewey, *Liberalism and Social Action*, 34. Note that the "tragic" mentioned here by no means has the same meaning as that which I give above in connection to Nietzsche. It has the banal and pejorative meaning linked to a disastrous event that should be avoided, while the Nietzschean "tragic" consists on the contrary of the affirmation of a conflict that is both insoluble and necessary; or, if one prefers, of a never definitively overcome *tension* between two tendencies.

29. Dewey, *Liberalism and Social Action*, 35.

30. Dewey, 35, 40.

31. See Milanese, "Dewey et le radicalisme politique," 85–87.

32. Dewey, *Liberalism and Social Action*, 35.

33. Dewey, "Liberalism in a Vacuum: A Critique of Walter Lippmann's Social Philosophy" (1937), in *The Later Works, 1925–1953*, vol. 11 (Carbondale: Southern Illinois University Press, 1987, 2008), 492.

34. Dewey, *Liberalism and Social Action*, 45: "In short, liberalism must become radical, meaning by 'radical' perception of the necessity of thorough-going changes in the set-up of institutions and corresponding activity to bring the changes to pass. . . . The process of producing the changes will be, in any case, a gradual one. But 'reforms' that deal now with this abuse and now with that without having a social goal based upon an inclusive plan, differ entirely from effort at re-forming, in its literal sense, the institutional scheme of things."

35. Dewey, 45: "For the gulf between what the actual situation makes possible and the actual state itself is so great that it cannot be bridged by piecemeal policies undertaken ad hoc."

36. Dewey, 45.

37. Dewey, 36.

38. Dewey, 36.

39. Dewey, 36.

40. Dewey, 57.

41. Dewey, 36–37.

42. Dewey, 54.

43. Dewey, 44.

44. Dewey, 37.

45. Dewey, 41.

46. Dewey, 53.

47. Dewey, 49–50.

48. Dewey, *Public and Its Problems*, 365.

49. Dewey, *Liberalism and Social Action*, 38–39.

50. Dewey, 39.

51. Dewey, 38.

52. Dewey, 51.

53. John Dewey, "The Economic Basis of the New Society" (1939), in *The Later Works, 1925–1953*, vol. 13 (Carbondale: Southern Illinois University Press, 1988, 2008), 321.

5. The Great Revolution: Switching Off Intelligence

1. See Ronald Steel, *Walter Lippmann and the American Century* (1980; New Brunswick, NJ: Transaction, 1999, 2008), 308.

2. Steel, 315–16.

3. Walter Lippmann, *The Good Society* (Boston: Little, Brown, 1937; repr., New Brunswick, NJ: Transaction, 2005), 3ff.

4. Lippmann, 1.

5. He cites the book by Ludwig von Mises, *Die Gemeinwirtschaft: Untersuchungen über Sozialismus* (Jena: Gustav Fischer, 1922); as well as the collection edited by Friedrich Hayek, *Collectivist Economic Planning* (London: Routledge and Kegan Paul, 1935). This is an important point because it shows that Lippmann's influence on neoliberalism is itself partially nourished by the Austro-American liberalism which today inspires a form of ultraliberalism. The challenge, which I will return to later, will thus be to measure the distance between actual *neo*-liberalism (that of Lippmann)—which is radically new in regard to the principles of classical liberalism—and contemporary *ultra*-liberalism, which, far from claiming some form of rupture with laissez-faire, instead adopts and hardens its path by specifically referring to Hayek.

6. John Dewey, "Liberalism in a Vacuum: A Critique of Walter Lippmann's Social Philosophy" (1937), in *The Later Works, 1925–1953*, vol. 11 (Carbondale: Southern Illinois University Press, 1987, 2008), 489–90, 66.

7. Lippmann, *Good Society*, 3.

8. Dewey, *Liberalism and Social Action* (1935), in *The Later Works, 1925–1953*, vol. 11 (Carbondale: Southern Illinois University Press, 1987, 2008), 41.

9. Lippmann, *Good Society*, 5.

10. Lippmann, 157ff.

11. This is the title of chap. 9 of *The Good Society*.

12. Lippmann, 163.

13. Lippmann, 161–62.

14. Adam Smith, *An Inquiry into the Nature and Causes of the Wealth of Nations* (1776; Oxford: Oxford University Press, 1976), 1:13.

15. Lippmann, *Good Society*, 177.

16. John Dewey, *Freedom and Culture* (1939), in *The Later Works, 1925–1953*, vol. 13 (Carbondale: Southern Illinois University Press, 1988, 2008), 182: "Production of the material means of a secure and free life has been indefinitely increased and at an accelerated rate. It is not surprising that there is a large group which attributes

the gains which have accrued, actually and potentially, to the economic regime under which they have occurred—instead of to the scientific knowledge which is the source of physical control of natural energies."

17. Smith, *Wealth of Nations*, 1:31: "That the division of labor is limited by the extent of the market."

18. Lippmann, *Good Society*, 164.

19. Lippmann, 162–63.

20. Lippmann, 167. Lippmann's radical thesis moreover leads him here to commit a strange anachronism wherein the English political revolution in the seventeenth century results from the debut of the industrial revolution in the following century.

21. Lippmann, 163.

22. Lippmann, 165, 168.

23. Dewey, *Freedom and Culture*, 180.

24. Lippmann, *Good Society*, 169.

25. John Dewey, *Human Nature and Conduct: An Introduction to Social Psychology* (1922), in *The Middle Works, 1899–1924*, vol. 14 (Carbondale: Southern Illinois University Press, 1983, 2008), 86–87.

26. I am of course leaving aside here, as well as in all the following pages, all the nuances that should be present in this overly simplistic reading of *The Wealth of Nations* to concentrate uniquely on the strategic utilization that Lippmann makes of Smith.

27. Smith, *Wealth of Nations*, 1:25.

28. Smith, 1:26–27: "But man has almost constant occasion for the help of his brethren, and it is in vain for him to expect it from their benevolence only. He will be more likely to prevail if he can interest their self-love in his favour, and shew them that it is for their own advantage to do for him what he requires of them. Whoever offers to another a bargain of any kind, proposes to do this: Give me that which I want, and you shall have this which you want, is the meaning of every such offer; and it is in this manner that we obtain from one another the far greater part of those good offices which we stand in need of. It is not from the benevolence of the butcher, the brewer, or the baker, that we expect our dinner, but from their regard to their own interest. We address ourselves, not to their humanity but to their self-love, and never talk to them of our own necessities but of their advantages."

29. Dewey, *Human Nature and Conduct*, 92. Once again, as for Lippmann, I am leaving aside here the complex question of the strength and limits of the Deweyan interpretation of Adam Smith's philosophy.

30. Dewey, 94.

31. Lippmann, *Good Society*, 176.

32. Lippmann, 15–16.

33. On the "providentialist hold" of Design theory on Adam Smith's ideas, see Didier Deleule, *Hume et la naissance du libéralisme économique* (Paris: Aubier-Montaigne, 1979), 114, which evokes a "finality inscribed in society by the 'invisible

hand' whose realization, with or without the conscious participation of the agents, actualized a premeditated Design."

34. Lippmann, *Good Society*, 177.

35. Lippmann, 169–71.

36. "Allocution de Walter Lippmann," in *Le Colloque Lippmann: Aux origines du néo-libéralisme*, ed. Serge Audier (Lormont: Le Bord de l'eau, 2008), 260.

37. Michel Foucault, *The Birth of Biopolitics: Lectures at the Collège de France 1978–79*, ed. Michel Senellart, trans. Graham Burchell (New York: Palgrave Macmillan, 2008), 119–20.

38. Lippmann, *Good Society*, 29.

39. Lippmann, 31.

40. Henri Bergson, *L'évolution créatrice* (1907; Paris: Puf, 2008), v–vi; trans. Arthur Mitchell as *Creative Evolution* (London: Macmillan, 1922, ix–x).

41. Bergson, *Creative Evolution*, 50–51.

42. Lippmann, *Good Society*, 31.

43. Bergson, *Creative Evolution*, 12.

44. Bergson, "Introduction à la métaphysique" (1903), in *La Pensée et le mouvant* (Paris: Puf, 2009), 211–12; trans. T. E. Hulme as *An Introduction to Metaphysics* (New York: Liberal Arts Press, 1949), 49.

45. Lippmann, *Good Society*, 31.

46. Bergson, *Creative Evolution*, 22.

47. Lippmann, *Good Society*, 30–31.

48. Except for maybe in book 4, which is very badly articulated in regard to the three preceding books, and takes a dramatic shift into the realm of "the intuition," of "the immaterial," and of "the spiritual." On the critique of this brutal metaphysical transition to intuition, see Dewey's attacks in "Liberalism in a Vacuum," commented on above.

49. Bergson, *Introduction to Metaphysics*, 52.

50. Bergson, 60–62.

51. Bergson, 52.

52. Lippmann, *Good Society*, 33–34.

53. Lippmann, 34.

54. Lippmann, 56.

55. Lippmann, 56.

56. Stephen Jay Gould, *The Structure of Evolutionary Theory* (Cambridge, MA: Harvard University Press, 2002), 14. See also the section "Darwin and Adam Smith," 121ff., where Stephen Jay Gould uses the article by Silvan S. Schweber, "The Origin of the 'Origin' Revisited," *Journal of the History of Biology* 10, no. 2 (1977): 229–316, to justify the thesis of the influence of Smith on Darwin. See Gould, 122: "Silvan S. Schweber (1977) . . . has traced the chain of influence upon Darwin from Adam Smith's school of Scottish economists—beginning in the early 1830's, and culminating in Darwin's intense study of these ideas as he tried to fathom the role of individual action during the weeks just preceding his "Malthusian" insight of September 1838."

57. All the expressions between quotation marks are indeed already found in Smith, *Wealth of Nations*, 25–27.

58. See the title of chap. 10 of *The Good Society*, 183.

6. Reforming the Human Species through Law

1. Louis Rougier, opening speech at the Lippmann Colloquium, in *Le Colloque Lippmann: Aux origines du néo-libéralisme*, ed. Serge Audier (Lormont: Le Bord de l'eau, 2008), 255.

2. Rougier, 255.

3. Pierre Bourdieu, "L'essence du néolibéralisme," *Le monde diplomatique*, March 1998, 3.

4. Rougier, opening speech, in Audier, *Le Colloque Lippmann*, 255.

5. Alexander Rüstow, in Audier, *Le Colloque Lippmann*, 319–20.

6. Walter Lippmann, *The Good Society* (Boston: Little, Brown, 1937; repr., New Brunswick, NJ: Transaction, 2005), 171–72. See also *Good Society*, 221: "But under the laissez-faire delusion it was supposed that good markets would somehow organize themselves or, at any rate, that the markets are as good as they might be. That is not true."

7. Lippmann, 182.

8. Lippmann, 183.

9. Lippmann, 203.

10. Rougier, opening speech, in Audier, *Le Colloque Lippmann*, 253–54.

11. See *The Good Society*, title of chap. 11.

12. See John Maynard Keynes, *The End of Laissez-Faire* (London: Hogarth, 1926), which refers to Jeremy Bentham, *Manual of Political Economy*: "Perhaps the chief task of economists at this hour is to distinguish afresh the *Agenda* of government from the *Non-Agenda*; and the companion task of politics is to devise forms of government within a democracy which shall be capable of accomplishing the *Agenda*."

13. Lippmann, *Good Society*, 212.

14. Lippmann, 284: "We have defined the liberal state as one in which social control is achieved mainly by administering justice among men rather than by administering men and their affairs by overhead authority. It follows that the temper of officialdom in a liberal society must be predominantly judicial."

15. John Dewey, "Liberalism in a Vacuum: A Critique of Walter Lippmann's Social Philosophy" (1937), in *The Later Works, 1925–1953*, vol. 11 (Carbondale: Southern Illinois University Press, 1987, 2008), 493.

16. Lippmann, *Good Society*, 283.

17. Lippmann, 283.

18. Lippmann, 283–84.

19. Rougier, opening speech, in Audier, *Le Colloque Lippmann*, 254.

20. Rougier, 254.

21. John Dewey, *Experience and Nature* (1925), in *The Later Works, 1925–1953*, vol. 1 (Carbondale: Southern Illinois University Press, 1981, 2008), 312. In this passage, Dewey cites and comments on Oliver Wendell Holmes, *Collected Legal Papers* (New York: Harcourt, Brace, 1920), reissued under the title *The Essential Holmes: Selections from the Letters, Speeches, Judicial Opinions, and Other Writings of Oliver Wendell Holmes, Jr.* (Chicago: University of Chicago Press, 1992), 118.

22. John Dewey, *The Public and Its Problems* (1927), in *The Later Works, 1925–1953*, vol. 2 (Carbondale: Southern Illinois University Press, 1984, 2008), 270.

23. See Lippmann, *Good Society*, 257.

24. See in particular John Dewey, *Theory of Valuation* (1939), in *The Later Works, 1925–1953*, vol. 13 (Carbondale: Southern Illinois University Press, 1988, 2008).

25. Holmes, *Essential Holmes*, 118, cited by Dewey, *Experience and Nature*, 312.

26. Dewey, *Experience and Nature*, 312.

27. Lippmann, *Good Society*, 203.

28. Lippmann, 206.

29. Lippmann, 206.

30. Lippmann, 256–57.

31. Lippmann, 209.

32. Lippmann, 210.

33. Lippmann, 319.

34. Lippmann, 321.

35. Lippmann, 372.

36. Lippmann, 334.

37. Dewey, "Liberalism in a Vacuum," 494.

38. Dewey, 494–95.

39. Dewey, 492.

40. Dewey, 495.

41. Dewey, 494.

42. Lippmann, *Good Society*, 378.

43. Lippmann, 337.

44. Lippmann, 356.

45. Lippmann, 358.

46. Lippmann, 358.

47. Lippmann, 266.

48. Lippmann, 358.

49. Lippmann, 20.

50. Michel Foucault, *The Birth of Biopolitics: Lectures at the Collège de France, 1978–1979*, ed. Michel Senellart, trans. Graham Burchell (New York: Palgrave Macmillan, 2008). On the relationships of continuity or rupture between these two versions of neoliberalism, see *infra*, my conclusion.

51. Lippmann, *Good Society*, 280.

52. Lippmann, 366.

53. Lippmann, 198–99.

54. Lippmann, 208.

55. Lippmann, 200–201.

56. Lippmann, 201–2.

57. Dewey, "Liberalism in a Vacuum," 490.

7. The Neoliberal Agenda: Toward a New Age of Biopolitics

1. On the distinction between *agenda* and *non-agenda* drawn from Bentham's utilitarianism, see again Pierre Dardot and Christian Laval, *La nouvelle raison du monde: Essai sur la société néolibéral* (Paris: La Découverte, 2009), 112, 143.

2. See Walter Lippmann, *The Good Society* (Boston: Little, Brown, 1937; repr., New Brunswick, NJ: Transaction, 2005), 165ff.; and John Dewey, *Freedom and Culture* (1939), in *The Later Works, 1925–1953*, vol. 13 (Carbondale: Southern Illinois University Press, 1988, 2008), 97ff., commented on below.

3. Michel Foucault, "La naissance de la médecine sociale" (1977), in *Dits et écrits II, 1976–1988* (Paris: Gallimard, 2001), 207–28.

4. Michel Foucault, *The Birth of Biopolitics: Lectures at the Collège de France 1978–1979*, ed. Michel Senellart, trans. Graham Burchell (New York: Palgrave Macmillan, 2008), 185.

5. Michel Foucault, *Discipline and Punish: The Birth of the Prison*, trans. Alan Sheridan (New York: Vintage Books, 1995).

6. John Dewey, "Creative Democracy—The Task before Us" (1939), in *The Later Works, 1925–1943*, vol. 14 (Carbondale: Southern Illinois University Press, 1983, 2008).

7. Dewey, *Freedom and Culture*, 151.

8. On these evolutions, see Jean Terrel's analyses in *Politiques de Foucault* (Paris: Puf, 2010), 85ff.

9. Foucault, "Naissance de la médecine sociale," and Foucault, "L'incorporation de l'hôpital dans la technologie moderne" (1978), in *Dits et écrits II, 1976–1988* (Paris: Gallimard, 2001), 508–21.

10. Michel Foucault, *"Society Must Be Defended": Lectures at the Collège de France, 1975–1976*, ed. Mauro Bertani and Alessandro Fontana, trans. David Macey (New York: Picador, 2003).

11. See Michel Foucault, *Security, Territory, Population: Lectures at the Collège de France, 1977–1978*, ed. Michel Senellart, trans. Graham Burchell (New York: Palgrave Macmillan, 2009), 45: "By definition, discipline regulates everything. Discipline allows nothing to escape. Not only does it not allow things to run their course, its principle is that things, the smallest things, must not be abandoned to themselves. . . . The apparatus of security, by contrast, as you have seen, 'lets things happen.' Not that everything is left alone, but *laisser-faire* is indispensable at a certain level."

12. Foucault, *Security, Territory, Population*, 47–48.

13. Foucault, *Birth of Biopolitics*, 319: "Liberalism . . . is imbued with the principle: 'One always governs too much'—or at least, one should always suspect

that one governs too much. Governmentality should not be exercised without a 'critique' far more radical than a test of optimization. It should not only question itself about the best (or least costly) means for achieving its effects, but also about the possibility and even legitimacy of its project for achieving effects."

14. See Foucault, *Security, Territory, Population*, 75: "From one direction, then, population is the human species, and from another it is what will be called the public. . . . The public . . . is the population seen under the aspect of its opinions, ways of doing things, forms of behavior, customs, fears, prejudices, and requirements; it is what one gets a hold on through education, campaigns, and conviction." The public "offer[s] a surface on which authoritarian, but reflected and calculated transformations can get a hold." Note that with this passing remark Foucault is himself sketching out an important connection, which would merit refinement, between his own concept of biopolitics and the Lippmannian theory of a necessary manufacture of consent.

15. Foucault, 73.

16. This point can explain and justify why Pierre Dardot and Christian Laval insist much more on neoliberal disciplines than on biopolitics. See *La nouvelle raison du monde*, 299ff.: "un nouveau système de disciplines."

17. By losing sight of the biological aspects of neoliberalism, and by also not discussing anything about his disciplinary program, Foucault sadly did not give us any indications on this subject, leaving his interpreters to imagine what his response would have been in his place. This silence clearly nourishes contemporary controversies about the real or supposed collusions that Foucault had with neoliberalism. On these polemics, see, for example, Serge Audier, *Penser le "néolibéralisme": Le moment néolibéral, Foucault et la crise du socialisme* (Lormont: Le Bord de l'eau, 2015), 42: "Foucault était-il vraiment anti-néolibéral?"; and Geoffroy de Lagasnerie, *La dernière leçon de Michel Foucault* (Paris: Fayard, 2012).

18. Lippmann, *Good Society*, 203.

19. Lippmann, 209. What we call today the problematic of care, central to partisans of radical democracy like Dewey or Jane Addams (see Alice Le Goff, *Care et démocratie radicale* [Paris: Puf, 2013]), is equally within the agenda of neoliberalism. As we will see in what follows in this chapter, the issue is thus of knowing what one understands by "care," and more generally by the policies of care in regard to education, health, and the environment. To say it more clearly: "care" does not immunize us, by being invoked, against the agenda of neoliberalism. As Foucault has shown in his critical pages of *The Birth of Biopolitics* about mothering and early childhood care (243-44), it can on the contrary actively contribute to it.

20. Lippmann, *Good Society*, 226.

21. Even if, as I will return to later on, the Foucauldian genealogy of classical liberals puts back into question this habitual presentation of things. Locke had gone somewhat in this direction. Later, starting from the end of the eighteenth century and under the impulse of Bentham's utilitarianism, public health policies started being launched. This is the theme of biopolitics, about which I will go into great detail in what follows in this chapter.

22. Lippmann, *Good Society*, 226.

23. See Serge Audier, ed., *Le Colloque Lippmann: Aux origines du néo-libéralisme* (Lormont: Le Bord de l'eau, 2008), 343, where Jacques Rueff declares: "I fully subscribe to Mr. Lippmann's text. He throws out the bases of a politics that, for my part, I qualify as liberal left politics because they tend to give to the most impoverished classes the most well-being possible. It is in this respect that I am rallying without any reservation to Mr. Lippmann's ideas." Positively adopting this idea, Audier openly sees "the hidden face of neoliberalism" concealed both by the ultraliberals and by their antiliberal adversaries—a hidden program that he would at last like to see recognized "with other doctrinal legacies" as being a full part of the "patrimony of the left" (Audier, *Le Colloque Lippmann*, 243).

24. See the start of chapter 3 of *The Good Society*, 22–23, which very clearly attacks the power of experts and in which Lippmann seems to renounce the positions he defended in *Drift and Mastery* (1914) and *Public Opinion* (1922).

25. Lippmann, *Good Society*, 228.

26. On the proximity between these analyses by Lippmann and the Kantian and even Husserlian conception of the market that the German ordoliberals have, see Foucault, *Birth of Biopolitics*, 120: "Competition is an *eidos*. Competition is a principle of formalization. . . . Just as for Husserl a formal structure is only given to intuition under certain conditions, in the same way competition as an essential economic logic will only appear and produce its effects under certain conditions which have to be carefully and artificially constructed." See also François Bilger, *La pensée économique libérale dans l'Allemagne contemporaine* (Paris: Libraire générale de droit et de jurisprudence, 1964), 47; and Rainer Klump, "On the Phenomenological Roots of German Ordnungstheorie: What Walter Eucken Owes to Edmund Husserl," in *L'Ordolibéralisme allemand: Aux sources de l'economie sociale de marché*, ed. Patricia Commun (Université de Cergy-Pontoise: CIRAC/CICC, 2003), 149–62.

27. Lippmann, *Good Society*, 213.

28. Lippmann, 213.

29. One could ask whether this promotion of conservation by new liberalism does not reappear in contemporary notions of "natural capital" and "ecosystemic services"—which are now imposed as the dominant norms of public policy on environmental issues. In the official international document Millennium Ecosystem Assessment, *Ecosystems and Human Well-Being: Biodiversity Synthesis* (Washington, DC: World Resources Institute, 2005), for example, one indeed finds a whole series of services (for supply, support, regulation) that have already been indicated by Lippmann. The "cultural services" provided by nature are not forgotten. Like all the partisans of conservation, Lippmann insists on the recreational value of preserved natural spaces that are essential for reconstituting a higher-performing workforce at a moment when urban environments are increasingly degraded.

30. Lippmann, *Good Society*, 226.

31. Lippmann, 226.

32. Lippmann, 182, 187.

33. See notably Herbert Spencer, *Social Statics* (London: Chapman and Hall, 1851); and Spencer, *The Man versus the State* (London: Williams and Norgate, 1884).

34. Lippmann, *Good Society*, 227–28.

35. John Dewey, "Liberalism in a Vacuum: A Critique of Walter Lippmann's Social Philosophy" (1937), in *The Later Works, 1925–1953*, vol. 11 (Carbondale: Southern Illinois University Press, 1987, 2008), 491.

36. See what Serge Audier asserts, "La face cachée du néo-libéralisme," in *Le Colloque Lippmann*, 71, 243. The entire sentence, which concludes his presentation, merits being cited: "Because liberalism cannot be reduced to an apology for the omnipresence of the market and for an asocial individualism—even if this also does form a part of its history; because it offers, on the contrary, tools to counterbalance these tendencies and to call into question or criticize those groups or individuals who prosper in situations of domination or inequality, it should fully form a part—along with other doctrinal legacies—of the patrimony of the left." Note that, in the paperback edition, Audier gives us a different text that is much more voluminous and which does not include this final sentence. See "Pour une autre histoire du 'néo-libéralisme,'" in *Le Colloque Lippmann: Aux origines du "néo-libéralisme"* (Lormont: Le Bord de l'eau, 2012).

37. Lippmann, *Good Society*, 165–66.

38. Lippmann, 161–62.

39. Dewey, *Freedom and Culture*, 180–81.

40. Lippmann, *Good Society*, 162.

41. See Dewey, *Freedom and Culture*, 131, criticizing the invocations of "the American way of life" by those who profess democracy while constantly betraying it.

42. Dewey, "Creative Democracy—The Task before Us" (1939), in *The Later Works, 1925–1953*, vol. 14 (Carbondale: Southern Illinois University Press, 1983, 2008).

43. Dewey.

44. Dewey.

45. Lippmann, *Good Society*, 163.

46. Lippmann, 163.

47. Lippmann, 163.

48. Lippmann, 165.

49. William Fielding Ogburn, in *Social Change with Respect to Culture and Original Nature* (New York: B. W. Huebsch, 1922), proposes a close dialogue in this book with the problem of dyschrony theorized by Graham Wallas and is interested, like him, in the political and social responses to "maladjustment." This text, which is important for both Lippmann and Dewey, would merit a very detailed study.

50. John Dewey, *Liberalism and Social Action* (1935), in *The Later Works, 1925–1953*, vol. 11 (Carbondale: Southern Illinois University Press, 1987, 2008), 54.

51. Dewey, 54.

52. Dewey, 53.

53. Dewey, *Freedom and Culture*, 96.

54. Dewey, 97.

55. Dewey, 97.

56. It is the subject of the following chapter of *Freedom and Culture*, entitled "The American Background," 99ff.

57. Dewey, *Freedom and Culture*, 97–98.

58. Dewey, 97.

59. Dewey, 165: The influence of science on both means and ends is not exercised directly upon individuals but indirectly through incorporation within culture.

60. Dewey, 87.

61. Lippmann, *Good Society*, 165.

62. Lippmann, 166.

63. Adam Smith, *An Inquiry into the Nature and Causes of the Wealth of Nations* (1776; Oxford: Oxford University Press, 1976), 18.

64. Lippmann, *Good Society*, 166, cited above.

65. Lippmann, 166.

66. Lippmann, 165–66.

67. Lippmann, 212ff.

68. Lippmann, 212ff.

69. Lippmann, 212ff.

70. Lippmann, 212–13.

71. Remember one of the older meanings of the term "handicap," which is historically linked to the lexical field of the equality of opportunities in competition: "The term handicap race was applied (late 18th century) to a horse race in which an umpire decided the weight to be carried by each horse, the owners showing acceptance or dissent in a similar way: hence in the late 19th century handicap came to mean the extra weight given to the superior horse" (*Oxford English Dictionary*). Except that here the meaning of the word is turned on itself: it is what biases the equality of opportunities instead of reestablishing it.

72. Lippmann, *Good Society*, 213.

73. This program of continual improvement of performances indicates that a more refined study should be conducted concerning not only the technical or ethical dimensions, but also the social and political ones, of the question of enhanced mankind in relation to both the new neoliberal agenda and the rise of genomic medicine.

74. See Daniel J. Kevles, *In the Name of Eugenics: Genetics and the Uses of Human Heredity* (Berkeley and Los Angeles: University of California Press, 1985), 173.

75. Kevles, 186, 193, 200. See also Ronald Steel, in *Walter Lippmann and the American Century* (1980; New Brunswick, NJ: Transaction, 1999, 2008), 207, which reminds us that Lippmann's articles on the subject, published in 1922 in *The New Republic*, denounced IQ tests as a naturalist and pseudo-scientific "system of social stratification."

76. Lippmann, *Good Society*, 212.

77. Lippmann, 212–13.

78. See Adam Smith, *Wealth of Nations*, 14, 17–18: "First, the improvement of the dexterity of the workman necessarily increases the quantity of the work he can perform. . . . Secondly, the advantage which is gained by saving the time commonly lost in passing from one sort of work to another, is much greater than we should at first view be apt to imagine it."

79. Lippmann, *Good Society*, 214. In the contemporary world of work like that of education and training, it is this acceleration of mobility, which was already theorized by Lippmann, that is leading to the abandonment of the idea of "profession" or of "status" for that of "jobs" and "employability." On this mutation and and its close link with neoliberalism, see Christian Laval, *L'école n'est pas une entreprise: Le néo-libéralisme à l'assaut de l'enseignement public* (Paris: La Découverte, 2003).

80. Lippmann, *Good Society*, 214.

81. On the notion of "adaptability" according to Dewey, or on its common synonym "flexibility," see notably *Human Nature and Conduct: An Introduction to Social Psychology* (1922), in *The Middle Works, 1899–1924*, vol. 14 (Carbondale: Southern Illinois University Press, 1983, 2008), 51–52, 70, as well as the texts from *Democracy and Education* commented on below

82. On the ambivalences of plasticity and flexibility, in particular within the context of neo-capitalism, and on the Hegelian conceptualization of this tension that continues today to produce its effects in the field of neurobiology, see respectively Luc Boltanski and Ève Chiapello, *Le nouvel esprit du capitalisme* (Paris: Gallimard, 1999) and Catherine Malabou, *Que faire de notre cerveau?* (Paris: Bayard, 2011).

83. Dewey, *Democracy and Education* (1916), in *The Middle Works, 1899–1924*, vol. 9 (Carbondale: Southern Illinois University Press, 1980, 2008), 49.

84. Dewey, 51.

85. Dewey, 51.

86. Dewey, 51.

87. See the title of the chapter, p. 46: "Education as Growth."

88. Lippmann, *Good Society*, 214.

89. Lippmann, 214.

90. On this point, see again Laval, *L'école n'est pas une entreprise*.

91. Dewey, *Freedom and Culture*, 181, already cited and commented on.

92. Lippmann, *Good Society*, 251.

93. Lippmann, 253.

Conclusion. Governing Life and the Living: Toward New Conflicts

1. See Hartmut Rosa, *Social Acceleration: A New Theory of Modernity*, trans. Jonathan Trejo-Mathys (New York: Columbia University Press, 2015).

2. Friedrich Nietzsche, *Human, All Too Human*, trans. R. J. Hollingdale (Cambridge: Cambridge University Press, 1986), § 282, p. 132.

3. I am following here the commentary about *The Genealogy of Morals* II § 12 made by Foucault in "Nietzsche, la généalogie, l'histoire" (1971), in *Dits et écrits I, 1954–1975* (Paris: Gallimard, 2001), 1004–24.

4. On this, Foucault's genealogy, as it is focused on the antinaturalism shown by the ordoliberals, will have told us nothing—to the point that the majority of scholars have themselves let the question go. With the notable exception of Pierre Dardot and Christian Laval who, in *La nouvelle raison du monde: Essai sur la société néolibérale* (Paris: La Découverte, 2009), 175 (*The New Way of the World*, trans. Gregory Elliott [London: Verso, 2013], 64), have clearly indicated—even if they have not gone as far as its evolutionary sources—the central place of adaptation in Lippmann's work: "The important word in Lippmann's vocabulary is *adaptation*. The *agenda* of neo-liberalism was guided by the need for constant adaptation of human beings and institutions to an inherently variable economic order, based on general, unrelenting competition." My own genealogy is in great part born from this incidental remark.

5. By holding on to not only "causes" or "identities," but also "status" and the particularly difficult social question of stability.

6. Again, see Foucault's reading of *Genealogy of Morals* II § 12 in "Nietzsche, la généalogie, l'histoire."

7. See Leona Miller and Jack Goldstein, "More Efficient Care of Diabetic Patients in County-Hospital Setting," *New England Journal of Medicine* 286 (1972): 1388–97.

8. This could explain how some official manuals for therapeutic education meant for caregivers borrow certain things from Foucault's lexicon. See, for example, Jean-François d'Ivernois and Rémi Gagnayre, *Apprendre à éduquer le patient* (Paris: Maloine, 2011).

9. On these themes, see my analysis of Dewey, *L'influence de Darwin sur la philosophie et autres essais de philosophie contemporaine* (Paris: Gallimard, 2016) in the review *Pragmata* 1 (2018): 439–53.

10. On this point, see again my book *Nietzsche et la vie: Une nouvelle histoire de la philosophie* (Paris: Gallimard, 2021), chap. 12.

Bibliography

Aristotle. *The Politics of Aristotle.* Translated by Peter L. Phillips Simpson. Chapel Hill: University of North Carolina Press, 1997.

Audier, Serge, ed. *Le Colloque Lippmann: Aux origines du néo-libéralisme.* Lormont: Le Bord de l'eau, 2008.

————. *Penser le "néolibéralisme": Le moment néolibéral, Foucault et la crise du socialisme.* Lormont: Le Bord de l'eau, 2015.

————. "Pour une autre histoire du 'néo-libéralisme.'" In *Le Colloque Lippmann: Aux origines du "néo-libéralisme."* Lormont: Le Bord de l'eau, 2012.

Bergson, Henri. *L'évolution créatrice.* 1907. Paris: Puf, 2008. Translated by Arthur Mitchell as *Creative Evolution* (London: Macmillan, 1922).

————. "Introduction à la métaphysique." 1903. In *La Pensée et le mouvant.* Paris: Puf, 2009. Translated by T. E. Hulme as *An Introduction to Metaphysics* (New York: Liberal Arts Press, 1949).

Bilger, François. *La pensée économique libérale de l'Allemagne contemporaine.* Paris: Librairie générale de droit, 1964.

Boltanski, Luc, and Ève Chiapello. *Le nouvel esprit du capitalism.* Paris: Gallimard, 1999.

Bourdieu, Pierre. "L'essence du néolibéralisme." *Le monde diplomatique,* March 1998, 3.

Carey, James W. *Communication as Culture.* 1989. New York: Routledge, 2009.

Chomsky, Noam, and Edward Herman. *Manufacturing Consent: The Political Economy of the Mass Media.* 1988. New York: Pantheon Books, 2002.

Dardot, Pierre, and Christian Laval. *La nouvelle raison du monde: Essai sur la société néolibérale.* Paris: La Découverte, 2009. Translated by Gregory Elliott as *The New Way of the World* (London: Verso, 2013).

Darwin, Charles. *On the Origin of Species by Means of Natural Selection.* 1859. London: Penguin Classics, 1985.

Deleule, Didier. *Hume et la naissance du libéralisme économique.* Paris: Aubier-
    Montaigne, 1979.
Dennett, Daniel. *Darwin's Dangerous Idea: Evolution and Meanings of Life.* New
    York: Simon and Schuster, 1995.
Devillers, Charles, and Henri Tintant. *Questions sur la théorie de l'évolution.* Paris:
    Puf, 1996.
Dewey, John. "Creative Democracy—The Task before Us." 1939. In *The Later Works,*
    1925–1953, vol. 14. Carbondale: Southern Illinois University Press, 1983, 2008.
———. *Democracy and Education.* 1916. In *The Middle Works, 1899–1924,* vol. 9.
    Carbondale: Southern Illinois University Press, 1980, 2008.
———. "The Economic Basis of the New Society." 1939. In *The Later Works,*
    1925–1953, vol. 13. Carbondale: Southern Illinois University Press, 1988, 2008.
———. *Experience and Nature.* 1925. In *The Later Works, 1925–1953,* vol. 1.
    Carbondale: Southern Illinois University Press, 1981, 2008.
———. "Experience and the Empirical." 1911. In "Contributions to A *Cyclopedia of*
    Education," in *The Middle Works, 1899–1924,* vol. 6. Carbondale: Southern
    Illinois University Press, 1978.
———. *Freedom and Culture.* 1939. In *The Later Works, 1925–1953,* vol. 13.
    Carbondale: Southern Illinois University Press, 1988, 2008.
———. *German Philosophy and Politics.* New York: Henry Holt, 1915.
———. *Human Nature and Conduct: An Introduction to Social Psychology.* 1922. In
    The Middle Works, 1899–1924, vol. 14. Carbondale: Southern Illinois University
    Press, 1983, 2008.
———. *Individualism Old and New.* 1930. In *The Later Works, 1925–1953,* vol. 5.
    Carbondale: Southern Illinois University Press, 1984, 2008.
———. "The Influence of Darwinism on Philosophy." 1910. In *The Middle Works,*
    1899–1924, vol. 4, 3–14. Carbondale: Southern Illinois University Press, 1977.
———. *Liberalism and Social Action.* 1935. In *The Later Works, 1925–1953,* vol. 11.
    Carbondale: Southern Illinois University Press, 1987, 2008.
———. "Liberalism in a Vacuum: A Critique of Walter Lippmann's Social
    Philosophy." 1937. In *The Later Works, 1925–1953,* vol. 11. Carbondale: Southern
    Illinois University Press, 1987, 2008.
———. "Practical Democracy: *The Phantom Public* by Walter Lippmann." 1925. In
    The Later Works, 1925–1953, vol. 2. Carbondale: Southern Illinois University
    Press, 1984, 2008.
———. *The Public and Its Problems.* 1927. In *The Later Works, 1925–1953,* vol. 2.
    Carbondale: Southern Illinois University Press, 1984, 2008.
———. *The Quest for Certainty: A Study of the Relation of Knowledge and Action.*
    1929. In *The Later Works, 1925–1953,* vol. 4. Carbondale: Southern Illinois
    University Press, 1984, 2008.
———. *Reconstruction in Philosophy.* 1920. In *The Middle Works, 1899–1924,* vol. 12.
    Carbondale: Southern Illinois University Press, 1982, 2008.
———. *Theory of Valuation.* 1939. In *The Later Works, 1925–1953,* vol. 13. Carbondale:
    Southern Illinois University Press, 1988, 2008.

d'Ivernois, Jean-François, and Rémi Gagnayre. *Apprendre à éduquer le patient.* Paris: Maloine, 2011.

Eldredge, Niles, and Stephen Jay Gould. "Punctuated Equilibrium: An Alternative to Phyletic Gradualism." In *Models in Paleobiology,* edited by T. J. M. Schopf. San Francisco: Freeman, Cooper, 1972.

Foucault, Michel. *The Birth of Biopolitics: Lectures at the Collège de France, 1978–1979.* Edited by Michel Senellart. Translated by Graham Burchell. New York: Palgrave Macmillan, 2008.

———. *Discipline and Punish: The Birth of the Prison.* Translated by Alan Sheridan. New York: Vintage Books, 1995.

———. "L'incorporation de l'hôpital dans la technologie moderne." 1978. In *Dits et écrits II, 1976–1988,* 508–21. Paris: Gallimard, 2001.

———. "La naissance de la médecine sociale." 1977. In *Dits et écrits II, 1976–1988,* 207–28. Paris: Gallimard, 2001.

———. "Nietzsche, la généalogie, l'histoire." 1971. In *Dits et écrits I, 1954–1975,* 1004–24. Paris: Gallimard, 2001.

———. *Security, Territory, Population: Lectures at the Collège de France, 1977–1978.* Edited by Michel Senellart. Translated by Graham Burchell. New York: Palgrave Macmillan, 2009.

———. *"Society Must Be Defended": Lectures at the Collège de France, 1975–1976.* Edited by Mauro Bertani and Alessandro Fontana. Translated by David Macey. New York: Picador, 2003.

Garetta, Guillaume. "Présentation" de John Dewey, *Après le libéralisme? Ses impasses, son avenir.* Translated by Nathalie Ferron. Paris: Flammarion, 2014.

Gautier, Claude. "*Le public et ses problèmes*: Le problème social de la connaissance." *Philosophical Enquiries: Revue des philosophies anglophones,* no. 5 (December 2015): 45–77.

Gayon, Jean, and Armand de Ricqlès. "Fonction." In *Les mondes darwiniens: L'évolution de l'évolution,* vol. 1, 137–61. Paris: Éditions Matériologiques, 2009, 2013.

Girel, Mathias. "James critique de Spencer: D'une autre source de la maxime pragmatiste." *Philosophie,* no. 64 (1999): 69–90.

Gould, Stephen Jay. *The Structure of Evolutionary Theory.* Cambridge, MA: Harvard University Press, 2002.

Hayek, Friedrich, ed. *Collectivist Economic Planning.* London: Routledge and Kegan Paul, 1935.

Holmes, Oliver Wendell. *Collected Legal Papers.* New York: Harcourt, Brace, 1920; rev. ed., *The Essential Holmes: Selections from the Letters, Speeches, Judicial Opinions, and Other Writings of Oliver Wendell Holmes, Jr.* Chicago: University of Chicago Press, 1992.

Huxley, Julian. *Evolution: The Modern Synthesis.* London: Allen and Unwin, 1942.

Jansen, Sue Curry. "Walter Lippmann, Straw Man of Communication Research." In *The History of Media and Communication Research: Contested Memories,* edited by David W. Park and Jefferson Pooley, 71–112. New York: Peter Lang, 2008.

————. "Phantom Conflict: Lippmann, Dewey, and the Fate of the Public in Modern Society." *Communication and Critical/Cultural Studies* 6, no. 3 (2009): 221–45.

————. *Walter Lippmann: A Critical Introduction to Media and Communication Theory.* New York: Peter Lang, 2012.

Jewett, Andrew. *Science, Democracy, and the American University: From the Civil War to the Cold War.* Cambridge: Cambridge University Press, 2012.

Kant, Immanuel. *"An Answer to the Question: What Is Enlightenment?"* London: Penguin UK, 2009.

Kevles, Daniel J. *In the Name of Eugenics: Genetics and the Uses of Human Heredity.* Berkeley and Los Angeles: University of California Press, 1985.

Keynes, John Maynard. *The End of Laissez-faire.* London: Hogarth, 1926.

Klump, Rainer. "On the Phenomenological Roots of German *Ordnungstheorie*: What Walter Eucken Owes to Edmund Husserl." In *L'ordolibéralisme allemand: Aux sources de l'économie sociale de marché,* edited by Patricia Commun, 149–62. Université de Cergy-Pontoise: CIRAC/CICC, 2003.

Lacorne, Denis. *L'invention de la République américaine.* Paris: Hachette Littératures, 1991.

Lagasnerie, Geoffroy de. *La dernière leçon de Michel Foucault: Sur le néolibéralisme, la théorie et la politique.* Paris: Fayard, 2012.

Lasch, Christopher. *The Revolt of the Elites and the Betrayal of Democracy.* New York: Norton, 1995.

Latour, Bruno. "Le fantôme de l'esprit public: Des illusions de la démocratie aux réalités de ses apparitions." In Walter Lippmann, *Le Public fantôme,* translated by Laurence Decréau. Paris: Démopolis, 2008.

Laval, Christian. *L'école n'est pas une entreprise: Le néo-libéralisme à l'assaut de l'enseignement public.* Paris: La Découverte, 2003.

Le Goff, Alice. *Care et démocratie radicale.* Paris: Puf, 2013.

Lippmann, Walter. *Drift and Mastery. An Attempt to Diagnose the Current Unrest.* 1914. Madison: University of Wisconsin Press, 2015.

————. *The Good Society.* Boston: Little, Brown, 1937. Reprint, New Brunswick, NJ: Transaction, 2005.

————. *The Phantom Public.* 1925. New Brunswick, NJ: Transaction, 1993, 2015.

————. *A Preface to Politics.* New York: Mitchell Kennerley, 1913.

————. *Public Opinion.* 1922. New York: Classic Books America, 2009.

Madelrieux, Stéphane. *La philosophie de John Dewey.* Paris: Vrin, 2016.

————. *William James: L'attitude empiriste.* Paris: Puf, 2008.

Malabou, Catherine. *Que faire de notre cerveau?* Paris: Bayard, 2011.

Manin, Bernard. *Principes du gouvernement représentatif.* Paris: Flammarion, 2012.

Milanese, Arnaud. "Dewey et le radicalisme politique dans les années 30: Entre critique et réappropriation." *Philosophical Enquiries: Revue des philosophies anglophones* 5 (December 2015): 79–120.

Millennium Ecosystem Assessment. *Ecosystems and Human Well-Being: Biodiversity Synthesis.* Washington, DC: World Resources Institute, 2005.

Miller, Leona, and Jack Goldstein. "More Efficient Care of Diabetic Patients in County-Hospital Setting." *New England Journal of Medicine* 286 (1972): 1388–97.

Mises, Ludwig von. *Die Gemeinwirtschaft: Untersuchungen über Sozialismus.* Jena: Gustav Fischer, 1922. Translated by J. Kahane as *Socialism: An Economic and Sociological Analysis* (New Haven, CT: Yale University Press, 1951).

Nietzsche, Friedrich. *Menschliches, Allzumenschliches, Kritische Studien-ausgabe,* vol. 2. Munich: Deutscher Taschenbuch Verlag, de Gruyter, 1993. Translated by R. J. Hollingdale as *Human, All Too Human* (Cambridge: Cambridge University Press, 1986).

Ogburn, William Fielding. *Social Change, with Respect to Culture and Original Nature.* New York: B. W. Huebsch, 1922.

Plato. *The Republic.* In *Plato in Twelve Volumes,* vols. 5–6. Translated by Paul Shorey. Cambridge, MA: Harvard University Press, 1969.

Rosa, Hartmut. *Social Acceleration: A New Theory of Modernity.* Translated by Jonathan Trejo-Mathys. New York: Columbia University Press, 2015.

Schudson, Michaël. "The 'Lippmann-Dewey Debate' and the Invention of Walter Lippmann as an Anti-democrat, 1986–1996." *International Journal of Communication* 2 (2008): 1–20.

Schweber, Silvan S. "The Origin of the Origin Revisited." *Journal of the History of Biology* 10 (1977): 229–316.

Smith, Adam. *An Inquiry into the Nature and Causes of the Wealth of Nations.* 1776. Oxford: Oxford University Press, 1976.

Spencer, Herbert. *The Man versus the State.* London: Williams and Norgate, 1884.

———. *Principles of Biology.* 1864. London: Chapman and Hall, 1899.

———. *Principles of Psychology.* London: Longman, Brown, Green, and Longmans, 1855.

———. *Social Statics.* London: Chapman and Hall, 1851.

Steel, Ronald. *Walter Lippmann and the American Century.* 1980. New Brunswick, NJ: Transaction, 1999, 2008.

Stiegler, Barbara. "Le demi-hommage de Michel Foucault à la généalogie nietzschéenne." In *Les historicités de Nietzsche,* edited by Bertrand Binoche and Arnaud Sorosina. Paris: Publications de la Sorbonne, 2016.

———. "Flux et Réalité: Une lecture croisée de Nietzsche et Bergson." *Quaestio: Yearbook of the History of Metaphysics* 17 (2017): 341–66.

———. "L'hommage de Stephen Jay Gould à l'évolutionnisme de Nietzsche." *Dialogue: Revue canadienne de philosophie* 54, no. 3 (2015): 409–53.

———. *Nietzsche et la biologie.* Paris: Puf, 2001.

———. *Nietzsche et la critique de la chair: Dionysos, Ariane, le Christ.* Paris: Puf, 2005.

———. *Nietzsche et la vie: Une nouvelle histoire de la philosophie.* Paris: Gallimard, 2021.

———. "Qu'y a-t-il de nouveau dans le *néo*-libéralisme? Vers un nouveau gouvernement du travail, de l'éducation et de la santé." In *Le nouvel esprit du libéralisme,* edited by Fabienne Brugère and Guillaume le Blanc. Lormont: Le Bord de l'eau, 2011.

———. Review of John Dewey, *L'influence de Darwin sur la philosophie et autres essais de philosophie contemporaine* (Paris: Gallimard, 2016). *Pragmata* 1 (2018): 438–53.

Sumner, William Graham. *The Challenge of Facts and Other Essays*. New Haven, CT: Yale University Press, 1914.

Terrel, Jean. *Politiques de Foucault*. Paris: Puf, 2010.

Trudel, Dominique. "Quelle nouvelle histoire pour la recherche en communication? Le cas de Walter Lippmann." *Communication* 29, no. 2 (2012).

Wallas, Graham. *The Great Society. A Psychological Analysis*. 1914. New York: Macmillan, 1916.

———. *Human Nature in Politics*. London: Archibald Constable, 1908.

Westbrook, Robert B. *John Dewey and American Democracy*. Ithaca, NY: Cornell University Press, 1991.

Zask, Joëlle. *Introduction à John Dewey*. Paris: La Découverte, 2015.

———. *L'opinion publique et son double: John Dewey, philosophe du public*. Paris: L'Harmattan, 1999.

Index

Barbara Stiegler is Professor at the University of Bordeaux Montaigne, France.

Adam Hocker is a bookseller, translator, and musician based in Berlin.

CPSIA information can be obtained
at www.ICGtesting.com
Printed in the USA
LVHW110336210422
716752LV00009B/1247

9 780823 299294